The Theology of Priesthood

EDITED BY

Donald J. Goergen, O.P.

and

Ann Garrido

CONTRIBUTORS

Benedict M. Ashley, O.P.

Stephen Vincent DeLeers

Donald J. Goergen, O.P.

Thomas F. O'Meara, O.P.

Paul Philibert, O.P.

Frank C. Quinn, O.P.

Thomas P. Rausch, S.J.

Jack Risley, O.P.

Kenneth Paul Wesche

A Michael Glazier Book

THE LITURGICAL PRESS
Collegeville, Minnesota

www.litpress.org

A Michael Glazier Book published by The Liturgical Press

Cover design by David Manahan, O.S.B. Illustration: Christ washing the feet of the Apostles. Manuscript detail, France, 12th–13th century. M.44, f.7. The Pierpont Morgan Library, Art Resource, New York.

1   2   3   4   5   6   7

Library of Congress Cataloging-in-Publication Data

The theology of priesthood / edited by Donald J. Goergen and Ann Garrido ; contributors, Benedict M. Ashley . . . [et al.].
    p.cm.
   Includes bibliographical references and index.
   ISBN 0-8146-5084-8 (alk. paper)
   1. Priesthood. 2. Catholic Church—Clergy. I. Goergen, Donald. II. Garrido, Ann, 1969– III. Ashley, Benedict M.

BX1912.T46 2000
262'.142—dc21

00-040558

Dedicated to

Dennis Zusy, O.P.
(1928–2000)
Preacher, Priest, Professor

For Erich —
with thanks to God
for the gifts you bring
to the Church — and to
your friends.

Churen
4/29/01
St. Catherine
of Siena

Contents

Preface   vii

1. *Issues for a Theology of Priesthood: A Status Report*   1
   PAUL PHILIBERT, O.P.

2. *Ministry, Ordination Rites, and Language*   43
   FRANK C. QUINN, O.P.

3. *The Ministry of Presbyters and the Many Ministries in the Church*   67
   THOMAS F. O'MEARA, O.P.

4. *The Place of Preaching in the Ministry and Life of Priests*   87
   STEPHEN VINCENT DeLEERS

5. *Priesthood in the Context of Apostolic Religious Life*   105
   THOMAS P. RAUSCH, S.J.

6. *The Minister: Lay and Ordained*   119
   JACK RISLEY, O.P.

7. *The Priesthood of Christ, the Baptized, and the Ordained*   139
   BENEDICT M. ASHLEY, O.P.

8. *Reflections on the Priesthood in "Eastern Orthodoxy"*   165
   KENNETH PAUL WESCHE

9. *Priest, Prophet, King: The Ministry of Jesus Christ*   187
   DONALD J. GOERGEN, O.P.

10. *In Conclusion: Ordained Leaders for the Body of Christ*   211
    PAUL PHILIBERT, O.P.

Contributors   219

Index   221

Preface

From March 12–14, 1999, the Walter Farrell Institute for Theological Reflection and the Aquinas Institute of Theology co-sponsored a colloquium in St. Louis on the theology of the priesthood. The Walter Farrell Institute, sponsored by the friars of the Dominican Central Province, had been conducting a seminar on this topic during the two previous years, which culminated in the colloquium.

The purpose of the seminar was to explore various facets of ordained ministry or the ministerial priesthood. This naturally called for an exploration of some aspects of lay ministry and the priesthood of all the baptized as well. It was not the purpose of the seminar or the colloquium to deal with the specific question of ordination and the ministry of women in the Church. That question would have required a colloquium of its own.

Those presenting major papers at the colloquium, which have been edited for publication here, were Benedict Ashley, Stephen DeLeers, Donald Goergen, Thomas O'Meara, Paul Philibert, Frank Quinn, Thomas Rausch, Jack Risley, and Kenneth Paul Wesche. Other participants and respondents included Charles Bouchard, Harry Byrne, Ann Garrido, Jay Harrington, Jim Karepin, Diane Kennedy, Marygrace Peters, Ed Ruane, Jerry Stookey, Mark Wedig, Dave Wright, and Dennis Zusy.

Paul Philibert, O.P., presents an overview of issues involved in the contemporary discussion on priesthood within the Roman Catholic tradition. His article thus serves as an appropriate introduction to this collection. Frank C. Quinn, O.P., addresses the significance of language as it pertains to priesthood and ministry and how the language we use is manifested in rites of ordination. Thomas F. O'Meara, O.P., situates the discussion on priesthood within the context of an expansion of ministry in the Church since Vatican II and the implications of this expansion for ministry in the future.

Stephen V. DeLeers cogently articulates a theology of priesthood grounded in Vatican II and post–Vatican II documents that focuses on the primacy of preaching. Thomas P. Rausch, s.j., then takes up the issue of diversity within ministerial priesthood as he reflects on priesthood as it has been experienced and understood within the context of apostolic religious life. Jack Risley, o.p., returns to the question of the relationship between ordained ministry and lay ministry, a topic that emerged frequently within the colloquium as a foundational theological issue.

The final three papers reflect on ordained ministry from very distinctive perspectives. Benedict M. Ashley, o.p., takes the letter to the Hebrews as his starting point. Kenneth Paul Wesche looks at priesthood through the glasses of an Eastern Orthodox priest. Donald J. Goergen, o.p., asks what insights African theology, specifically African christology, might offer a contemporary Catholic theology of priesthood. Paul Philibert then provides us with a concluding reflection as well.

It would be instructive if we could present the discussion and interaction within the colloquium as well as the major papers, since many insights emerged in the course of our communal reflection. However, that is not easy to capture. Our hope is that these papers may stimulate others to reflect further as we all in the Church attempt to understand church, ministry, and priesthood more deeply.

I thank all the participants in the colloquium for making it a positive and valuable experience. I thank Aquinas Institute of Theology in St. Louis for its support and sponsorship of the colloquium. And I especially thank Ann Garrido who has been so helpful as co-editor in preparing the material for publication.

Donald J. Goergen, o.p.

1

Issues for a Theology of Priesthood: A Status Report

PAUL PHILIBERT, O.P.

Introduction: Context

In half a century, the Roman Catholic Church has gone from an almost universally accepted understanding of priesthood as hierarchical leadership instituted by Christ and attested in the Scriptures to the recognition of serious historical and theological challenges to the Counter-Reformation understanding of ordained leadership. In addition, statistical accounting for the demographics of ordained leadership in the universal Church has become a matter of great political sensitivity. Vatican congregations are clearly reluctant to accept that a sea of change is taking place in the demographics of ministry worldwide. So, for example, *L'Osservatore Romano* (31 July 1996) featured an article that claims a 75 percent increase in seminarians and priests worldwide in the period between 1975 and 1995. On the other hand, the Kenedy Directory showed that the number of U.S. Catholics grew by nearly a million in 1996, while there were 974 fewer priests and 1,481 fewer nuns than in the year before (CNS, June 6, 1997).

Furthermore, there is a competition between two visions of the priest: the idea of the priest as essentially a cultic leader in the celebration of the sacraments, and, on the other hand, the understanding of the priest as an effective pastoral leader of a community of people whom he knows well and is able to serve with personal sensitivity. The articulation of a theology of priesthood cannot avoid the significance of these volatile dynamics of Catholic experience. Although Vatican II chose to replace *sacerdos*

1

with *presbyter* as the technical term for the ordained minister, not everyone in the Church has been willing to accept the council's theological recasting of this terminology. Some imagine that Vatican II itself is responsible for a diminution in recruiting and retaining priests in service. Others feel about the council what Chesterton averred about Christianity: it hasn't failed, it's just not been tried.

Let me remark upon some of the concrete conditions in our own country that influence the exercise of presbyteral leadership and that probably have an impact upon attracting vocations to priesthood. The following is a list of issues that should be addressed pastorally:

1. *The current ritual experience of the Church:* Many Catholics experience Sunday worship as the fulfillment of an impersonal legal obligation. One theologian somewhat jokingly described the Church as a "multi-national religious corporation with retail shops called parishes where people can go to satisfy their obligation for Sunday worship." Roman Catholics must deal with parishes of one or two thousand families (or even more), while the typical Protestant parish consists of less than one thousand people. For many years, sociologists estimated weekly Sunday church attendance by Catholics in the United States at 45 percent. Recent studies show that a more realistic estimate is about 28 percent.[1] Sunday worship has become a "buyers' market" in the sense that the great majority of Catholics currently feel free to judge when and where the liturgy is fulfilling and satisfying to them. This evidence implies that most Catholics do not weigh their participation in the corporate worship of a stable concrete community to be a significant factor or a personal responsibility.

2. *The failure to integrate liturgy with life: Lumen gentium* (§ 34) describes the liturgical life of the laity as follows: "For all their works, if accomplished in the Spirit, become spiritual sacrifices acceptable to God through Jesus Christ: their prayers and apostolic undertakings,

[1] William D'Antonio et al., *Laity—American and Catholic: Transforming the Church* (Kansas City, Mo.: Sheed & Ward, 1996). Jim Davidson and colleagues at Purdue University, in *The Search for Common Ground: What Unites and Divides Catholic Americans* (Huntington, Ind.: Our Sunday Visitor Press, 1997), have studied the generational differences of three groups in the Church, showing progressive declines in church attendance in the younger groups from pre–Vatican II Catholics to Vatican II Catholics to post–Vatican II Catholics (see chs. 3 and 4). See also Richard A. Schoenherr and Lawrence A. Young, *Full Pews and Empty Altars: Demographics of the Priest Shortage in United States Catholic Dioceses* (Madison: University of Wisconsin Press, 1993).

family and married life, daily work, relaxation of mind and body, even the hardships of life if patiently born. In the celebration of the Eucharist, these are offered to the Father—along with the body of the Lord."[2] It would be news to most Sunday Catholics that what they came to offer to God was themselves and their life's integrity. The failure to communicate this vision lays unreasonable (and erroneous) theological expectations upon the priest/liturgist as the one who must carry the weight of the laity's burden of spiritual involvement. Even more troublesome, this scenario reinforces the faulty vision that only what the priest does at Mass really matters.

3. *The social status of the presbyter:* Since the 1970s the social status or occupational prestige of Roman Catholic clergy has diminished, due to a number of factors that include the upward social mobility of Catholic laity, a more highly educated laity in the Church, and the relative decrease of the priest's practical power as social leader of the parish community. For some decades now it has been recognized that vocations flourish when priests enjoy a higher socioeconomic status relative to the mainstream of the social group.[3] This is no longer the case for most U.S. Catholic communities, even though it would have been the case fifty or a hundred years ago. Often enough, Vatican statements or talks by conservative bishops contrast the abundance of vocations in the Third World with the scarcity in North America and northern Europe, but without taking note of the sociological differences. Whatever else may be at work, socioeconomic status has a significant role to play in the availability of vocations to priesthood.

4. *Competing images of the Catholic priest:* In the pre–Vatican II Church, most Catholics took for granted that the pastor was "the lord of his own parochial domain." In those days, there were not very many lay people with any kind of theological education in the parish. There were few instances of laity as professional catechists, liturgists, or administrative assistants or pastoral associates. This has mostly changed. Today the image of the priest is probably best described as

[2] Texts of the Vatican documents cited in this essay are taken from *Vatican II: Constitutions, Decrees, Declarations,* ed. Austin Flannery (Dublin: Dominican Publications, 1996).
[3] See Joseph H. Fichter, *Religion as an Occupation: A Study in the Sociology of Professions* (Notre Dame, Ind.: University of Notre Dame Press, 1966); and Robert M. Brooks, "Sociological Dimensions of the Seminary," *Seminary Education in a Time of Change,* ed. James M. Lee and Louis J. Putz (Notre Dame, Ind.: Fides Publishers, 1965).

a generative mentoring pastor—one whose responsibility is to maintain harmony while bringing into cooperation the rich and diverse gifts of all the members of the community.[4] (Concomitant with this shift in the image of priest should be a shift away from a focus upon the priest's identity and toward a focus on the priest's generativity. The role of pastor and animator of the local church's varied charisms is far more demanding than the role of liturgical presider alone.)[5]

5. *New biblical foundations:* The biblical theology of ministry and priesthood has developed tremendously in the twentieth century, and particularly in the period following Vatican II. Later in this chapter we will refer to some key findings of this biblical research and theology. However, for the moment, it is clear that the notion of Jesus ordaining twelve apostles as bishops who then proceeded immediately to ordain helpers who became priests, and so on, is a fundamentalist distortion of New Testament sources. The emergence of the Church's ordained leadership and the theology of apostolic succession is a gradual and complex tradition. The Church has nothing to fear from addressing apostolicity in solid historical terms. It is a mistake to cling to expressions of apostolicity that are fundamentalistic in tone and that do not identify the heart of the Church's present responsibility to maintain its apostolic character.[6]

6. *Feminism:* The role of the priest in Catholic communities in North America must be considered against the two-fold reality that women are the evident majority of regular communicants at Sunday Mass, and that women are the decided majority among those serving as lay ministers in the Church. (Murnion states that roughly 80 percent of those doing professional ministry in the Catholic Church today are laity, and roughly more than 80 percent of that pool of lay

---

[4] Scott Appleby coins the phrase "orchestra leader" to suggest the generative mentoring pastor in chapter six of Jay Dolan et al., *Transforming Parish Ministry: The Changing Roles of Catholic Clergy, Laity, and Women Religious* (New York: Crossroad, 1989) 89–90.

[5] See Paul J. Philibert, "Generativity and Priests' Morale: Another Look at the Issue," *White Paper of the National Federation of Priests' Councils* (January 1990).

[6] Avery Dulles uses an interesting description: "Apostolic succession does not mean a historical replacement of the dead by the living, though the term might seem to suggest this. Rather, it signifies aggregation into the presently existing and living apostolic body." In *The Priestly Office: A Theological Reflection* (Mahwah, N.J.: Paulist Press, 1997) 34.

ministers are women.)[7] Issues touching women in Church leadership roles run the gamut from the demand for women's ordination
to episcopacy and priesthood, on the one hand, to a much less startling concern for women to have job security, just compensation,
and a voice in pastoral decision-making, on the other hand. Such
questions circumscribe the role of the priest in ways previously unknown. For women with concerns of this kind, an exclusive male
priesthood can seem an affront, and their relationship with male
incumbents in the priestly role can be clouded with resentment
and hostility.

7. *Signs of dysfunction:* Sadly, one of the most publicized features of
   Catholic priesthood in the popular culture has been repeated accu-
   sations of sexual misbehavior or sexual abuse of women or minors
   by priests (or bishops). As has been noted occasionally, these incidents of misbehavior are roughly parallel to incidents of male misbehavior by any other comparable population of North American
   males. However, this fact neither excuses the behavior of men whose
   lives are said to be consecrated to God in the service of the gospel
   nor diminishes the shock and scandal created by the multiple and
   public instances of priestly misbehavior.

These pastoral tensions describe contextual factors within which a
discussion of priesthood must be conducted. The Church has an old
habit of speaking triumphantly about its ministers, whether popes or
bishops or priests. Whatever questions arise relative to the role of the
presbyter in the Church, we must be frank about the changing circumstances and the limitations of the persons who are serving in these roles.
    Since the Synod of Bishops on the Priesthood in October 1990, Pope
John Paul II has taken every opportunity to affirm priests in their role of
gospel service, clarify what the Church asks of them, and reinterpret their
vocation to ordained ministry as a gift from God and a great and noble
calling. Clearly the topic of presbyteral leadership is high on the Vatican's
agenda. In PDV (§74),[8] the pope instructs priests that "the concern . . .
to find . . . someone to replace him in priesthood" is a duty of charity
toward his own local church. Then the pope goes on to speak of the "fair

---

[7] See Philip J. Murnion and David DeLambo, *Parishes and Parish Ministers: A Study
of Parish Lay Ministry* (New York: National Pastoral Life Center, 1999). The pastoral
trends discovered in 1992 remain essentially the same.

[8] John Paul II, *Pastores Dabo Vobis: I Will Give You Shepherds: Post-Synodal Apostolic
Exhortation* (Washington, D.C.: United States Catholic Conference, 1992) §74, 201.

distribution of the clergy" that would give from priest-rich dioceses to priest-poor dioceses. Within this post-synodal reflection on the state of the Church's priesthood, we can find almost every form of imaginative rethinking except the rethinking of the nature and conditions of priestly service as it is now canonically established.

So what is that canonically established understanding of priesthood? To review this question, we turn to *The Catechism of the Catholic Church*[9] and its account of the sacrament of holy orders.

The Church's Magisterial Teaching

The catechism has an article devoted to "the Sacrament of Holy Orders" (§§1536–1600). There this sacrament is defined as follows: "Holy Orders is the sacrament through which the mission entrusted by Christ to his apostles continues to be exercised in the Church until the end of time; thus it is the sacrament of apostolic ministry. It includes three degrees: episcopate, presbyterate, and diaconate" (§1536).

In subsequent paragraphs, the word *order* is explained as meaning incorporation into a moral body. "Integration into one of these bodies in the Church was accompanied by a rite called *ordinatio*. . . . Today the word *ordination* is reserved for the sacramental act that integrates a man into the order of bishops, presbyters, or deacons." This is more than an election, designation, delegation, or institution by the community, "for it confers a gift of the Holy Spirit that permits the exercise of a sacred power which can come only from Christ himself through his church." Ordination is also a consecration—a setting apart. The laying on of hands with the consecratory prayer is the visible sign of ordination.

The priesthood of the Old Covenant is considered to be a prefiguring of the ordained ministry of the New Covenant. The Israelite priesthood was instituted to proclaim God's word and to restore communion with God through sacrifices and prayer. "Everything that the priesthood of the Old Covenant prefigured finds its fulfillment in Christ Jesus, the 'one mediator between God and men'" (§1544). The redemptive sacrifice of Christ accomplished on the cross is made present in the eucharistic sacrifice of the Church, which is realized today through the ministerial priesthood without diminishing the uniqueness of Christ's priesthood (§1545).

The catechism goes on to distinguish between two participations in the one priesthood of Christ: that of the baptismal priesthood of the faithful in which each participates "according to his own vocation, in Christ's

---

[9] *The Catechism of the Catholic Church* (Washington, D.C.: United States Catholic Conference, 1994). (Abbreviated as CCC.)

mission as priest, prophet, and king. Through the sacraments of Baptism and Confirmation the faithful are 'consecrated to be . . . a holy priesthood'" (§1546). The priesthood of bishops and priests differs essentially from that of the lay faithful:

> While the common priesthood of the faithful is exercised by the unfolding of baptismal grace—a life of faith, hope, and charity, a life according to the Spirit—the ministerial priesthood is at the service of the common priesthood . . . the ministerial priesthood is a means by which Christ unceasingly builds up and leads his church (§1547).

The catechism explains that Christ, as head of his body, shepherd of his flock, and high priest of the redemptive sacrifice, provides for the Church the ecclesial service of ordained ministers. The Church describes this by saying that "the priest, by virtue of the sacrament of Holy Orders, acts *in persona Christi capitis*" (§1548). The catechism then quotes the text of Aquinas (*ST* III, q. 22, a. 4c): "Christ is the source of all priesthood: the priest of the old law was a figure of Christ, and the priest of the new law acts in the person of Christ." (The phrase *in persona Christi* derives much of its authority from its use in the theological writings of Thomas Aquinas.)

The catechism's theological explanation of ordained ministry focuses upon the presence of Christ as head of the Church being made visible in the midst of the community of believers. Ignatius of Antioch is cited to say that "the bishop is the *typos tou Patrou:* he is like the living image of God the Father" (§1549).

The catechism goes on to explain that the Holy Spirit's power in the priest does not guarantee freedom from human weakness or even sin, even though the power of the Spirit can work within a sinful minister (§1550). Further, priesthood is ministerial—it is a service "for the good of men and the communion of the church" (§1551). The ministerial priesthood not only represents Christ the Head before the Assembly, but also acts in the name of the whole Church in presenting the prayer of the Church to God. This does not mean, however, that priests are merely delegates of the community. "It is because the ministerial priesthood represents Christ that he [the priest] can represent the Church" (§1553). (Note here the descending imagery that pictures the priest as the representation of Christ and, by consequence, as one able to represent the whole Church aggregated to Christ by baptism.)

The catechism then defines the three degrees of the sacrament of holy orders. Chief place is held by bishops who express "the unbroken succession going back to the beginning and [who] are regarded as transmitters of the apostolic line" (§1555). The fullness of the sacrament of holy orders is conferred by episcopal consecration and confers "together with the office of sanctifying, also the offices of teaching and ruling" (§1558). Through episcopal consecration, the grace of the Spirit is given and a sacred character impressed so that bishops take the place of Christ as teacher, shepherd, and priest and act as his representative. Bishops are thus constituted "true and authentic teachers of the faith and have been made pontiffs and pastors" (§1558). The collegial nature of the episcopal order is signified by the Church's practice of having several bishops participate in the consecration of a new bishop. "In our day, the lawful ordination of a bishop requires a special intervention of the bishop of Rome, because he is the supreme visible bond of the communion of the particular Churches in the one Church and the guarantor of their freedom" (§1559). Though each bishop is the legitimate pastor of only one local church, he is also responsible with the other bishops for the apostolic mission of the universal Church.

Priests are described as co-workers of the bishops. The catechism cites *Presbyterorum ordinis* (§2) as follows: "the function of the bishops' ministry was handed over in a subordinate degree to priests so that they might be appointed to the order of priesthood and be co-workers of the episcopal order for the proper fulfillment of the apostolic mission" (§1562). By their "own particular sacrament of priestly ordination, priests are anointed by the Holy Spirit and signed with a special character to be configured to Christ in such a way they are able to act in the person of Christ the Head" (§1563). While not having the same degree as the pontifical office, priests are associated with bishops in sacerdotal dignity after the image of Christ and are consecrated to preach the gospel and shepherd the faithful as well as to celebrate divine worship "as true priests of the New Testament" (§1564).

Priests share in the universal dimensions of the mission that Christ entrusted to the apostles (§1565); in celebrating the Eucharist, they act in the person of Christ and proclaim Christ's mystery (§1566), and together with their bishop they constitute with their fellow priests "a unique sacerdotal college [presbyterium] dedicated . . . to a variety of distinct duties" (§1567). In a certain sense they represent the bishop and can exercise their ministry only in dependence on and in communion with him. The unity of the presbyterium finds liturgical expression in the imposition of hands by priests after the bishop during the rite of ordination of priests (§1568).

The catechism conveys the current magisterial teaching that only a baptized male may validly receive ordination. The explanation is given as follows:

> The Lord Jesus chose men *(viri)* to form the college of the twelve apostles, and the apostles did the same when they chose collaborators to succeed them in their ministry. . . . The church recognizes herself to be bound by this choice made by the Lord himself. For this reason the ordination of women is not possible (§1577).[10]

The catechism acknowledges that the Eastern churches have accepted a discipline that allows married men to be ordained as deacons and priests. Nonetheless, ordained bishops and priests of the Latin Church "are normally chosen from among men of faith who live a celibate life and who intend to remain celibate 'for the sake of the kingdom of heaven'" (§1579). In addition, holy orders configures the ordained by an indelible character "so that he may serve as Christ's instrument for his church" (§1581).

The catechism's final consideration of the theology of priesthood has to do with the grace of the Holy Spirit proper to this sacrament. By this grace, the priest is configured to Christ as priest, teacher, and pastor, of whom the ordained is made a minister. The gift of grace of presbyteral ordination is described in §1587: "To stand without reproach before your altar . . . , to proclaim the gospel of your kingdom; to fulfill the ministry of your word of truth; to offer you spiritual gifts and sacrifices; and to renew your people by the bath of rebirth."

In an earlier section of the catechism, the ecclesial ministry of the Church is identified as being intrinsically linked to service (§876), collegial in character (§877), and marked by a personal character so that each one who is ordained as minister is called personally (§878). The text of the catechism is concerned to give a careful explanation of the Church's conventional understanding of its sacramental tradition with respect to holy orders. No mention is made of earlier historical practice or of controversies concerning the Church's present discipline. All in all, the vision of Church as imaged in the texts of the catechism suggests the following characteristics:

- a hierarchical society that traces the warrant for its organizational structure back to the very words of Christ in Scripture and to the most ancient traditions of the apostolic church;
- that understands its ministers of sanctification and governance as sacramental beings, that is, acting in the name of and in the power

[10] The catechism does not allude to the theological argument of nuptial imagery that was developed in *Mulieris dignitatem* (1988). It relies exclusively on the argument of the weight of tradition in the Church's practice. We will review the argument proposed in *Mulieris dignitatem* later in this chapter.

of Christ, and thus marked by a tremendous awareness of their un-
worthiness and their nobility;

- functioning within a tightly knit ecclesiastical structure that is hierarchical in nature and in which each person voluntarily and knowingly accepts an ordered place;
- expressed in a world of Christian faith within which there will always be abundant candidates to fit within the ecclesiastically established criteria of male and celibate priesthood;
- expressive of a structure of continuity between Old Covenant priesthood and New Testament ministry (by way of the biblical image of
"prefiguring"); and
- expressive of relative lack of concern for the validity of, the needs
of, and its relation to the wider *Oikumene* (the ecumenical church).

Against this background, we now may raise certain questions that
have developed in theology and Church life that will help us to critically
appropriate this portrayal of ordained ministry in the Catholic Church as
articulated by *The Catechism of the Catholic Church*.

Priesthood in Traditional Piety

Later in this chapter, I will describe the central orientations of Vatican II's theology of priesthood, which took *presbyter* as the central term
for the ordained minister-assistant to the bishop. Before turning to that,
however, I turn briefly to a source that had great currency in priests' li-
braries just before the council, the *Daily Breviary Meditations* by Bishop
Joseph Angrisani, published in 1954 with a letter of recommendation by
Archbishop Giovanni Montini (the later Pope Paul VI). This is a document from a given era, of course. But it discloses basic attitudes toward
the role, piety, and spirituality of the priest as seen in a pre-conciliar theology and spirituality. This book went through several editions in all the
European languages and can be considered a representative example of
pre-conciliar piety in Europe as well as America.

Among this text's dominant factors are an emphasis upon the priest's
sacral character, a reticent attitude regarding the laity as a separate (and
inferior) class of Christians, a fear of sexuality and affectivity, and a worldview without any passion for innovation or improvisation.

Angrisani views the priest as a morally weak creature called to a sublime vocation.[11] The body is a burden; it is the soul that is in communi-

---

[11] Joseph Angrisani, *Daily Breviary Meditations,* vol. 3 (New York: Benziger Brothers, 1954) 22–3. Subsequent references to this volume are given with page indications in parentheses.

cation with God. Along with this spiritual dualism, there is (as we shall see) a two-level universe in which the invisible supernatural is what matters, even though we find ourselves exiled in the visible and natural.

Another point of major concern for Angrisani is innocence. He fails to see that anything is gained through experience or the lessons of life. The laity are regarded as a threat to the priest's integrity (414). In addition to a general suspicion of the corrupting influence of laity, there is a particular paranoia about the corrupting influence of women (492).

Another dimension that is strongly emphasized in these meditations is the superior holiness of the ordained. Along with his insistence upon superior holiness goes the curious teaching that the priest is in some sense a scapegoat for the people whom he serves (31).

Angrisani describes a total dedication on the part of the priest. He desires to motivate priests to be tremendously generous in their self-giving to their ministry and to the Church. But his theological vision is dualistic, fearful of the natural world, elitist in its conception of holiness, and an image of priesthood which is more sacral than service-oriented, more focused on the supernatural privilege to the person of the priest than on the corporate reality of the Church as a whole. It was largely to redress this kind of piety that the council document *Presbyterorum ordinis* was composed. But first, how did this pre-conciliar popular piety concerning priesthood come about? That is our next point.

Historical Contributions to the Theology of Holy Orders

A brief citation from Raymond Brown can set the scene for the historical quest about the meaning of priesthood in Christian experience:

> It is striking that while there are pagan priests and Jewish priests on the scene, no individual Christian is ever specifically identified as a priest [in the text of the New Testament]. The Epistle to the Hebrews speaks of the high priesthood of Jesus by comparing his death and entry into heaven with the actions of the Jewish high priest who went into the Holy of Holies in the Tabernacle once a year with a blood offering for himself and for the sins of the people (Heb. 9: 6-7). But it is noteworthy that the author of Hebrews does not associate the priesthood of Jesus with the Eucharist or the last supper; neither does he suggest that other Christians are priests in the likeness of Jesus.[12]

The concept of priest as received in the New Testament is derived from Old Testament priesthood. Therefore, it seems necessary to say a few

[12] Raymond E. Brown, *Priest and Bishop: Biblical Reflections* (Paramus, N.J.: Paulist Press, 1970) 13.

words about priesthood as it existed in Israel. The story of Heli in 1 Samuel gives us a place to situate our analysis. The Israelite priest was a consultant who could speak authentically about the meaning of the Torah; in addition he was a sanctuary attendant. He was responsible for the good order, cleanliness, and regular ritual functions of the sanctuaries (whether at the national shrines where the people gathered to meet God in the ark or in local "high places"). The priestly roles, therefore, included teaching the Torah and the Law, offering sacrifice, and exercising prophecy. Their function before the people was to discern God's presence and God's will. Later, the prophets would usurp this oracular function. Only gradually will priesthood become linked with acts of sacrifice established at regular times in the ritual of the temple.[13]

Note that there is controversy in the post-exilic period over priesthood. The Levites, who were established as a tribe with priesthood as an inherited role and responsibility, came to be disinherited of this role. (One theological interpretation explained that it was because of Aaron's rebellion at Meribah.) In any event, once Jerusalem became David's royal city, the priest Zadok appeared on the scene. His ancestry is obscure and some scholars suggest that he may have been the priest of the city before it was conquered by David. In any event, his descendants thereafter remained the priestly class in Jerusalem until the Temple was destroyed in 587 B.C.E.[14]

There is no pre-exilic evidence for a high priest. After the exile, however, the temple worship was organized with a high priest as the leader and authority of those who exercised the functions of priesthood, which included teaching and sacrifice. Gradually the teaching functions became the property of the scribes and Levites (who, after the Exile, become cantors and servants of the priests).[15] The high priest coordinated the temple service, oversaw the service of the priests, and stood as the chief religious authority of the people, a role of enormous prestige.

Recent decades have given considerable attention to "intertestamental studies" that focus on the various movements that developed in the transition between Israel and Christianity. Some authors read into New Testament witness to John indications of a movement surrounding the Baptist, parallel to the prophetic and apocalyptic movements in first-century Palestine. Particularly notable among these are the Essenes, de-

---

[13] Nathan Mitchell, *Mission and Ministry: History and Theology in the Sacrament of Order* (Wilmington, Del.: Michael Glazier, 1982) 39 and passim.

[14] John J. Castelot, "Religious Institutions of Israel," *The Jerome Biblical Commentary,* ed. Raymond Brown (Englewood Cliffs, N.J.: Prentice-Hall, 1968) 707 (76:20).

[15] Ibid., 708–10 (76:27–38).

vout people who withdrew to the desert and who dissociated from the temple and its priesthood. One characteristic of their religious practices was ritual bathing, a central feature of John the Baptizer's program of preaching. To the degree that Jesus fell under the cultural sway of John's religious movement, there might be some explanation for Jesus' attitude of "spiritual worship" (John 2) and his relative independence from the Temple of Jerusalem.[16] John P. Meier, among others, imagines that Jesus found John's message convincing, accepted John's baptism, and thus received from God his distinct prophetic mission as a wandering preacher, proclaiming the reign of God. Jesus felt deeply the activity of God bursting in upon human life, and in the midst of his ministry came to understand in full human cognizance his role as Son of God.[17]

Raymond Brown and others draw different conclusions from the key text of Hebrews. On the one hand, some scholars see the text from Hebrews indicating a deliberate rejection by Christians of the whole institution of priesthood.[18] On the other hand, Avery Dulles has written recently:

> If the concept of priesthood in Hebrews is taken as a starting point, it becomes apparent that other New Testament authors such as Paul understood Jesus as a priestly figure, even though they do not use the term. They consider the death of Jesus on the cross to be a religious sacrifice. Indeed it becomes apparent that the idea of priesthood is pervasive in the New Testament descriptions of Jesus as the one who bore the sins of many and allowed his body to be broken and his blood poured forth on behalf of others.[19]

In a New Testament context priesthood is analogical, not univocal. *Priest* does not have the same meaning for Aaron, Zadok, Christ, and the presbyter of the post-second-century Church. The term is not equivocal either; it is not completely discontinuous with the shared meanings and relationships of those noted above. But the idea of priest as one whose office is to perform rites and make sacrifices is very different for the Christian world than it is for the Israelite or pagan world.

We might summarize the ministry of the first leaders of the Church as continuing to proclaim the reign of God as Jesus did, preaching his

---

[16] Mitchell, *Mission and Ministry,* 80–7

[17] John P. Meier, *A Marginal Jew: Rethinking the Historical Jesus,* vol. 2 (New York: Doubleday, 1991).

[18] Thus Mitchell, *Mission and Ministry.* Also see Tibor Horvath, *The Sacrificial Interpretation of Jesus' Achievement in the New Testament* (New York: Philosophical Library, 1979); and Thomas F. O'Meara, *Theology of Ministry* (New York: Paulist Press, 1983).

[19] Avery Dulles, *The Priestly Office: A Theological Reflection* (Mahwah, N.J.: Paulist Press, 1997) 5–6.

resurrection, and inviting believers to faith in anticipation of the fulfillment of Jesus' promise of everlasting life. Brown indicates that four principal roles in the New Testament "funneled into the Christian priesthood, namely, the disciple, the apostle, the presbyter-bishop, and the celebrant of the Eucharist."[20]

While all Christians are called to be disciples of Jesus, those who are principally concerned with leadership and ministry are bound in a special and paradigmatic way by the demands of discipleship. The gospels show us exaggerated demands in the parabolic sayings of Jesus that indicate that nothing can interfere with a disciple's response to the call issued in the name of the reign of God. "It is almost a monomaniacally consuming vocation, occupying all the interest of the disciple and allowing no competitive diversion."[21] However, it is the role of the apostle that shapes the ministry for others. Jesus gathered the Twelve around him as chosen disciples. He commissioned them to internship in the service of preaching and healing after the pattern of his own example. Brown comments, "in the Jewish notion of apostolate the one sent . . . represents the one who sends, carrying not only the sender's authority, but even his presence to others."[22] In that sense, the apostle is similar to a personal ambassador (cf. 2 Cor 5:20) who both speaks and deals with authority and who has the confidence of his Master. The apostle represents the Master in plenipotentiary fashion where the Master cannot be physically present.

When the idea of presbyter-episcopos emerges, he is a residential figure living among those for whom he cares. In some texts of the New Testament, presbyters and bishops were undifferentiated, together responsible for pastoral care of the churches. "We do not seem to have in the New Testament (with the possible exception of III John) the situation found in the letters of Ignatius of Antioch, where there is a single bishop with the presbyters as his helpers."[23] Presbyter-bishops took up where the Pauline apostles left off, becoming responsible for the care of the churches founded by the apostles. Their role is the task of "organizing, stabilizing, and preventing dangerous innovation" (Titus 1:9). This activity complements the service of the apostle; the presbyter-bishop must censor and correct "so that he may be able to give instructions in sound doctrine and confute objectors . . . (Titus 1:9-11; cf. Acts 20:30)."[24]

[20] Brown, *Priest and Bishop,* 21.
[21] Ibid., 22.
[22] Ibid., 28.
[23] Ibid., 35, n. 20.
[24] Ibid., 37.

Finally, Brown speaks of the one who presided at Eucharist. He summarizes much in these words: "There is simply no compelling evidence for the classic thesis that the members of the Twelve always presided when they were present, and that there was a chain of ordination passing the power of presiding at the Eucharist from the Twelve to missionary apostles to presbyter-bishops."[25] We do not know how one got the right to preside and whether it was a permanent commission. A more plausible idea than a chain theory of apostolic succession is that "sacramental powers were part of the mission of the Church and that there were diverse ways in which the Church (or the communities) designated individuals to exercise those powers—the essential element always being church or community consent (which was tantamount to ordination . . .)."[26] The Didache seems to have been written just at the turning point at which presiding became the exclusive privilege of bishops and presbyters. In any case, says Brown, "by the end of the second century, if not earlier, the blending of the diverse New Testament roles has been carried through in its essentials, and the full-blown concept of the Christian priest emerges as the result."[27]

Transformations in Ministry

Two important factors led to the transformation of the apostolic Christian communities. The first of these was the delay in the return of Christ the Lord. As noted above, a presupposition of most New Testament literature is the imminent return of Christ to restore all things to God the Father. When Christ did not return, the Church had to begin to think in terms of organizational continuity. The second great surprise was the widespread and rapid growth of the Church, particularly among the Gentiles in those areas where Paul and other apostles preached throughout the Mediterranean world. In the early second century, the move from a fluid understanding of ministries (note above the practical identity of *presbyter* and *episcopos*) to a fixed expectation of leadership under the direction of the three ministries of bishop, presbyter, and deacon was one of the results of this organizational restructuring.

Ignatius of Antioch (d. 109–110) gives the first written witness to the monoepiscopate, that is, the leadership of one bishop in a diocese assisted by priests and deacons. The understanding of *episcopos* and *presbyter* as *sacerdos* is not sudden but gradual. Hervé Legrand summarizes an important body of research:

[25] Ibid., 41.
[26] Ibid., 41–2.
[27] Ibid., 43.

The perception of the president of the Eucharist as an explicitly sacerdotal figure is not attested before the beginning of the third century (Hippolytus, Tertullian, Cyprian). On the other hand, with all the witnesses we note that it is a fact, and most often it is axiomatic (Clement, Ignatius, Justin, Tertullian, Hippolytus, Cyprian and the canonical tradition deriving from Hippolytus) that those who preside over the life of the church preside at the eucharist.[28]

Thomas O'Meara offers two reasons why the permanent ministers came to be thought of as priests:

First, there was the natural desire in the midst of *sacerdotes* functioning in the cult of the emperor or in the cults imported from Egypt to have a priesthood. More important were the images and words of the Old Testament. In a largely gentile church, two centuries removed from the writings of Hebrews and I Corinthians, the Old Testament was read historically. An inspired page no longer struck Christians as a forecast of fulfillment in Christ but as a divine prescription.[29]

Clement of Rome and Cyprian of Carthage looked with admiration to the hierarchy of the Jewish temple, even though the early Christians had considered the sacrifice of Christ as the termination of a priestly hierarchy. The benefit of this move toward sacerdotalization of the clergy was the reinforcement of structure and order for the Church. There was a loss, however, in the move away from the pragmatic involvement of the laity in the Church's evangelization and ministry and toward a spiritualization of their life and faith that made them more observers than participants in the Church's cult and ministry.

Beginning in the fourth century, monasticism became a great source of strength for the Church. Monks were first of all an extra-canonical and non-clerical movement.[30] But by the sixth century, monasticism became a force for missionary expansion and along with that went a clerical ministry for the missionaries. Some bishops, like Augustine of Hippo, favored a communal life for their priests. Without going into detail here, we can say that by the end of the first millennium, the monastery set the tone for the Church.[31]

[28] Hervé Legrand, "The Presidence of the Eucharist according to the Ancient Tradition," *Worship* 53 (1979) 407. In the following pages, I follow the lead of O'Meara, *Theology of Ministry,* ch. 5: "The Metamorphoses of Ministry," 95–6.

[29] O'Meara, *Theology of Ministry,* 101–2.

[30] See Kevin Seasoltz, "A Western Monastic Perspective on Ordained Ministry," *A Concert of Charisms: Priesthood in the Context of Religious Life,* ed. Paul Hennessy (Mahwah, N.J.: Paulist Press, 1997) 25–60.

[31] O'Meara, *Theology of Ministry,* 105–6.

St. Augustine is usually acknowledged as establishing the tradition of common life for the clergy of a diocese. For Augustine in his diocese as for Canons Regular, the fundamental pastoral act is preaching. Not much pastoral ministry beyond that is described within this model, although obviously the normal pastoral work for the care of souls must have been part of the life of Augustinian presbyteral service.[32]

Benedictine monastic life is related to priesthood essentially in terms of the liturgical needs of the monastic community. Priesthood rarely came early in the life of a monk in the early days and it was given through the initiative of the abbot. It was not conferred as an ecclesiastical honor, but responded to a pragmatic need of the community. The purpose of ordination was to enable the monk to celebrate Mass, and no pastoral work outside the monastery was attached. Jean Leclercq calls this "an *ascetic* as distinct from a *pastoral* priesthood, but it could as readily be called a *contemplative* one. To allow the monk to say Mass alone was to give him more freedom for a life of solitude and prayer."[33] The sacramental ministry of monks, then, enjoys the special concession not to exercise a pastoral charge among the people, but to celebrate the sacraments within the monastic enclosure.

Ordained ministry was further transformed by the influence of the Hierarchies of Pseudo-Denys. Hierarchy came to be taken for granted in public and Church life in the thirteenth century. All offices were seen in a hierarchical relationship. Aquinas was deeply influenced by Denys.

> Aquinas sees three sacred activities in the church: the minister purifies, the priest illumines and purifies, the bishop brings to perfection and illumines in a special way. If monks are on a rung beneath this hierarchy of active office, Aquinas argued that his Dominican friars should approach episcopal rank for they are the Pope's preachers.[34]

When the Dionysian hierarchy is applied to the church, all diversity is seen in a vertical direction. Ministry (which literally means service) becomes swallowed up by authority.

By reason of a hierarchical worldview in which earthly officeholders are supposed to mirror (even sacramentalize) the structure of celestial relationships between God and the angelic hierarchies, Aquinas (as spokesman for a medieval worldview) saw the bishop not only as an authority in law and jurisdiction, but as a principle of supernatural life:

---

[32] David Power, "Theologies of Religious Life and Priesthood," *A Concert of Charisms,* ed. Paul Hennessy, 68–70.

[33] Ibid.

[34] O'Meara, *Theology of Ministry,* 111. Cf. Aquinas, 4 Sent. 24, 3, 2.

the bishop illumines and animates other Christians. This aspect of medieval thought seems to be deeply entrenched in the current expressions of a theology of holy orders.[35]

Aquinas articulated the theological model for priesthood within the mendicant tradition.

> Religious [by reason of their state of life] are committed by vow to a lifelong pursuit of the perfection of charity and are taken up with observances, prayer, study, and discipline that lead to their own holiness. Ordination, however, is ordered to the service of others in ministry and requires that one be able to lead others on the way of charity.[36]

Aquinas defined priesthood principally as the power to consecrate the body and blood of Christ in the Eucharist acting *in persona Christi*. Aquinas did not equate the relation of the minister to Christ with representing Christ in his own personality, however, but rather with representing Christ's action in the priest's sacramental and ritual action.

The relationship of priesthood to religious life in the mendicant tradition suggests that for the clerical religious, priesthood is an office that serves to allow the religious to fulfill the ministerial demands of the charism undertaken in their profession.[37] In the mendicant situation, ordination to priesthood arises out of pastoral necessity, "as the needed authorization to preach and to hear confessions in their mission among Christ's poor, an authorization that comes in a particular way through papal jurisdiction."[38]

Positively, the principles of Dionysian hierarchy helped stabilize the ministry of the Church in difficult times. Yet ministry is thus formally limited to bishops and priests and tends to be reduced to the administration of the sacraments. Priesthood comes to be defined as *potestas in corpus eucharisticum;* other functions recede into the background. As the Middle Ages proceed through increasing political and social crisis (especially the years of the Black Plague), the idea of absolute ordination—ordaining people independently of a pastoral charge so that they will be able to celebrate the Mass—increases. Chancery priests, ordained to say Masses for dead nobility by benefice, became more frequent (along with the multi-

---

[35] For a treatment of Denys' influence and ideas see Andrew Louth, *The Origins of the Christian Mystical Tradition: From Plato to Denys* (Oxford: Clarendon Press, 1981). The hierarchical ideas of Denys are evident in the texts from CCC cited above.

[36] Power, "Theologies of Religious Life and Priesthood," 71.

[37] See Paul J. Philibert, "Priesthood within the Context of Religious Life," *Being a Priest Today,* ed. Donald Goergen (Collegeville: The Liturgical Press, 1992) 73–4.

[38] Power, "Theologies of Religious Life and Priesthood," 72–3.

plication of clergy who scarcely understood the Latin words they said). One result was an increasing loss of contact between the clergy and the laity. Civil law also increased privileges allotted to the clergy. The seeds for chaos and crisis were being planted.

Luther and the Protestant Reformation brought about another new moment in priesthood. "They challenged celibacy and monasticism so that they might abolish the class system within the church. Luther preached the priesthood of all the baptized and the dignity of every human occupation."[39] Luther found a warrant for ministry and priestly dignity in the New Testament for all the baptized.

Bernard Cooke reminds us that Luther's teaching about the basic or common priesthood of all believers was fundamental to his revision of Church order. This was not a new teaching, of course, but its significance had been obscured by centuries of treating bishops and presbyters as the sacerdotium of the Church. In addition, medieval practice had deprived the laity almost entirely of any active role in the celebration of Eucharist. So Luther made a great contribution by calling attention to the New Testament teaching on universal priesthood.[40] Some commentators even saw in the decrees of Vatican II a vindication of Luther's fundamental interests in Church reform.[41]

Parallel to Luther's reform, John Calvin struggled to create a Christian city where life and worship would be transformed and sanctified. In Calvin's reform, there would be neither hierarchy, sacrifice, nor mediator. While Calvin drew from the New Testament four ministries— pastor, deacon, elder, and teacher—in time the pastor absorbed the others. For him, the service of the word was central and the minister of the word presided at Eucharist.[42]

[39] O'Meara, *Theology of Ministry,* 114. Regarding the problem of illiterate priests and priests without pastoral ministries, see William Wright, "From 'Clerk-in-orders' to 'Pastoral Minister': The Reformation of Ordained Ministry," *Priesthood: The Hard Questions,* ed. Gerald Gleeson (Newton, N.S.W.: E. J. Dwyer, 1993) 31–2.

[40] Bernard Cooke, *Ministry to Word and Sacraments: History and Theology* (Philadelphia: Fortress Press, 1976) 594–5.

[41] See Jaroslav Pelikan's response to the Constitution on the Sacred Liturgy in *The Documents of Vatican II,* ed. Walter Abbott and Joseph Gallagher (New York: Guild Press, 1966) 181: "In fact, several of its fundamental principles represent the acceptance, however belated, of the liturgical program set forth by the Reformers: the priesthood of all believers; the requirement 'that the faithful take part knowingly, actively, and fruitfully.'" See also Joseph Ratzinger, *Theological Highlights of Vatican II* (New York: Paulist Press, 1966) 175–6.

[42] O'Meara, *Theology of Ministry,* 115; Cooke, *Ministry to Word and Sacraments,* 598–9, 146.

One result of the reformation emphasis was the development of a new understanding of the pastoral role of the Catholic priest. Along with this came a great centralization in liturgy, canon law, catechetics, and administration codified by the reforms of the Council of Trent. The Church came to be seen as emanating from papal authority, leading to a purely vertical interpretation of the hierarchical principle and a consequent de-emphasis of the active and apostolic purpose of the non-ordained.[43]

The Church's increased efficiency is expressed in a new wave of missionary activity, the blossoming of seminaries, and the development of new religious orders. The missions grew and moved into every area of the world, but "the faith was propagated in the seventeenth century as the extension of Rome. The ministry was tied to a certain form of education, to celibacy, to Western rituals. The leaders of the new churches of Africa, Asia, and South America were papal vicars, and local ministry never really surfaced."[44]

The Reformation helped to bring about a modern world that opened up sympathetically to the Enlightenment. The autonomy of secular social structures and, later, scientific theories such as evolution (seemingly hostile to Christian theology) became dominant forces in society. In the face of cultural hostility, the Church turned inward. The French Revolution (in its multiple expressions) led to the expulsion of religious and priests from their religious houses and parishes. Understandably, bishops, priests, and religious began to feel victimized by society.

The spirituality of the French School (shaped by the Oratorians and the Sulpicians) became dominant. The seventeenth century was dealing with a reaction to the Protestant Reformation, with the need to reform the clergy in Europe (especially in France), and with the influence of Pietism throughout Europe. The basic theological intuition of the French School is the intimate union between the priest and Christ the mediator. Olier, the founder of the Sulpicians, wrote of the special union of the priest with Christ, priest and victim, that pervades the entire life of the priest. Priests are, in his words, "in Jesus Christ and with Jesus Christ . . . both priests and victims for the sins of the world."[45] Thus in the Sulpician view, the presbyter is a sacramental representation of Christ not only in his liturgical action, but in his pastoral ministry and in his person.

---

[43] O'Meara, *Theology of Ministry,* 118.

[44] Ibid., 119–20. We might note that to this day there is surprisingly little ferment for inculturation in theology and popular piety. The most notable exceptions are the localized movements in some of the African churches (particularly Zaire) and the developments in North American Latino centers of pastoral and liturgical studies like the Mexican American Cultural Center.

[45] Ibid.

The mystical identification of the priest with Christ in the Sulpician model is a major factor leading to the strong emphasis upon the transformation of the ordained priest into a different and consecrated person, whose own experience and emotions are sacramental symbols of Christ's love for and generosity toward the Church, and whose holiness demands a separation and distinctness from the ordinary currents of social life. A figure representative of this spirituality is the Curé d'Ars. John Paul II frequently refers to him as an exemplar for priests.[46]

However, such a model of ministry is inward and hidden, not evangelizing and public. Theological romanticism leads to a quiet conviction that one is loved and blessed by God, even though the circumstances of life are conflictual. But this romantic theology is otherworldly, mystical, and ultimately pessimistic about social existence.

This examination of transformations in ministry offers these two insights: (1) it gives us an idea of the many transformations that priestly ministry has experienced through the centuries, and (2) it explains how the pre-conciliar theology (exemplified by the meditations of Bishop Angrisani seen above) came to be what it was. Of course, the next question is: what were the hopes of the Second Vatican Council and where is the development of its renewal at present?

The Council's Decree on Priestly Life and Ministry

Vatican II's document on priesthood came from the fourth session of the council, which began in September 1965. An immense amount of work lay before the conciliars, including Schema 13 (which became *Gaudium et spes*). Paul VI set a tone of hope and optimism in an opening address in which he said, among other things: "In this world the Church is not an end but a means. It serves all humankind."[47] As with other topic areas, the draft text submitted to the council met with great criticism. Much work was done (by Yves Congar among others) to develop the text that finally became *Presbyterorum ordinis*.[48] In the following paragraphs I will attempt to indicate the major theological positions of *Presbyterorum ordinis,* following the text in its own development.

Acknowledging that all the faithful are made a holy priesthood in the Spirit, PO 2 says: "Therefore there is no such thing as a member [of

[46] John Paul II, *Gift and Mystery* (New York: Doubleday, 1996) 57: "Saint John Mary Vianney astonishes us because in him we can see the power of grace working through human limitations." CCC also cites the Curé d'Ars in §1589.

[47] Ratzinger, *Theological Highlights of Vatican II,* 138.

[48] *Fifty Years of Catholic Theology: Conversations with Yves Congar,* ed. and into. by Bernard Lauret (Philadelphia: Fortress Press, 1988) 3–5.

the church] who does not have a share in the mission of the whole body." Immediately, however, PO goes on to indicate that the Lord appointed certain men as ministers with "the sacred power of order, that of offering sacrifice and forgiving sins, [who] exercised the priestly office publicly in behalf of men and women in the name of Christ." Designating priests as "co-workers with the episcopal order," PO 2 teaches that priesthood is conferred by the anointing of the Holy Spirit, which "so conforms them to Christ the Priest . . . that they are able to act in the person of Christ the head." Since priests are apostles, they fulfill the sacred task of offering the gospel to all peoples "so that all who belong to [the People of God], sanctified as they are by the Holy Spirit, may offer themselves 'a living sacrifice, holy and acceptable to God.'"

Priests of the New Testament are set apart within the People of God, but not so as to be separated from the people. They are dispensers of "a life other than that of this earth" (§3). They would be pastorally ineffective, however, if they remained aloof from their circumstances. The first task of priests is to preach the gospel of God to all (§4). Their ministry of the word is exercised in different ways according to the needs of different circumstances. However, preaching the word within the celebration of Mass is particularly important because "there is an indivisible unity between the proclamation of the Lord's death and resurrection, the response of the hearers and the offering itself."

PO 5 teaches that priests are made sharers in Christ's priesthood; they act as ministers of Christ, who through his Spirit exercises his priestly role for our benefit in the liturgy. The liturgy is the center of the life of the Church and priests must "teach the faithful to offer the divine victim to God the Father in the sacrifice of the Mass and with the victim to make an offering of their lives" (§5). Finally, priests participate in Christ's role as pastor and head in the exercise of a ministry to build up the Church. Their objective is to lead all believers to active charity and to liberty. "Very little good will be achieved by ceremonies, however beautiful, or societies, however flourishing, if they are not directed toward training people to reach Christian maturity" (§6). The poor and the weak are particularly commended to the pastoral care of priests.

PO 7 indicates the special relationship of priests as co-workers and assistants with the bishop, and the parallel relation of priests to the presbyterium of priests who, with the bishop, make up the ministerial family of a local church. PO 8 exhorts priests, whether diocesan or regular, to assist one another as fellow-workers in the service of truth. It exhorts hospitality and kindness and the sharing of goods.

PO 9 reminds priests that they were themselves reborn in the font of baptism and are thus related as brothers to all the baptized. Their relations with the lay faithful should be one of service: "to be sincere in their appreciation and promotion of lay people's dignity and of the special role the laity have to play in the church's mission" (§9). PO 10 and 11 are concerned about the pastoral distribution of priests, cooperation for missions, and the importance of fostering vocations.

PO 12 and 13 return to the three-fold structure of analyzing priestly ministry (prophet, priest, and pastor) and analyze how each one of these ministries leads to growth in holiness. PO 14 and 15 exhort to unity, harmony, humility, and obedience.

PO 16 addresses celibacy. The council recommends the continuation of the norm of ecclesiastical celibacy for priests and bishops. However, it acknowledges the distinct and different discipline of the Eastern churches. A comment is appropriate here, perhaps. At the time of the debate over PO, Paul VI forbade public discussion of celibacy, decreeing that only written opinions would be accepted but no further debate on that topic was allowed in the conciliar assembly. Thus it is interesting to note, in an early response to the council by Joseph Ratzinger, the following observation: "In view of the shortage of priests in many areas, the Church cannot avoid reviewing this question [of celibacy] quietly. Evading it is impossible in view of the responsibility to preach the gospel within the context of our times."[49]

PO 17 to 21 deal with the topics of voluntary poverty, the interior life, study, and social security. While some of these texts are of continuing interest, they do not bear immediately upon the theology of priesthood. PO ends with a conclusion and exhortation (§22) that acknowledges how much cultural change can lead to a sense of the "apparent fruitlessness" of pastoral work and to "bitter loneliness" for priests. However, PO urges that we remember that God is still at work in the world. The Holy Spirit of God, "urging the church to open new avenues of approach to the modern world, also suggests and fosters suitable adaptations of the priestly ministry." Priests are cooperating in God's hidden plan (Eph 3:9); therefore, they must walk by faith until the work of God is revealed. The last word of PO is a testimony of thanks to all the priests of the world.

---

[49] Ratzinger, *Theological Highlights of Vatican II,* 178. The Latin American episcopate at the council strongly expressed their concern about the catastrophic situation of the Church in their region and urged a married clergy in Latin America: see Henri Fesquet, *The Drama of Vatican II* (New York: Random House, 1967) 693.

Two Commentaries

A 1966 commentary on the work of the council by Joseph Ratzinger made the following observations about PO:

> Luther's protest against the [medieval] Catholic notion of priesthood was really based on the fact that in the Catholic view the priesthood was almost exclusively a sacrificial priesthood. . . . The medieval view saw the priesthood fundamentally as an office charged with conciliating an offended God. The incontestable weakness of this position was that in its effort to find universal concepts, it gave insufficient attention to the special historical character of the NT priesthood. It went too far in conforming Christian priesthood to the general idea of priesthood as found in the history of religions.[50]

Ratzinger stresses how PO understands priesthood as pertaining to all believers. It moves beyond a one-sided emphasis on priesthood as sacrament. It shows how the priestly ministry of the ordained is ordered to the service of praise and obedience of the People of God. "This means that the eucharist is not simply a self-centered act of consecration and sacrifice performed by the priest, as though it were irrelevant whether lay people participated in it or not."[51]

Ratzinger praises the phrase "presiding over" to describe the leadership of the priest in eucharistic celebration: "It is the priest's task to serve as a *pater familias* . . . and to say grace over the Lord's supper on behalf of God's own household."[52] Thus a seamless unity is achieved that draws into one the preaching of the gospel, the sacrifice, the consecration of the offering, the animation of the assembly, the glorification of God, and the exchange and sharing at the table of the Lord. Priestly ministry can no longer be imagined as exclusively ritual in its focus, but also concerned with leadership in the whole of life. Ratzinger then concludes that the perspectives of PO should have far-reaching consequences for ecumenical dialogue and for growth in the spiritual self-awareness of Catholics.

Edward Schillebeeckx published a similar brief commentary on the decrees. His observations about PO include the following:

> This decree transcends the traditional image of the priest, which was defined by his liturgical relation to the eucharist. It draws a pastoral image of him which does not deny his function in religious worship, but incorpo-

---

[50] Ratzinger, *Theological Highlights of Vatican II,* 176.
[51] Ibid., 177.
[52] Ibid.

rates it in a larger entity; the prophetic service of the word and the pastoral leadership and guidance of the church community are thus reappraised.[53]

PO takes the spirituality of the priest out of its former monastic framework and roots it in official ministry. On another topic, "for the first time since the Middle Ages, a Council document admits that celibacy is not of the essence of priesthood," even as it recognizes the affinity between ministry and celibacy and advocates the continuation of the canonical practice for the Latin church.[54] In some way, then, the document ceases to surround the priest with an aura of mystification, but begins to treat him as a real human being. PO offers a nuanced discussion of the collaboration between priest and layman.

Schillebeeckx makes reference to a controversy in which the French Dominicans were deeply involved, the "worker-priest" movement. He notes that the decree gives its blessing to a priestly life in which manual work is used as an expression of pastoral presence. "Compared with the condemnation of the association between priesthood and manual work— almost on the very eve of the Council—this is really unbelievably new."[55]

Summary Ideas

To conclude this reflection on the text of the council's decree, it seems evident that a certain number of developments appeared within PO that are of great theological significance. Among the most important, in my view, are the following:

- the ministry of the priest is three-fold, modeled on the witness of the New Testament, that is, prophetic, priestly, and pastoral;
- the ministry of the word stands as the source of the cultic action of the community, and great emphasis is placed upon this ministry as fundamental to the presbyter's responsibilities;
- the priesthood of the ordained, which differs "essentially and not only in degree" (LG 10) from the common priesthood of the faithful, is interrelated and ordered to the priestly action of the people who "are invited and led to offer themselves, their works and all creation in union with Christ" (PO 5);
- PO does not define priesthood in terms of power, but of responsibility (or ministry); and

[53] Edward Schillebeeckx, *The Real Achievement of Vatican II* (New York: Herder & Herder, 1967) 42.
[54] Ibid., 43.
[55] Ibid., 44.

- finally, the goal of the priest is the development of the Christian maturity of the people, which includes leading them to the full expression of their own capacity to build community and to become agents of charity and evangelization in the world (PO 6).

The explicit teaching of a relation between the two priesthoods of laity and ordained is an emphasis with great potential for further development. As Daniel Donovan says:

> The hierarchy is not a hierarchy of grace but of service. The common priesthood and its sacrifice have to do with life . . . the ministerial priesthood does not fit in at a particular point on the scale of holiness, but is rather of a different order. By definition it is a ministry, a service, through which Christ the one priest continues to sanctify and build up his priestly community.[56]

Some Particular Critical Points

There are three critical points on which extended discussion is needed. These are the following: (1) the questionable adequacy of PO's image of priestly service, (2) the theological questions surrounding the phrase *in persona Christi,* and (3) the right of a local church to Eucharist. Let me examine these in some detail.

Priesthood, Ministry, and Religious Life

John O'Malley, S.J., has raised a question that has implications for ecclesiology. What, he asks, is the vision of priestly identity in PO? His answer is as follows: PO describes priestly ministry in terms of three essential components: (1) it is a ministry to the faithful, (2) taking place in a stable community of faith, (3) done by the clergy in hierarchical union with the bishops.[57] These conditions describe the situation of diocesan clergy, but not that of religious clergy. For example, with respect to ministry to the faithful, it is above all religious who are the missionaries and evangelizers of the Church; that often puts them in the situation of extending ministry to unbelievers—those who are not among the faithful. The imagination, perseverance, and creativity required for the constant reinvention of the evangelical mission are thus not communicated very well by PO's text or vision.

---

[56] Daniel Donovan, *What Are They Saying About the Ministerial Priesthood?* (Mahwah, N.J.: Paulist Press, 1992) 8.

[57] John W. O'Malley, *Tradition and Transition: Historical Perspectives on Vatican II* (Wilmington, Del.: Michael Glazier, 1989) 128–9; see John W. O'Malley, "One Priesthood: Two Traditions," *A Concert of Charisms,* ed. Paul Hennessy, 13–14.

As to the second aspect, ministry taking place in a stable community of faith, regular clergy are commonly involved in a variety of ministries that are not related to the territorial parish. The first example, of course, would be the itinerant preacher whose mission it is to go from place to place to evangelize, catechize, and preach. However, we can also think of those clerical religious who are engaged in research, scholarship, writing, and scientific collaboration, none of which characteristically is rooted in a parochial site. A different kind of distance from PO's vision can be noted relative to monastic foundations, which, while stable, are not parochial. Reflection on the history of religious orders would lead to countless examples showing the insufficiency of PO's description.

Third, as to "ministry done by clergy in hierarchical union with the order of bishops," religious need to examine both their history of exemption and the current apostolic needs of communities of regular clergy to have international, inter-diocesan, and multicultural ministries. The present elaboration of the code and the context of PO do not at all assure that the religious ordinary (the major superior of clerical religious) has maintained the recognition and jurisdiction that developed historically or that this autonomy is adequately protected at present.[58]

The Council of Trent designated preaching as the *praecipuum munus* of the bishop[59] and thus contributed to the revival of this ministry of the word of God. Nonetheless, reacting to Protestant attacks on Roman practices, Trent focused more on the sacraments than anything else, and "for Trent the sacrament of orders relates to office and hierarchy, and it confers the power to administer the sacraments, most especially to confect the eucharist."[60] So ultimately the prophetic dynamic of preaching became secondary to the ritual dynamic of sacramental celebration.

At Trent, there were practically no abbots present and the only voting members were bishops. The Tridentine bishops were concerned to strengthen their authority within their dioceses and with pastors in their parishes. This led to the consequent development of a pattern of "parochial conformity," establishing a pattern according to which the parish is seen as the site of all ministries. Clearly Trent contributed to this inclination. Yet, says O'Malley,

> From the sixth century even until long after the Council of Trent the parish church was only one element in a vast and lumbering array of other institutions like monasteries, priories, shrines, manor chapels, oratories,

[58] Seasoltz, "A Western Monastic Perspective," 25–6.
[59] O'Malley, *Tradition and Transition,* 155.
[60] Ibid.

guilds, confraternities, third orders, sodalities, schools, and collegiate churches (to which list "retreat houses" would at a certain point be added) where in one way or another Christians satisfied their devotion.[61]

O'Malley goes on to point out that both the Dominicans and the Jesuits were founded precisely to do ministry in exceptional ways. He develops the argument that their mandate or mission to ministry comes not from ordination, but from their charism. Addressing the tenuous significance of PO's conviction that priestly ministry is done under the scrutiny of the bishop, O'Malley reminds us that the Jesuits, for example, received the charge from Pope John Paul II, in his allocation to the General Congregation of the Jesuits, to be committed to ministries like "ecumenism, the deeper study of relations with non-Christian religions, and the dialogue of the Church with cultures," and "the evangelizing action of the Church to promote justice, connected with world peace."[62] Further, religious orders and congregations have been the ones to have a special ministry toward "orphans, young vagrants, prostitutes, the alienated—or, on the other hand, those laity seeking to devote themselves to God and their neighbor in more challenging and unconventional ways."[63]

O'Malley argues for a better integration of our understanding of priesthood and ecclesiology by rooting the discussion in a more adequate historical framework. We need to achieve a better integration of the non-parochial aspects of apostolate with the apostolate as expressed in parishes. O'Malley ends up noting the healthy "division of labor" that has prevailed for centuries between diocesan and regular clergy. Diocesan clergy have ministered primarily in parishes. Religious did this also, of course, but they were founded precisely to express the ministerial priorities of their own particular charism. Therefore, the teaching of Vatican II on the topic of priesthood has to be reviewed and enlarged to acknowledge this division of labor and its significance in interpreting the theology of priesthood.[64]

Elsewhere I have written that in the light of *Perfectae caritatis,* "the identity of the priest who is also a religious is derived more fundamentally from his religious charism than from his ordination."[65] In this sense the priestly office of the regular clergy is in the service of a more fundamental religious identity, which is the following of Christ according to

[61] Ibid., 159.
[62] Ibid., 163, n. 86.
[63] Ibid.
[64] Ibid., 171. See Paul Philibert, afterword in *A Concert of Charisms,* 184–97.
[65] Philibert, "Priesthood within the Context of Religious Life," 88.

the charism of his religious family. Regular clergy maintain practices of religious discipline and spirituality that have been developed precisely to form a quality of faith and a spirit of ministry identifiable as pertaining to a particular religious charism. As just noted, this charism frequently carries religious clergy beyond the confines of the parishes; indeed, a crisis we now must face is how to free many regular clergy from parishes (where they do not belong) so as to send them on mission to their priority ministries deriving from the original inspiration of their institute.

Both the *Lineamenta* for the synod on religious and *Vita consecrata* indicate that the fundamental responsibility of regular clergy, as of all religious, is to bring to the church in the locales where they minister the full force and spirit of the charism of their institute.⁶⁶ This question deserves the careful surveillance of religious at a time in which the shortage of diocesan clergy frequently occasions the invitation for regular clergy to supply priestly services in diocesan parishes.

This question about PO's understanding of the identity of priests may also be related to a lingering tendency to overemphasize the cultic. The novelty of reestablishing the three-fold dynamic of presbyter as prophet, priest, and pastor was such that the council itself did not carry through on the power of this insight. O'Malley's challenge, therefore, is to address this problem and to carry out a thorough-going application of PO's theological insights about priestly identity that would explore the full riches of the prophetic and pastoral dimensions of presbyteral ministry.

Priestly Representation: In persona Ecclesiae et Christi

Both *Lumen gentium* and *Presbyterorum ordinis* clearly state that the priest acts *in persona Christi*. Some contemporary Roman documents also use the expression that the priest represents the people *in persona Ecclesiae*.⁶⁷ As we have seen above in *The Catechism of the Catholic Church,* Roman documents in the post-conciliar period have used these formulas to ground their argument against women's ordination, and *Mulieris dignitatem* states that the priest acting *in persona Christi* represents nuptial imagery or, as David Power puts it, "the ordained represents Christ as bridegroom to the church's bride,"⁶⁸ and thus the ordained must have a

---

⁶⁶ *Lineamenta: The Consecrated Life and Its Role in the Church and in the World* (Washington, D.C.: United States Catholic Conference, 1994) esp. §§39 and 40. Also *Vita Consecrata: Post-Synodal Apostolic Exhortation of the Holy Father John Paul II* (Rome: Vatican Press, 1996) esp. §§30 and 48.

⁶⁷ David N. Power, "Church Order: The Need for Redress," *Worship* 71 (1997) 296–7, esp. 300.

⁶⁸ Ibid., 299. See *Christifideles Laici: Post-Synodal Exhortation of His Holiness John Paul II* (1988) §51: "This is a practice that the Church has always found in the expressed

physical resemblance to the maleness of Christ in order to realize the symbolic dynamics of this imagery. But, as David Coffey has pointed out, Rome is cautious about referring to the priest's status *in persona Ecclesiae,* since "it would make the priest simply a delegate of the community."[69] As Coffey says, it is desirable for the priest to be a delegate of the community in some sense, but it is more important that he be called by God and appointed by legitimate authority.

Coffey posits a dialectical relationship between the two expressions. He speaks of the phrase *in persona Christi* as representing a descending theology, having as its point of departure God's initiative and as its term human experience. On the other hand, the phrase *in persona Ecclesiae* represents an ascending theology, beginning from ecclesial experience and rising to the sphere of God. These are two complementary ways of doing theology, both having foundations in the New Testament. Coffey notes that, given the conservatism of the Roman magisterium, this dialectical relationship probably explains their practice of assigning primacy to the phrase *in persona Christi* over the phrase *in persona Ecclesiae* in their theological statements.[70]

Elements that might be thought to pertain only to the descending approach may usually be discovered in an ascending approach as well. Let me cite Coffey's example:

> The best example I can give . . . centers on the role of the Holy Spirit in the incarnation. In the traditional descending Christology, derived ultimately from St. John's gospel, there is no essential role for the Holy Spirit

---

will of Christ . . . who called only men to be his apostles; a practice that can be understood from the rapport between Christ, the Spouse, and his Bride, the Church." It is interesting to observe, however, that historian Henri Fesquet reported the following statement of council theologian Jean Daniélou, later a cardinal of the Church: "I am partisan to the idea that the Council authorize the ordination of deaconesses without delay, indeed before the end of the Council. As for an eventual female priesthood, there is no basic theological objection to it." See Henri Fesquet, *The Drama of Vatican II* (New York: Random House, 1967) 707. Daniélou was undoubtedly considered one of the premiere patristic historians of this century. Schillebeeckx argues: "Why . . . must the fact that, given the culture of the time, Jesus chose twelve men as apostles, in this connection suddenly acquire a theological significance while at the same time the similar fact that this same Jesus for the most part, and perhaps even entirely, chose only married men is not allowed any theological significance . . . ?" John Bowden, *Edward Schillebeeckx: In Search of the Kingdom of God* (New York: Crossroad, 1983) 86.

[69] David Coffey, "Priestly Representation and Women's Ordination," *Priesthood: The Hard Questions,* ed. Gerald Gleeson, 80.

[70] Ibid., 81.

in the incarnation, though the Spirit is recognized to be present to Jesus, and indeed present "without measure." But in ascending Christology, based on the synoptic tradition, the Holy Spirit bestowed creatively on Jesus by the Father is the very spirit of sonship for him, anointing him only-begotten Son of God.[71]

Applying this to our two phrases, it becomes clearer how the phrase *in persona Christi* is linked to a descending theology and evokes God's call and the transforming power of the sacramental grace of holy orders. Yet taking the perspective of an ascending theology, *in persona Ecclesiae* is seen as an indispensable prerequisite, a foundation of the condition of acting *in persona Christi*. *In persona Ecclesiae* is a necessary stage toward the acquisition of the status of one acting *in persona Christi*. A general New Testament principle, indeed, is that "ascending theology is the presupposition of descending theology, not vice versa."[72]

Analogically we are speaking here of the priest as a "sacrament"— and so we can apply to his symbolic person the traditional terms of *sacramentum* (sign), *res et sacramentum* (symbolic reality), and *res* (grace). Following Coffey and Edward J. Kilmartin, this leads us to say that the sign value of the priest is his action in the name of Christ, to draw the community together; his symbolic reality is to lead the community to respond to God's word and enter into encounter with God through the Christian sacraments; and the grace *(res)* of the priest-as-sacrament is to animate the community's transformation into a new creation made one in Christ the head. This insight leads to understanding the priest's representation of Christ as indirect rather than direct. That is to say, the priest does not represent Christ apart from the assembly, but precisely as one within the assembly, drawing Church to become aware of its graced destiny. Although his leadership is essential, its goal is to unite himself with the Church rather than to stand out over against the Church.[73]

[71] Ibid. This same argument is developed again in David Coffey's "The Common and the Ordained Priesthood," *Theological Studies* 58 (1997) 209–10.

[72] Coffey, "Priestly Representation," 81.

[73] Ibid., 82. Here Coffey quotes Kilmartin as concluding: "The priest first represents (denotes) the Church in its sacramental activity and secondly represents (connotes) Christ the Head of the Church." E. Kilmartin, "Bishop and Presbyter as Representative of the Church and Christ," *Women Priests: A Catholic Commentary on the Vatican Declaration,* ed. Leonard Swidler and Arlene Swidler (New York: Paulist Press, 1977) 296. Coffey goes on to distance himself from the phrase "connotes" used by Kilmartin as being too weak to express the fullness of the christological representation involved.

Note that Dulles and Ratzinger disagree explicitly with this position: "The church . . . requires an official ministry that stands with Christ and represents him to the

In a more recent article, Coffey cites the German theologian Georg Hintzen as follows to explain the ascending sacramentalism of the priest:

> Saying *"in persona Christi et Ecclesiae"* shows that we need to understand the ministry of the official priest "sacramentally," i.e., *in genere signi:* the priest is the sacramental real-symbol for both Christ the high priest and God's priestly people of the Church. On the level of sacramental rite, he presents in the sign that which in this external sign-reality happens (or is to happen) inwardly: the communio of head and members in their common surrender to the Father;—surrender of the high priest (which has opened again for human beings the way to the Father) and the answering surrender of human beings (who follow Christ on his way to the Father). In the one person of the priest the unity of the *totus Christus, caput et membra,* finds at the same time its symbolic expression.[74]

Coffey adds that the priest represents Christ sacramentally, making visible and active in the Church an invisible reality (Christ the head), while to his representation of the Church, which is already visible, he adds "headship, apostolate, or leadership to the action of this group of believers, in order to constitute them as Church in the full sense." Apart from this presbyteral ministry, believers are only a human group, unable to represent the Church fully. The priest's representation, however, by no means renders the people's action superfluous, "for just as their faith is positive and active, so is their priesthood."[75] A simpler way to underline the central truth here is expressed by Albert Rouet, who says:

> If we come back to the question of the content of this work that is liturgy, the following becomes clear: 1) it is for the sake of resurrection life, 2) it is for transformation, because it is conversion, and 3) its purpose is to bring corporate life into being, for it is building up the Body of Christ. The liturgy is the art of living.[76]

This entire discussion about priestly symbolism must be kept within the essential theological context of what priestly leadership is about. Priests are neither liturgical dramatists nor supernatural bankers. They are lead-

---

community." Dulles, *The Priestly Office,* 22. See also Donovan, *What Are They Saying About the Ministerial Priesthood?* 71–2.

[74] Coffey, "The Common and the Ordained Priesthood," 233, citing and translating Georg Hintzen, "Das gemeinsame Priestertum aller Gläubigen und das besondere Priestertum des Dienstes in der oïkumenischen Diskussion," *Catholica* 45 (1991) 44–77.

[75] Ibid., 234.

[76] Albert Rouet, *Liturgy and the Arts,* trans. Paul Philibert (Collegeville: The Liturgical Press, 1997) 6.

ers of a people whose lives are brought into unity with the sacrifice of Christ and lifted to God in the gift of this rite that is a sacrament of encounter with God. Rouet again is emphatic: "[The people's] profane moments are not empty; liturgy deciphers the secret fullness of the ordinary. Preparation for liturgy is an exercise in waiting, watching in order to move subtly toward the integration of ordinary experiences of life with the heart of life."[77] Or again: "So liturgy is about the truth of being human, what it is that makes humanity really live and what helps it to enter into the true human vocation to divine life."[78]

Coffey responds to an objection made to his thesis that the priest is a dialectical sacramental symbol (in the sense just described). This objection argues that the priest's representation of Christ places him into the very character of Christ "identifying himself with Christ's own words and gestures."[79] Imagine the Mass as a sacred drama with the priest playing the role of Christ. The Roman declarations about the priest representing Christ in his maleness and the explanation that this is based upon the nuptial imagery required by the biblical tradition reinforce the idea that the institution narrative within the Mass is the critical and essential moment within which the sacrament is confected.

This theological perspective runs into serious difficulties, however, as Coffey explains again. It isolates the institution narrative—the moment of consecration—from the rest of the liturgical action. It ignores the structure of the Eucharistic Prayers, composed, as they are, of a variety of elements within which the institution narrative is but one moment and the *epiclesis* (the invocation of the Holy Spirit) is another. Further, turning the Mass into a sacred drama isolates the priest as the principal actor and separates him from the faithful, turning them into an audience (even if they participate as in "living theater").[80]

Coffey argues that an examination of the Eucharistic Prayers reveals that they are not structured as a drama. Even though the priest uses the words of Christ at the institution narrative, he does not play his part as in a theater piece. The Eucharistic Prayer is not drama, but narrative. The priest speaks throughout in the third person. Even in the pronunciation of the words of the consecration, the priest is continuing the narrative,

[77] Ibid., 82.
[78] Ibid., 168.
[79] Coffey, "Priestly Representation," 83.
[80] Ibid. Coffey says, "If the priest acts as representative of the church, it is the 'apostolic church' that he represents, which stands in historical and ontological continuity with that of the apostles" (82). Therefore, the priest acts not "in the person" but "in the name" of the apostles in order to express the Church's apostolic fidelity.

which always includes, "On the night before he died, Jesus took bread and said to his disciples . . . ." The priest maintains his direct representation of the Church and his identity as its minister throughout the sacred action.

Coffey's conclusion is that St. Thomas is incorrect at this point in implicitly suggesting that the priest's way of acting *in persona Christi* at the moment of consecration is exclusively christological and descending, as opposed to pneumatological and ascending (as well). The priest's representation of Christ when he acts *in persona Christi* remains indirect. "His direct representation is of the church, and it includes his commission to celebrate the liturgy by virtue of apostolic succession."[81] Coffey summarizes by saying that the priest in logical (not temporal) order acts *in persona Ecclesiae* where *"Ecclesiae"* means the earthly church; then he acts *in persona Christi,* where *"Christi"* designates Christ the head; and finally he acts either *in persona Ecclesiae* or *Christi* where *"Ecclesiae"* and *"Christi"* each has the same designation—"the whole church or the whole Christ, head and members."[82]

David Power covers much of the same ground as Coffey in his article in *Worship* entitled "Church Order: The Need for Redress." Power also agrees that it was Thomas's view that in reciting the words of the institution narrative within the canon, the priest consecrates and sacrifices. He then adds, "at best, from this point of view, the rest of the Canon seems an ornament to the words of Christ."[83] Power disagrees that it is possible that the intention of the Church should be for the priest to go back and forth representing Christ in the historical words of the narrative and then immediately changing to represent the Church in the rest of the prayers. Citing the very important article by P.-M. Gy on the role of the "We" in the Eucharistic Prayer, Power says, "surely liturgical scholars have done enough to show by careful literary and theological investigation that the supper narratives cannot be taken out of the context of the prayer through which they were incorporated into liturgy."[84]

The Eucharistic Prayers were meant to be prayed in the person of Christ acting within his body; the Last Supper narrative is always drawn into these prayers by indirect locution. This commemorative act of the Church is realized through proclamation, rite, and prayer. To interpret

[81] Ibid., 84.

[82] Ibid., 88.

[83] Power, "Church Order," 301.

[84] Ibid., 303; where Power cites Pierre-Marie Gy, "Le 'nous' de la priere eucharistique," *La Maison-Dieu* 191 (1992) 7–14 (abridged in *Theology Digest* 41 [Summer 1994] 129–31).

that the priest, in saying the words of Christ in the institution narrative, acts in a different voice from the rest of the prayer is to misconstrue the role of the ordained minister and the relation of the Church to Christ. When the priest recounts the words of Christ within the celebration, he does so as "one with the church, in formulating its corporate prayer." Thus, in Power's view: "There is no single and immutable way of relating ordained ministry to Christ, to church, and to the originating event of the passion. Yet, all interpretations are obviously set within a common tradition."[85]

Power's argument therefore situates the use of the phrases *in persona Christi* and *in persona Ecclesiae,* but also points to the need for further thought on the theological expression adequate to the mystery. He goes on to say:

> It is only in and through the *koinonia* of life and sacrament that one can truly speak of Christ's presence in the church. He is not there as it were to form *koinonia* out of those who gather. He is present in the very being of this communion, as it is lived and sacramentally celebrated.[86]

This leads Power to stress the sacramentality of the Church.

Why do we need to look for any other enfleshed sacrament of Christ, when the Church itself is the sacrament of Christ? To conceive that the phrase *in persona Christi* means that the priest sacramentalizes Christ in some kind of "figural representation" beyond the idea of working through the power of Christ given to the Church "is to take from the sacramentality of the church as a communion."[87] It is after all at the table of the Lord that the Church is most itself as the sacrament of Christ. The specific role of the priest is to lead the People of God to the precise moment in which their reality as a sacrament of Christ is most clearly embodied. Power cautions against transferring authority from the canon of the word to the canonical authority of the bishop, from an obedience to all the gifts of the Spirit to the control of the episcopal charism, and "from a Eucharist focused on the common table of the one Body to a Eucharist enthralled with the ritual performance of the bishop or the presbyter."[88]

In summary, this discussion of the phrase *in persona Christi* leads to the following synthetic reflections:

- the sacramental work that is the focus of the priest's mediation is the work of the people, who as body of Christ are the principal graced

[85] Ibid., 304.
[86] Ibid., 307.
[87] Ibid.
[88] Ibid., 308.

reality in the moment of sacrament: remember Aquinas's insistence that the deepest spiritual reality *(res)* of the Eucharist is the *communio amoris* that is the effect of the people's celebration;

- an ascending theology that is both pneumatological as well as christological is closer to the contemporary retrieval of biblical understanding and closer to the structure of the apostolic communities than an exclusively christological and descending understanding of *in persona Christi;*

- the leadership of the priest is both *in persona Ecclesiae et Christi,* as shown, in such a way as to make the literalization of the nuptial metaphor awkward and implausible: one member of the body is not the bridegroom vis-à-vis the bridal figure given to the rest of the members;

- the ascending and pneumatological reading of *in persona Christi et Ecclesiae* renders the service theme of the presbyter and the leadership of the body clearly, in such a way as to emphasize the social reality of the priest's relation to the people and of his pastoral leadership within the community of the people.

Therefore, it seems clearer that the ministry of the ordained priest is marked by the following dynamics: (1) The presbyter is called to a service linked to prophecy (word), priesthood (ritual presidency), and pastoring (administrative ability and care); thus the embodiment of the word of God in all three of these ways flows into the sacred action of sacramental rites. (2) This presbyteral leadership is generative in its purpose, having as its focus the realization of and the empowerment of those who carry the grace of the body of Christ, celebrated in the sacraments, out toward the transformation of the world. (3) Nothing in an ascending and pneumatological reading derogates from the graced power, the great dignity, or the totalizing demands of the role of presbyter as conceived through the ages; but this orientation is a corrective to priestly triumphalism and to a consecrated elitism that can be dangerous for ecclesiology. The radical consecration in any Christian's life is, of course, baptism.

The Right of the Local Church to Eucharist

The shortage of priests within many communities in northern Europe and North America has caused some theologians to reflect on the implications of the present Vatican discipline requiring male celibate candidates for ordination. Absolutizing these disciplinary requirements effectively means leaving many communities without a resident presider at Eucharist. (The Center for Applied Research in the Apostolate

[CARA] estimates that 16 percent of North American parishes currently lack a resident priest, for example. The situation is even more dramatic in parts of Europe.)[89] The Vatican's response to this crisis in pastoral leadership has been to urge more aggressive recruitment for priestly vocations, urge the distribution of priests from places where numbers are higher to places where the need is greatest, and to sanction and oversee the development of *Sunday Worship in the Absence of a Priest.*[90]

This latter practice is both impressive and dangerous. Yves Congar expressed well both of these dynamics in an extended interview recorded during his years of hospitalization in Paris. Asked about Sunday assemblies without priests, Congar responded:

> In a way they're magnificent. . . . What is magnificent is that the laity are now setting to work. The gospel and the Church continue, where the absence of a priest could have created a void, a kind of gulf into which what remains of Christianity could disappear. So . . . I encourage the laity to take initiatives in communities which have no priest—to share the Word of God, to distribute the eucharist and so on.[91]

But Congar goes on to caution about a serious difficulty, that is, the "Protestantizing" of the people's understanding of what Church is. Such assemblies are very close to what Protestant worship is—Christian assembly, communal praise, confession of the same faith together. But that is not what the Mass is. "Like us, [the Orthodox] would certainly accept that it is better than nothing, but they themselves would bear extremely powerful witness in the opposite direction."[92]

Closer to home, parishes that experience Sunday services without a priest often find that their people confuse the Word Service with the Mass. Sometimes lay leaders have testified to their assembly's preference for their liturgies over Mass led by a priest who scarcely knows them or

---

[89] *The CARA Report* 2 (Spring 1997) 5. In Europe as a whole, 36 percent of parishes have no resident pastor; in the Middle East, 25 percent.

[90] The 1988 Vatican decree authorizing these celebrations was implemented in the dioceses of the United States five years later. See the introduction to *Sunday Celebrations in the Absence of a Priest* (New York: Catholic Book Publishing Co., 1994) 15, §8: "In circumstances in which there is no reasonable opportunity to provide for the celebration of Mass, local bishops may judge it necessary to provide for other Sunday celebrations in the absence of a priest, so that in the best way possible the weekly gathering of the faithful can be continued and the Christian tradition regarding Sunday preserved."

[91] *Fifty Years of Catholic Theology,* 48–9.

[92] Ibid., 50.

who can't communicate effectively or lead with pastoral sympathy. (This is another argument for seeing how the prophetic and the pastoral aspects of presbyteral leadership needs to be linked to the cultic.)

We have noted above the problem of inadequate catechesis about the nature of the Eucharist as well as the centrality of themes about Eucharist in *Lumen gentium* and *Presbyterorum ordinis* (among other documents of Vatican II). But the Church has not done well in communicating this rich eucharistic theology to the laity. De facto, some studies show that in some cases people are happier with the priestless Sunday because the lay pastoral leader is more in touch with their needs and more competent in pastoral leadership than the priests to whom they have been previously exposed.[93] This creates not just administrative, but solid theological problems for the Church, since it means regularizing communities in which people estimate the benefit of Sunday worship more in terms of their own spiritual comfort, rather than in terms of the sacramental realism that we have tried to describe above.[94]

Edward Schillebeeckx set about to address precisely this situation in his 1980 book *Kerkelijk ambt*.[95] Schillebeeckx, following a historical reconstruction of apostolic church practice, enunciates the principle: "The ancient church and (above all since Vatican II) the modern church cannot envisage any Christian community without the celebration of the eucharist."[96] The link between local church and Eucharist is essential: in the pre-Nicene Church there is evidence that any community with at least twelve fathers of families had the right to liturgical presidency. In the view of the ancient Church, a shortage of priests was an ecclesiastical

---

[93] See, for example, Ruth Wallace, *They Call Her Pastor: A New Role for Catholic Women* (Albany: State University of New York Press, 1992). One sample testimony of this kind is cited on page 72, speaking of a lay woman pastor: "[She] is not afraid to get out and minister, to get out and work at things and not sit back and give orders to somebody else to do the work. . . . Priests we have had don't take the initiative. They put themselves on a pedestal and let somebody else do the work. Right now we are getting more total community effort than we ever have because she is so active."

[94] See Gerard Austin, "Communion Services: A Break with Tradition?" *Fountain of Life,* ed. Gerald Austin (Washington, D.C.: Pastoral Press, 1991) 213: "Since baptism is the gateway to all the sacraments and gives one the right to a sacramental life, is not the proliferation of communion services on Sunday a denial of what is due baptized men and women?" Austin then goes on to cite William Marravee as follows: "What in fact appears to be most characteristic of the present situation is that less importance is being ascribed to the integrity of the eucharist and to the eucharistic dimension of the local community than to the maintaining of a male celibate ordained ministry."

[95] Edward Schillebeeckx, *Ministry: Leadership in the Community of Jesus Christ* (New York: Crossroad, 1981).

[96] Ibid., 72.

impossibility. So, he concludes, the present "so-called shortage of priests" must be criticized in the light of ancient practice and because the present situation arises out of conditions imposed upon the ministry on grounds that are not ecclesiologically valid today. "Even now there are more than enough Christians, men and women, who in ecclesiological and ministerial terms possess this charisma."[97] He cites as examples catechists in the missions and pastoral workers in Europe and elsewhere who would be prepared to take presbyteral leadership provided that this does not entail being clerical or entering into a clerical system.

Additional points could be developed; for example, the question of how the current notion of "character" relates to the leadership of the presbyter. Schillebeeckx's view would tend toward thinking that at present we reify a metaphor, in the sense that the anointing of the Spirit that empowers presbyteral leadership is metaphorically called an indelible marking of the person (yet no mark can be seen). But Roman documents have proceeded to make this "mark" of the spiritual powers given in ordination paramount in their understanding Christian priesthood and speak of it as a *datum ab origino.*[98]

Considering the right of local churches to celebrate their unity in Christ through the Eucharist, I find the tendency of some recent Vatican documents mystifying and unhelpful. Put comparatively, recent Vatican documents tend to overdramatize and oversacralize the ordained minister, when it is Christ—directly accessible to each believer by faith and through the Spirit—who is the Ur-sacrament: the Source of all holiness. Beyond that, the Church is the sacrament of Christ alive in the world, and the celebrations of the seven sacraments even in their ritual expression are realizations of the reality and powers of the Church-as-sacrament. To dramatize Holy Orders as the creation of a distinct priestly-sacramental personality suggests that the central issue is the sacramental powers and holiness of the bishop, then of the priest, because from them comes forth the sacraments that create the Church. This turns the ecclesiological reality on its head. Schillebeeckx resists this topsy-turvy theology, and in doing so he has come under fire repeatedly from the Congregation of the Faith. Yet he has played an invaluable role, for his research and theological writings have clarified issues that others have allowed to be coopted by the prevailing Roman theology.

John Bowden summarizes the chief postulates of Schillebeeckx's position by saying: (1) the community has a right to priests; (2) the decisive element in presbyteral leadership is recognition by the community;

[97] Ibid., 73.
[98] Ibid., 71–2.

but (3) problems arise when ministry is no longer related to the local church, but to a priestly power to confect the Eucharist.[99]

This simplistic summary runs into difficulty with, among other issues, the parish-centered ecclesiology that we examined above in the writings of John O'Malley. That is, Schillebeeckx's reflections do not examine the complex tangle of presbyteral ministries that have evolved under the banner of clerical religious life. But Schillebeeckx's argument undoubtedly articulates one of the dimensions of a worldwide crisis in Church administration from the perspective of the Church's grass roots.

Although the Congregation of the Faith has disallowed certain of the formulations of Schillebeeckx's *Ministry* book, his argument for seeing Church order from below stands as a vivid problematic for pastoral theology.[100] He has argued that critical communities (which we would call here small ecclesial communities) find that they must operate at times outside conventional solutions, and has made the distinction of practice *praeter ordinem ecclesiae* as opposed to *contra ordinem*.[101] To conclude this brief review of the topic, Schillebeeckx's ideas have forced theologians to keep in mind the important practical ramifications of distinguishing between the core elements of Christian faith and *koinonia*, on the one hand, and the historically conditioned solutions of the Church's disciplinary norms, on the other.

As regards the theology of priesthood, this discussion shows us the necessity of conceiving the ministry of the presbyter as a service to concrete communities of faith, always contextualizing the "powers" of the ordained within a larger reality, that is, the incessant gift of the Spirit of Jesus to the Church that has listened to the word of God and come together in witness and mutual service. Such communities do not come about autonomously apart from the celebration of the sacraments, but the sacraments are themselves celebrations of the whole dynamic of life within such communities constituted in the Spirit of Jesus. At the very least, Schillebeeckx puts us on our guard against a disembodied sacramentalism. His theology calls for a careful revisioning of ecclesiology, especially on the topic of the genesis of the local church in the dialectic between word and sacrament.

[99] Bowden, *Edward Schillebeeckx,* 76–7.

[100] Various treatments of Schillebeeckx's conflicts with the Congregation of the Faith exist; for example, Ted M. Schoof, ed., *The Schillebeeckx Case* (New York: Paulist Press, 1980); Peter Hebblethwaite, *The New Inquisition? The Case of Edward Schillebeeckx and Hans Kung* (San Francisco: Harper & Row, 1980); *Journal of Ecumenical Studies* 19 (1982) 244–67.

[101] See Edward Schillebeeckx, *The Schillebeeckx Reader,* ed. R. J. Schreiter (New York: Crossroad, 1984) 200–1.

The New Story

Twenty years ago Thomas Berry wrote a remarkable pamphlet in which he claimed that much of the confusion among Christians today derives from the fact that we have lived for so long with the "old story" of God's mastery in Genesis, that all of our instincts for thinking about the world are couched in that rendition of reality. However, Enlightenment humanism and scientific technology have gradually robbed the old story of its power and credibility. We have, little by little, entered a new world in which we ourselves have taken mastery over the leadership of the cosmos (in our own view). From time to time, traumatic experiences (like war, genocide, AIDS, or the threat of extra-terrestrial cataclysm) cause us to react with fear, conscious that we are not masters of such realities. But our real challenge is to develop a "new story"—a telling of the mastery of God in the midst of our new technological and cybernetic reality that is believable and worthy of our enthusiasm.[102]

A parallel predicament exists in ecclesiology and in particular in the theology of holy orders. Returning to the introduction to this paper, we are faced with the need to reconceptualize the very idea of how episcopal and presbyteral leadership works in a society where the number of nominal Catholics is growing and the ranks of the clergy (male, celibate, life-time committed) continue to diminish. At issue is not just the question of facing the defeat of an old model. More relevant is the goal that John XXIII posed for the council, *aggiornamento,* the necessary updating to bring the Church into a new age. Part of the new story will be, of course, to reappropriate with new insight the constitutional and foundational moments of the Christian Church as these are disclosed to us through the work of biblical retrievals. John Meier's *A Marginal Jew,* for example, renders us more aware of the powerful role of the religious movements surrounding the appearance of Jesus, particularly the importance of the Baptist and his circle. Meier's and others' biblical studies reinforce the importance of being able to calculate an ascending as well as a descending christology, ecclesiology, and sacramentology. To do that would be to contribute an important part to the new story.

Another part of the new story, however, has to do with the "signs of the times." In the midst of tremendous institutional transitions, God is giving us signs of a new generosity on the part of many laity, a responsiveness of even non-Christians to many of the ideals of Christian spirituality, and some of the raw materials for a renewed vision of human community (even as community becomes a global, planetary term).

---

[102] Thomas Berry, *The New Story* (Chambersburg, Pa.: Anima Books, 1978).

We can note the escalating demands for good preaching, good celebration, and human realism in community-building among church-
goers. The prevailing dominance of juridical and canonical concerns in
the education, government, and direction of the Catholic clergy has created an emphasis upon maintenance rather than mission—upon not losing any of the traditions of priestly culture rather than upon reaching out
to find the most effective ministers. But for preachers to be effective,
there must be a poetic and ecstatic element in their work. For the animation of the liturgy to be life-giving, there must be some element of
shaman in the one who leads. For pastoral leadership to be authentic,
there must be dialogue, real engagement with people, and a deep and
empathic concern that is, in part, learned by apprenticeship. Too often
we ask seminarians to fulfill the demands of the academic and pastoral
program of priestly formation without constructively engaging their images of God, of the Church, of spirituality, or of pastor. While both dynamics are needed, we should be more concerned about introducing
candidates for life-long service as presbyter to mature and adequate (full-
some) images of God and of the Church than to a repertory of erudite
theological categories and arguments.

What will the New Story be? Perhaps the answer to that question
will flow from the responses and dialogue of Catholic pastors and leaders to this book. In any case, this chapter, summary as it is, hopes to
demonstrate the rich resources for the development of a revitalized theology of orders (and of Church Order). The potential is rich, the possibilities are large.

2

Ministry, Ordination Rites, and Language

FRANK C. QUINN, O.P.

The Language of Ordained Ministry in the Roman Catholic Church

Foreword

This essay treats the images and metaphors used of ordained ministry, especially that of bishop and presbyter, from the standpoint that such images and metaphors need revitalization today in order to be heard in all their richness. We often tend to treat them literally—and this has affected much writing in the area of the theology of ordination. The first part of this essay deals with confusion in English over the use of several terms and speaks to the two different universes of discourse relative to the language of ordained ministry. A brief section on the nature of metaphor concludes this first part, since some still consider it mere decorative language rather than the vital, truth-seeking language of liturgy.

The last section of the paper begins with a consideration of the particular sacerdotal metaphors used of Christ and his Church, since such metaphors later play a role in the prayers and formulae of the ordination rites. There follows a consideration of the differences between the pre–Vatican II and post–Vatican II ordination rites for presbyter as well as bishop through an analysis of the changes in metaphorical usage vis-à-vis

---

*Scripture quotations in this article are taken from the New Revised Standard Version Bible, Catholic edition, © 1989 by the Division of Christian Education of the National Council of Churches of Christ in the USA. Used by permission. All rights reserved.

each of these orders. Such analysis points to a change in our understanding of these two ministries.

Introduction: Words Used of Ordained Ministry

In writing about ordained ministry in the Roman Catholic Church, authors use images canonized by long usage and often assume that their readers clearly understand how such language is being used. But it is not always clear what authors mean or whether they themselves have even questioned the meaning of the words they are using. Think, for example, of the word "priest." What does a particular author mean when using the term? Is it always clear from the context of the article? Is the reader left with a number of questions such as: Is "priest" being used as a name for official ministers, with no other connotation? Is it meant to refer to a member of a cultic priesthood engaged in ancient "sacrifice," a *sacerdotium*? a wisdom figure (elder) advising a leader? the middle rank in the three grades of the sacrament of order/s? the two ranks of order that, in contrast to the deacon, are privileged to lead the assembly in eucharistic worship?

Because of the many issues surrounding "ordained" ministry in the Roman Catholic Church today—and this includes much more than simply the issue of who may be ordained—it is important, when writing about this topic, that we employ descriptive terms knowledgeably. The metaphorical language of Christian ministry is rich because such ministry, in all its varieties, bears the weight of twenty centuries of evolution. Moreover, since ministry is not only a complex of social functions but is rooted in the mystery that is Christ Jesus, simplistic explanations are not suitable.

Confusion in English Usage

One point that needs to be made at the outset is that in English there is not available the variety of terms that we find in Latin or Greek to distinguish between cultic service in a temple and the non-cultic ministries of word, worship, and service that arise in Christianity and that are rooted in the ministry of Jesus. This is particularly the case with the English word "priest." This word can refer either to the Greek/Latin *presbyteros/us* or to the Greek/Latin *hiereus/sacerdos.* The first usage, which is a literal translation (from the Old English *preost*) of *presbyterus,* means "elder," advisor, wisdom figure. The second usage, based on the fact that there is no English noun for either *hiereus* or *sacerdos,* means cultic or temple official, the one who offers sacrifice, etc. The first usage is without sacral overtones; the second is entirely sacral.

It may be argued that *priest,* because of its etymology, should carry both meanings. But it seems to me that this is practically impossible.[1] When the word *priest* is used, people ordinarily think of cultic officials such as those in Jewish or pagan temples. Moreover, *priest* is now used in official Catholic rites to refer to the liturgical ministry of both bishop and presbyter, and there it is used to designate those sacramental activities that both may carry out. It would seem appropriate, then, to translate the Latin/Greek *presbyterus/os* by the English word *presbyter.* This would allow the word *priest* to stand for sacerdotal realities. Unfortunately, there is not general agreement to this solution on the part of official Roman agencies such as the congregations for worship and doctrine.

Sacerdotal versus Ministerial Terminology

Cultic Language

In the first century of our era, the language of cult would have been ingrained, since temples, ritual sacrifices, hereditary priesthood, and even the selling of meat remaining from the animals sacrificed were part of the fabric of Jewish and pagan religion. The world of cultic or ritual sacrifice[2] generated a whole series of sacral terms: the particular types of ritual activities that could be called "sacrifice" (such as holocaust, communion offering, covenant rite, etc.), the location where sacrifices were carried out (temple, altar, Holy of Holies), the designation of those who acted on behalf of the people (the sacred officials or *sacerdotium,* the priesthood, hierarchy, etc.). The heart of a society's worship centered on the cultic worship of the gods through offerings of animals, grains, incense; it was led by (hereditary) officials, and occurred either inside or outside temples, in locations where some kind of divine epiphany had taken place.

Ritual "sacrifice" portrays a fundamental attitude of humanity toward the divine powers beyond it, of creature to creator. Sacrifice is celebrated, as indicated above, for a number of reasons: gestures of devotion and reverence and offering to the gods, the need to placate chthonic powers or to ward off dangers, and so on. Such activity speaks of mediation between

---

[1] Note that the *Random House Dictionary* defines priest as "a person whose office it is to perform religious rites, and esp. to make sacrificial offerings."

[2] I speak of "cultic or ritual" sacrifice to remind us that any notion of sacrifice at the time of Jesus was in terms of worship, whereas today sacrifice is generally a secular concept. On this see Robert J. Daly, *The Origins of the Christian Doctrine of Sacrifice* (Philadelphia: Fortress Press, 1978) 3–4. Daly bases his remarks on an earlier work by Royden Keith Yerkes, *Sacrifice in Greek and Roman Religions and Early Judaism* (London: Adam and Charles Black, 1953).

humanity and divinity. In this context (cultic) priests (=sacerdotal officials) are mediators between the gods and the people. The latter usually remain outside the sacred precincts and the temples where sacrifice is carried out.[3]

As noted above, sacrificial language is sacred language. In Greek *(hieros)* and Latin *(sacer)*, the root of the many words expressing this activity means "holy, whole." The cultic official who offers sacrifice is *ho hiereus. Hierarchy,* of course, is based on this root. In Latin, *sacer* forms the root of many words still used in English today: sacrifice *(sacri-ficium)*, sacerdotal *(sacer-dotalis)*,[4] sacrament *(sacra-mentum)*. Whether in Greek or Latin, it is clear that all of these terms have to do with the holy, that place where humanity comes into contact with the *fascinans tremendum.*

The problem for our age is that sacrifice in popular use is not a sacred, cultic term, but is used in a secular way.[5] It bears negative rather then positive connotations. Furthermore, there is an almost absolute concentration on the death of an animal or person and of having to give something up. We do not ordinarily think of the ritual killing of an animal, for example, as a necessary condition for cultic, sacrificial action. Robert Daly notes that these misperceptions have

> been the point of departure for some very common but erroneous explanations of sacrifice, that is, those theories of sacrificial atonement which emphasize the suffering and death of the victim or the destruction of the material being offered. These theories, which raise serious theological problems, are in this respect totally without scriptural foundation.[6]

The Language of Christian Ministry

The New Testament does not speak of its ministers or its rituals in cultic and sacral ways. It reserves such terms to Christ, the true and only mediator between God and humankind, and to Christ's body, the baptized.[7] As a consequence (1) in Christianity literal sacrificial terminology is transformed into metaphor used of Christ and his body the

---

[3] It is very important that we recognize the lack of a role for the assembly if we conceive of all Christian liturgy as literally and only "sacrificial."

[4] Unfortunately, only the adjectival form "sacerdotal" has come over into English, not the noun, *sacerdos.*

[5] Yerkes, *Sacrifice in Greek and Roman Religions,* 2.

[6] Daly, *The Origins of the Christian Doctrine,* 3.

[7] The growing spiritualization of (cultic) sacrifice allowed this transference of terms to take place. The inner heart of sacrifice, "the internal religious/ethical dispositions with which one offers sacrifice or takes part in sacrificial worship," could be shifted to the person and acts of Jesus and the ethical life of Christians. See Daly, *The Origins of the Christian Doctrine,* 139 and passim.

Church[8] and (2) Christian "liturgy" and Christian ministry are not conceived of as cultic in character, even though it is evident such events as the Last Supper bear profound cultic (=sacrificial) overtones.

The names for Christian ministry are functional and relational, rather than sacred or cultic. Such designations as apostle, prophet, and teacher do not have specific application to a place or a community, while *episkopos* (overseer), *presbyteros* (elder), and *diakonos* (one who serves) refer more clearly to resident ministries of oversight and service. The worship Christians engaged in was daily prayer, the breaking of the bread (the "meal"), the thanksgiving, "hymns, psalms, and spiritual songs," the word, the bath, etc. Although Jewish Christians might have continued to attend the temple, where sacrificial rituals were carried out, Christian worship itself was at first a domestic phenomenon. Christians used tables rather than altars, presided over the assembly rather than served in the Holy of Holies, gave thanks (the "sacrifice of the lips") rather than drawing the blood of animals.

Such an application of sacred and cultic language to the life and activities of the Christian community involved a transformation of the concepts of sacrifice, cultic officials, and cultic places. There was transference of language literally referring to cultic ritual activity to the arena of daily life and ethical conduct. Christ and his body, ethical service, including care for others, such as the taking up of collections for the Jerusalem community, were all described in terms of sacrifice and priesthood. Paul refers cultic places—temple—to the baptized who are temples of the Holy Spirit. He also refers to the baptized as the living stones making up the one temple, the body of Christ, the heavenly Jerusalem. The great Temple, visible in Jerusalem until its destruction, is simply made metaphor for a greater spiritual edifice.

There was, then, a re-appropriation, a re-pristinization, of the metaphors of sacrifice. Actual cultic activity, which spoke of the distance between the gods and the people, was applied to human life and human relationships, which spoke of the breaking down of the distance between God and the baptized in Christ Jesus. The "a-ha" moment, the metaphoric surprise, is the turning on its head of the entire universe of sacrifice.

Contemporary authors such as Gordon Lathrop[9] and David Power[10] make the claim that we need to recover the note of metaphoric surprise

---

[8] Think of such metaphorical statements as "Christ is high priest of the new covenant," "Christ's death on the cross is a sacrifice," "Christ is the altar of sacrifice," etc.

[9] Gordon Lathrop, *Holy Things: A Liturgical Theology* (Minneapolis: Fortress Press, 1993).

[10] David Power, "Words that Crack: The Uses of 'Sacrifice' in Eucharistic Discourse," *Worship* 53 (September 1979) 386–404.

in our contemporary use of cultic language vis-à-vis Christian liturgy and ministry. The reason for this is that over the course of time metaphors have been turned into literal statements. In different periods of Christian history Christian sacramental ministry has been understood in various ways, in dependence on contemporary concepts of the Church and its sacraments. One author points out, for example, that from the Counter-Reformation to Vatican II Catholic liturgy and its ministers were considered primarily in cultic and sacrificial ways. Sacrifice, priesthood, etc., were literally applied to Christian realities.[11] In other words, Christian ordained ministry was conceived as a literal continuation of the hereditary sacerdotal ministry of the Old Testament and the Jewish temple.

Recovering Metaphoric Speech

Introduction

> It is truly right and just,
> our duty and our salvation,
> that we should always sing your glory, Lord;
> but we praise you with greater joy than ever
> in this Easter season when Christ became our paschal sacrifice.
> By offering his body on the cross,
> he brought to completion the sacrifices of old.
> By commending himself into your hands for our salvation,
> he showed himself the priest, the altar, and the lamb of sacrifice.
> Therefore, the universe resounds with Easter joy,
> and the choirs of angels sing the endless hymn of your glory.[12]

In this meditation upon the meaning of Christ's death and resurrection we find the theology of the paschal mystery of Jesus revealed not in propositional statement but through metaphor and symbolic language. This is language of commitment, not of theoretical explanation. It is also language that seemingly promotes contradiction. Furthermore, it is language that cannot be explained away or substituted for by other expressions, especially if it is to continue to exercise its metaphoric "surprise."

Note the seeming contradictions: *"when Christ became our paschal sacrifice"*—Christ is not a paschal sacrifice, the latter being a fully developed

---

[11] I refer to the book by Paul Bernier, *Ministry in the Church: A Historical and Pastoral Approach* (Mystic, Conn.: Twenty-Third Publications, 1992), in which the author proposes six ways of thinking about Christian ministry in the course of our history—models dependent, of course, on the way each period viewed God, Christ, and the Church.

[12] Easter Preface V, *The Roman Sacramentary* (Washington, D.C.: International Commission on English in the Liturgy, 1998).

ritual of temple offering and home celebration in the spring of the year. *"By offering his body on the cross"*—the language is that of temple priests offering (unwilling) ritual victims to God in a temple setting. The reality of Christ's death was the execution of a seeming blasphemer that took place outside the walls of the Holy City, thus purposely removed from the holy temple and all religious, ritual activity. *"He brought to completion the sacrifices of old"*—again, a contradiction, since what is being expressed are two different realities, one the history of religions and the innumerable rituals offered to God over the ages, the other the meaningless and cruel execution of a human being. *"He showed himself the priest, the altar, and the lamb of sacrifice"*—of course, Christ was none of those. And thus, in the midst of literal contradiction we find ourselves immersed in profound and emotional meaning, unattainable by any other means, because what is being insisted upon is that Jesus Christ is all of these in a way the literal realities could never be.

In our age metaphor and symbol can all too often fall prey to a literalization that explains metaphor away or, in terms of theological language, that too easily turns metaphor into propositional statement. This truth is well expressed by Gordon Lathrop in his discussion of sacrifice as metaphor in terms of Christian life and liturgy:

> We have become numb to the surprise of this [metaphorical] use of sacrificial language for what is no sacrifice. Perhaps we do not recognize the ordinary reference of these words because of the absence of ritual slaying from our daily experience, though in many parts of the world cultic violence is very much alive. Perhaps Christian catechesis has brought us to use the terminology of sacrifice quite univocally of Jesus' death and of Christian response, so that the words come to seem *thoroughly Christian words, empty of any other reference.*[13]

Lathrop continues:

> Ecumenical intuition has been that the death of Christ, the meaning of Christian worship, and the orientations of Christian ethics are all deeply connected. "Sacrifice" has been valued as one important way to talk about that connection. The surprise has been missing, however. Christian worship is not sacrifice. Neither was the death of Christ, at least when it is looked at as an historical event. Neither is the moral life. . . . Christ's death was a public execution . . . it was thoroughly alien to the sacred cultic exchange.[14]

---

[13] Lathrop, *Holy Things,* 140, emphasis mine.
[14] Ibid., 141.

Metaphor Today

Contemporary writing about metaphor, analogy, symbolic speech, etc., is so vast and so pertinent to many fields that it is impossible to deal with it in any comprehensive way in this brief paper. Consequently, the following reflection will only attempt to present a few ideas about metaphor, its meanings, and its importance in modern theological discourse.

Negative Approach to Metaphor: A Mere Literary Device

In rhetorical usage metaphor has often been considered as a merely decorative device: "metaphor is treated as a 'trope' whereby an author substitutes a 'strange' word where the reader might logically expect an ordinary or familiar one."[15] In this sense metaphor does not create or contribute "anything *new* in language."[16] Speaking of metaphor this way implies that a substitution of a more fanciful kind has been made for a plainer and even clearer term. Thus, any confusion can be cleared up by restoring the original. For example, "Juliet is the sun" can be made clear by saying, "Juliet is an important person in my own life."[17]

This approach to metaphor is found in the writings of philosophers and theologians of the past, who tended to treat metaphor as a weak and fanciful form of analogy. But before this, according to David Burrell, Aristotle linked apt analogy and good metaphor.[18] Burrell goes on to note that the medievals did not follow Aristotle. Instead, they tended to distinguish "properly" analogous expressions from metaphors, associating the latter with poetic (i.e., fanciful) expression.[19] But according to Burrell, it was not Thomas Aquinas[20] but Cajetan who, in developing a theory of analogy, "tended to further separate analogy from metaphor."[21]

Metaphor and Simile

In contemporary usage metaphor is a form of analogy. "The function of analogy . . . is to make clear the unfamiliar and the unexplained

---

[15] Nathan Mitchell, *Liturgy Digest* 4:1 (1997) 94.

[16] Ibid.

[17] Ibid.

[18] David Burrell, "Analogy," *The New Dictionary of Theology,* ed. Joseph A. Komonchak, Mary Collins, and Dermot A. Lane (Collegeville: The Liturgical Press, 1991) 15.

[19] Ibid.

[20] His attention to the "art of recognizing and distinguishing among analogous uses" prevented him from developing a complete theory of analogy. See ibid., 16.

[21] Ibid.

by means of that which is already familiar and already explained."[22] Metaphor is often compared to simile in order to illustrate different forms of analogy. But there is quite a difference between the two. Simile[23] makes the analogy clear. We find similes abounding in the language of mystics telling of their experiences and in the language of Scripture and the psalms: "like a deer that yearns for running streams, so my soul yearns for the Lord my God." But simile can be turned into metaphor. Note the following passage from Isa 26:17-18:

> *Like* a woman [*simile*] with child,
> who writhes and cries out in her pangs
> when she is near her time,
> so were we [simile] because of you, O Lord;
> we were with child [*metaphor*], we writhed,
> but we gave birth only to wind.

Metaphor operates at a different level: "Metaphors have a direct quality absent from similes. They hide their analogical character."[24] Metaphor declares not likeness, but identity: "The Lord is my shepherd," "This is my body." The danger, especially in theological discussion and popular piety, is that metaphoric statement can be taken literally. This is particularly the situation when origin or cultural situation is forgotten. For example, Thomas Fawcett points to the lack of outrage today in terms of atonement theories (e.g., Christ is a ransom for many).[25]

Despite this, Fawcett writes, "the danger inherent in metaphors is the price that is paid for symbolic power." For metaphor operates on the level, not simply of understanding, but of decision: "A metaphor . . . insists on being taken seriously at the deepest level, that of personal commitment."[26]

Metaphor as Commitment

Metaphor is so much part of our speech, though often unrecognized, that it exists at all levels of human discourse, from the most trivial to the supremely important. Therefore it is important to disavow any ideas that metaphor is simply weak analogy, a decorative device in sentence

---

[22] Thomas Fawcett, *The Symbolic Language of Religion* (Minneapolis: Augsburg Publishing House, 1971) 48.

[23] "Analogy is self-evidently present in the use of similes. One thing is said to be like another." Ibid., 50.

[24] Ibid., 52.

[25] Ibid.

[26] Ibid., 53–4.

construction. Little of the contemporary literature on metaphor contin-ues to promote this outdated idea. "Indeed, what Aquinas famously de-scribed as the language proper for theological discourse—viz., analogy—resembles quite closely the strategies of metaphor analyzed by modern scholars."[27]

The purpose of metaphor is neither to make a comparison between two realities perfectly clear nor to explain away the differences. When so done, metaphor is turned, as noted above, into naïve identification of the two terms or even into strict, propositional statement, as seems to be happening today to such metaphors as "Christ is priest, prophet, and king," and especially in the last few years to the scriptural bridegroom imagery used of Christ and applied to contemporary male presbyters.

It is important to note that metaphor works at the level of discourse. This means that the sentence is the basic unit rather than individual words or phrases. In other words, although metaphor belongs to the realm of analogy, it is not to be explained (away), as if each term can be analyzed for its meaning and the metaphor either forgotten or turned into something more literal. The "is" is always part of metaphorical usage, joining the two members. One must speak not of words used metaphorically, but of "metaphorical statements."[28] Such statements are jolting because absurdity is the basic strategy of metaphor: "The absur-dity is revealed as an absurdity for a literal interpretation. . . . Thus metaphor does not exist in itself but in an interpretation."[29] Metaphor discloses new meaning by abolishing or canceling literal reference; it demonstrates both a new world and a new way of being in the world.

Conclusion

This brief examination represents an attempt to treat one facet of theological discourse that particularly belongs to the areas of Scripture, worship, and sacramental and liturgical theology. Some questions that arise even from this brief survey center on the way various writers treat metaphor today in their analysis of ordination in the Catholic Church, the role of the laity, etc. Some seem to be literalizing metaphor and cre-ating propositional statements that, on examination, may cause more problems than they solve. Two areas of consideration, with which we will conclude this reflection, are the eucharistic meal and eucharistic "sacrifice."

[27] Mitchell, *Liturgy Digest,* 5.
[28] Ibid., 94.
[29] Ibid., 95.

Eucharistic Meal

One of the strongest uses of metaphor in all Christianity centers on the Last Supper and Jesus' words. The application of bread and wine, already part of Jewish history, to Jesus himself "was a startling innovation which opened up an entirely new range of meaning, sharpened the disciples' understanding of the events about to take place, and has been the means whereby countless Christians have been able to share in the bond of union thus made possible."[30] At the same time, too easy identification (losing metaphor) has led us along a "history of metaphysical speculation and bitter argument at the propositional level."[31] Further, the domestication of often startling and shocking speech, for example, such cannibalistic language as "eating his body" or "drinking his blood," profoundly affects the way in which we approach sacraments such as the Eucharist.[32]

Eucharistic Sacrifice

We began this essay noting the metaphorical rhetoric of an Easter preface, which ranged through a universe of sacred, cultic, sacrificial language and applied all to Jesus Christ, who was/is literally not part of such a universe. It is in this area of the cultic that we have most literalized metaphor. David Power notes:

> What is most lacking in an appreciation of eucharistic language is attention to the creative and transformative power of metaphor. This shows up in a particularly poignant way in regard to the image of sacrifice. Much of the acrimony surrounding the nature of the Eucharist as sacrifice might have been avoided had the metaphorical nature of Christian sacrificial language been noted.[33]

Power points out the non-cultic language used of Christian Eucharist and its ministers. When cultic metaphors began to be used of the Christian minister, "at first this meant nothing more than what was meant by designating the prayer of the blessed gifts a sacrifice. It was strictly in association with his role of eucharistic and community presidency that the term was applied to him."[34] Power goes on to note that already in the

---

[30] Fawcett, *The Symbolic Language of Religion,* 53.

[31] Ibid.

[32] The strong sense of such language is evoked in Margaret Visser, *The Rituals of Dinner: The Origins, Evolution, Eccentricities, and Meaning of Table Manners* (New York: Penguin Books, 1991) 35–7.

[33] David N. Power, *The Eucharistic Mystery: Revitalizing the Tradition* (New York: Crossroads, 1992) 320.

[34] Ibid., 321.

writings of John Chrysostom there is a tendency to employ terms such as *sacrifice* or *priest* "in a more mythical than metaphorical sense."[35]

But despite an early turn to what might be called a mistaken "history of religions" approach to Christian rites and ministries, Power insists that, today, there is a need to demythologize the language of priesthood and sacrifice. "In this context, it is the power of the Christian use of the language of sacrifice as a language of reversal that has to be brought again to the fore." And, he warns us, "By failing to renew itself, the language of liturgy may fail to convey the power of Christ's death to liberate people from the harm and the sorrow that jeopardize their existence."[36]

It is dangerous, therefore, to explain (away) metaphor. Yet this always remains a danger for Christian theology and Christian faith. In this instance we lose not only understanding, but the need for decision. "A metaphor . . . insists on being taken seriously at the deepest level, that of personal commitment."[37]

Metaphors Used of Christ, the Baptized, and the Ordained

History tells us that words used to explore the meaning of Christ and his people, words and expressions that are clearly metaphorical, often end up being used literally. When this happens much of the original meaning is diluted. Moreover, the various relationships sustained by originally metaphorical usage, such as the relationship between Christ and the baptized, the Church and the Eucharist, the laity and the ordained, are weakened. The original connections are not sustained. Hierarchy becomes a sacred ranking, descending from top to bottom, rather than a principle of relationship of ministers to people, the former acting as Christ, the servant to the latter. Recent use of words such as *sacrifice* and *priest* and *temple* has been strongly shaped by the history of religion's definitions of these terms. There is need then to recover the metaphorical character of language used for Christ and the Church, as well as the many images that help us understand the nature of Christian ordained ministry.

Let us briefly explore some of the ways in which Christ, Church, and Eucharist have been described:

(1) Christ is named a priest in the letter to the Hebrews. But this "priest" sits at the right hand of God and leads his people home. The Levitical priesthood is ended; another priesthood arises in the line of Melchizedek (Ps 109:4). This allows the author of Hebrews (chapter 7)

---

[35] Ibid.
[36] Ibid., 322–3.
[37] Fawcett, *The Symbolic Language of Religion,* 54.

to discover a prototype on the fringes of Judaism and before the inauguration of the official Israelite priesthood. Jesus' priesthood is universal. "Melchizedek represents an authentic religious value outside Israel; he was taken into the history of salvation and was to enjoy an extraordinary position in it."[38]

And yet, Jesus was not a *sacerdos,* a (cultic or ritual) priest. He belonged to no sacred *sacerdotium.* Yet, following Hebrews we speak of him as priest and even as the High Priest. Such use of sacerdotal metaphor allows us to understand Christ's role as mediator in a most profound way, which does not have the same power when we use sacerdotal language literally of Christ. For when we attribute everything that the *sacerdotium* represents to Christ, "paradoxically, it shows Christ effectively taking up [again] the work in which the old priesthood failed."[39]

(2) Christ's "priesthood" is exercised not in a temple, but in his body on the cross. Here we turn the language of sacrifice on its head by naming Christ's execution a sacrifice. Literally, this is impossible because his murder was not a cultic action done by a priesthood in a temple. And so his death on the cross, so strongly emphasized in Hebrews in cultic sacrificial terms, is understood and grappled with metaphorically. Metaphors help us to make sense of a senseless act.

(3) Eucharist is very easily spoken of as sacrifice in Catholic circles; yet at the same time it must emphatically be stated, *"the Eucharist is not a sacrifice"* in the history of religions' sense, as if it were like other literal ritual sacrifices. The metaphorical claim of Eucharist as sacrifice relates the contemporary Christian meal directly to the "sacrifice" of Christ, his once-for-all death on the cross—the sacrifice of Calvary. But when we call the Eucharist a cultic sacrifice in its own right and literally, we tend to distance the Eucharist from Calvary and allow it to be understood as an independent "sacrifice," a tragic misreading of the Eucharist that played a role in the Protestant Reformation.

At the same time it should not be forgotten that the Passover themes dominating the synoptic accounts of the Last Supper and the words of Jesus over the cup direct our attention to Hebrew ritual practice in temple and home. The difference, of course, is that the Passover sacrifice in John and the words of Jesus concerning the new covenant in his blood are directly referred not simply to events in Israel's history, but to the very person of Jesus himself. As Xavier Léon-Dufour wisely observes:

---

[38] A. Gelin, "The Priesthood of Christ in the Epistle to the Hebrews," *The Sacrament of Holy Orders* (London: Aquin Press, 1962) 37–8.

[39] Ibid., 39.

"In Christ's death on the cross cultic activities have passed over into personal events."[40]

(4) "In the Greek and Latin New Testaments we find the classical terms for those who perform sacred rites (the Greek *hiereus,* the Latin *sacerdos*) applied not to the apostles nor to any other ministerial subgroup, but to all the baptized."[41] Such metaphorical use of sacerdotal language is appropriated from the description of the Jewish people in the Old Testament as a royal and priestly people. Such application is inevitable when one realizes the powerful connection we find in Paul's theology of the body of Christ. If the head is priestly then so is the body. It is not surprising that one of the earliest additions to the baptismal rite was the anointing of the head following on the water baptism, symbolizing and ritualizing the neophyte's participation in the one royal priesthood of Jesus.

(5) Because of the application of sacrificial terminology to the eucharistic meal,[42] further cultic or sacral metaphors are also used of the ministers of the table (or, increasingly, the altar).[43] Over time such metaphoric language tended to be taken literally. Even worse, the eucharistic "sacrifice" and the "priestly" ministry cease to be related to the priesthood of Jesus and the baptized. The Church forgets that such language is "first christic and ecclesial (that is, baptismal), and then episcopal."[44] If it is recognized that such priestly language is primarily about Jesus and his Church, then the application to the ordained is healthy. But, as Aidan Kavanagh notes, "A baptismal element needs to be introduced into our contemporary discussion of ministry . . . worship and the ordained ministries operate within the overarching sacramentality of the Church and *as functions of it.*"[45]

---

[40] Xavier Léon-Dufour, *Sharing the Eucharistic Bread: The Witness of the New Testament,* trans. Matthew J. O'Connell (New York/Mahwah, N.J.: Paulist Press, 1987) 197.

[41] Thomas J. Talley, "Priesthood in Baptism and Ordination," *Worship: Reforming the Tradition* (Washington, D.C.: Pastoral Press, 1990) 1.

[42] See Chapter 14 of the Didache. It can be asked whether the language of pure sacrifice that is found there primarily refers to the hearts of the participants rather than to the table rite. However, the quotation from Mal 1:11, which is so important with regard to the use of sacrificial terminology for Christian sacrament, is very much in evidence in this chapter.

[43] "Very quickly, however, the sacrificial understanding of the eucharist led to the more specific application of sacerdotal terminology to those who presided over the rite," Talley, "Priesthood in Baptism and Ordination," 1.

[44] Aidan Kavanagh, "Unfinished and Unbegun Revisited: The Rite of Christian Initiation of Adults," *Worship* 53 (July 1979) 337.

[45] Ibid., 334, emphasis mine. Kavanagh goes on to remind us "that Holy Orders are rooted in baptism never seems to cross our minds. . . . The church baptizes to

One indication that the notion of Eucharist as "sacrifice" is key to application of sacral language to Christian ministers is found in the history of the presbyterate. As presbyters became eucharistic presiders sacerdotal language was applied to them, as it was to the bishops before them. By the high Middle Ages, in fact, when bishops ceased to be regarded by most theologians as part of the sacrament of orders, presbyters were thought of as the sole subjects of the *sacerdotium,* since both they and the bishops are equal in their power to "confect" the Eucharist. And for centuries eucharistic confection becomes key to the theology of the sacrament of orders. Aidan Kavanagh writes well of the dangers inherent in this confinement of sacerdotal language solely to the presbyterate:

> The association of priesthood with the presbyterate among the western churches has presbyteralized not only the ministry but the very sacerdotality of the Church as well. This turn has lent a certain ruthless logic to the pernicious perception of ordination to the presbyterate as the only way of achieving true Christian status, or even "first-class citizenship," in the Church. Our various seminaries are full of people seeking this apparent yet nonexistent "honor."[46]

Questions

When we admit the fact that sacerdotal language in Christianity is metaphoric in nature, a number of questions may be asked: (1) What are the dangers in simply identifying Christian ordained ministry with (cultic) priesthood? (2) When acknowledged in its full metaphorical power is there really a difference "in essence" between the "priesthood" of the baptized and that of the sacramentally ordained? That is, is there a difference in the "priesthood" of either, since there is only one priesthood, that of Jesus Christ, in which the baptized and ordained share? (3) Is it not interesting that the language of the sacred, when used of Christianity, is (at least in origin) always metaphorical? Think of the cultic sphere and its application to Christians: temple—the *ecclesia* is a temple; the altar—the eucharistic table is an altar; cultic priests—Christ/bishop/presbyter are "priest"; sacred—Christian ministry is sacred ministry; sacrifice—Christ's death on the cross is a sacrifice/the eucharistic meal is a sacrifice. And on and on. Modern authors are reminding us that we need to reencounter the shock, the surprise of these statements. In perceiving their wrongness we acknowledge their richness of meaning—ambiguous

---

priesthood: it ordains only to executive exercise of that priesthood in the major orders of ministry" (335).

[46] Ibid., 336.

and multivalent. (4) Finally, is part of the contemporary discussion and disagreement about ordination, the meaning of priesthood, and the role of women in the Church due to a refusal to take metaphor (and symbol) seriously and on their own terms?

Ordination Rites—Before and After Vatican II

Introduction

Many changes have occurred in Christian ordination rites since the first clear evidence of their existence in the *Apostolic Tradition,*[47] attributed to Hippolytus of Rome ca. 215 C.E. The simple Roman structure of election, prayer with handlaying, and presiding at the Eucharist by the one ordained bishop has given way, over time, to many additional rites originating in different locations and cultures. These rites reflect changes in ideas about ordained ministry. There is a shift from identification of those with the appropriate charism to the choice of those who had "embarked on an ecclesiastical career and who, after a certain type of training and a certain apprenticeship in lower orders, had been chosen by their ecclesiastical or civil superiors for advancement."[48] There is the change from recognizing local leadership in a sober way to "increasingly elaborate" rites concerned with conferring sacramental authority.[49] There is the tendency in northern European countries to treat the images and metaphors of the restrained Roman prayers literally. Thus, for example, such expressions as "the dew of heavenly unction" in the ordination prayer for bishops was turned into an actual physical anointing of the candidate.[50] And most strikingly there is a growing emphasis on the sacral character of the ordained. Sacerdotal and sacrificial metaphors begin to dominate the more pastoral metaphors of service and oversight.

A theological shift also occurs in the consideration of those to whom the sacrament of order(s) pertains. As scholastic theologians develop a theology of the sacrament of order, trying to discern the specific characteristics of each order, the notion of a bishop being ordained—in fact, of having the fullness of ordination—is deemphasized and ignored. The language of consecration is used for making a bishop. A theology of order evolves, primarily based upon one's proximity to eucharistic con-

---

[47] See, for example, Gregory Dix, ed., *The Apostolic Tradition* (London: SPCK, 1968).

[48] H. B. Porter, *The Ordination Prayers of the Ancient Western Churches* (London: SPCK, 1967) 78.

[49] Ibid.

[50] Ibid., 79.

secration. Since there is no difference between a bishop confecting the sacrament and a presbyter doing the same, no difference is perceived between them with regard to order, although with regard to jurisdiction enormous differences exist. In terms of the sacrament of order bishops and presbyters are equal because both equally confect the Eucharist. In fact, the word *sacerdos* is used principally of presbyters in the high Middle Ages rather than of bishops as such.

The limitation of a theology of order to the ordained minister's relationship to eucharistic confection—not, please note, to oversight of people and ambo and table—along with the practice of "absolute ordination" by clerical religious orders, testifies to a vision of orders quite different from that of the early Church. This vision was sustained by a complex ritual of ordination, made up of a number of ordination rites from various locales and cultures, which particularly focused on the "power" given to the minister to consecrate. This was the ordination rite that remained in place until 1969.

Presbyteral Ordination Rite: Structure and Texts

Pre–Vatican II

In the Roman Pontificals of the past millennium we find the rites of ordination for doorkeepers, exorcists, lectors, acoltyes, subdeacons, deacons, presbyters, and bishops. Theological arguments over whether all of these pertain to the sacrament of orders, or whether just subdeacon, deacon, and presbyter are to be so identified, occupy the minds of the school men. It is clear that, however the major and minor orders are divided, there are seven, not eight, and the bishop is generally not considered part of the seven.[51] And so in recent pre–Vatican II pontificals, although we find the title *De Ordinatione Presbyteri* heading the ordination rite for presbyters, relative to making bishops the title of the rite is *De Consecratione Electi in Episcopum*!

In the rite for ordaining a presbyter one might say that the candidate is ordained several times, since the complex ritual contains several ritual elements that were considered, in different churches, to ordain. Among the many ritual elements let us note the following:

---

[51] See, for example, St. Thomas Aquinas, *Summa Theologiae* III, q. 40, a. 5. "Is the episcopate an Order?" Thomas answers that since the sacrament of order is related to the Eucharist and since the bishop has no power superior to the priest, the episcopate is not an order. However, in terms of certain sacred actions, such as ruling the mystical body (the People of God), the episcopacy is an Order (a hierarchical rank). But since it is not part of the sacrament there is no character involved.

1. The Litany of the Saints.
2. The rite of handlaying by bishop and presbyters, followed by two prayers, the preface dialogue and the prayer of ordination in which the presider prays to God: "Give them the dignity of the presbyterate." The emphasis here is on the priestly ministry of presbyters, but in the second rank after the high priests, the bishops.
3. The imposition of priestly garments: once vestments cease to be related to formal secular dress, they begin to acquire sacred characteristics, indicating particular offices in the church.
4. Anointing of hands, preceded by prayer, while the candidate kneels and the "Veni creator spiritus" is sung.
5. The conferring of the utensils of this office ("Porrectio instrumentorum"), the chalice with wine and the paten with the host. The formula is: "Receive the power to offer sacrifice to God, and to celebrate mass for the living and the dead. In the name of our Lord Jesus Christ. Amen." The addition of this rite to the presbyteral ordination rites might be due to similar conferrals that developed in the other, "minor orders." Ironically, it was this rite, with its emphasis on giving the power to offer the sacrifice of the mass that was considered to be the moment of ordination! In its "Decree for the Armenians," St. Thomas' "On the Articles of Faith and on the Sacraments" was taken over almost *verbatim* by the Council of Florence [1439]. Relative to the moment of ordination of a presbyter the decree reads: "The sixth sacrament is that of order, whose *matter* is that which is conferred by its administration; thus the priesthood [*sacerdos*] is conferred by the handing over of the chalice with the wine and the paten with the bread; the diaconate by giving the book of Gospels; the subdiaconate by giving the empty chalice covered by the empty paten; and similarly for the others by the assignment of the things pertaining to their office. The *form* for a priest is this: 'Receive the power of offering sacrifice in the Church for the living and the dead, in the name of the Father and of the Son and of the Holy Spirit.'"
6. Following communion, a second imposition of hands on each ordinand, with the words; "Receive the Holy Spirit; whose sins you forgive, they are forgiven, and whose sins you retain they are retained."

From this brief examination we can conclude that sacerdotal images predominate in the hybrid ordination of a presbyter. With the emphasis on an indicative formula and a giving of utensils supplying the "form and matter" of the sacrament, there is emphasis on being given a power to do something. One's role in the church as minister is nowhere emphasized. The prayer with handlaying that constituted the Roman rite of ordination receives little attention from theologians and so the epicletic gesture of handlaying, of beseeching God to send the Holy Spirit upon this particular minister of the church, is for all purposes ignored, as it is in other sacraments of the western church, especially the eucharist.

Post–Vatican II

The first edition of the revised presbyteral ordination rite evidenced a profound difference in comparison to the medieval rite. Most important, due in part to the intervention and clarification of Pius XII, the moment of ordination has nothing to do with handing over utensils. Instead, the ancient Roman tradition of ordaining through handlaying and epicletic prayer is once more the central rite of the sacrament and, consequently, the subject of theological study. Several of the other northern European rites have been abandoned; the rest are now found under the rubric "Explanatory Rites." As such, they no longer bear the weight given to them by medieval theologians.

Here is the outline of the rites of ordination:

1. The Litany of the Saints.
2. Handlaying with prayer. This prayer, as the pre–Vatican II prayer, is drawn from the Leonine Sacramentary and compares the candidates to the Levites of the Old Testament, the elders to whom was extended the spirit of Moses, and the sons of Aaron who shared in their father's priestly power. In New Testament terms they are related to the apostles' companions who preached the gospel. As contemporary ministers they are fellow workers with the bishop and their mission is to see to the spread of the gospel to the ends of the earth. In this first translation of the rite of ordination of presbyters both *sacerdos* and *presbyterus* are represented by the English word *priest.* As a consequence, it is not always easy to know what meaning is intended without resorting to the Latin. Finally, it should be noted that the so-called essential formula in the prayer, approved by Pope Paul VI, was translated as "Almighty Father, grant to these servants of yours the dignity of the priesthood," even though the Latin clearly states: "grant to these servants of yours the dignity of the presbyterate."
3. Explanatory rites:[52]

---

[52] We find this designation in several of the new revisions of the sacraments, such as baptism. Such terminological precision indicates that these rites unfold the meaning of what has already occurred in the central rites of the sacraments. In the case of ordination, as we have seen the central rite is not a formula conferring a power, but an epicletic prayer for the Holy Spirit.

3.1. Clothing with vesture, with no formula.

3.2. Anointing of hands with chrism with the formula: "The Father anointed our Lord Jesus Christ through the power of the Holy Spirit. May Jesus preserve you to sanctify the Christian people and to offer sacrifice to God." Chrismation is, not surprisingly, related to sanctification and to sacerdotal activity.[53] But it should be remembered that, in baptism, the first post-baptismal rite of chrismation is that done unto the royal priesthood of Christ. Furthermore, it is a christening of the head. It would seem that the chrismation of the hands in the ordination rites needs to be related to this first—and much more important—"explanatory" rite in baptism.

3.3. Presentation of the Gifts with the formula: "Accept from the holy people of God the gifts to be offered to him. Know what you are doing, and imitate the mystery you celebrate: model your life on the mystery of the Lord's cross." Clearly a different meaning than that implied in the formula for the *porrectio instrumentorum* is intended here. There can be no confusion now that this minor rite constitutes any part of ordination itself.

3.4. Kiss of peace.

The second typical edition of the "Rites of Ordination" was promulgated from Rome in 1989. The green book version was published by ICEL in 1993. In this edition of the ordination rites the sequence of ordinations is restored to an earlier order: bishops come first, then presbyters, followed by deacons. For centuries the sequence had been arranged in an "ascending" order!

Unfortunately, the Roman Congregation of Worship has not accepted the ICEL green book edition of the new version. As a consequence, at the moment of this writing a translation still awaits approval. Ironically, objections from the congregation were often to the translation of the Latin *presbyterus* by the English *presbyter,* which makes for total clarity in understanding what the prayers are saying. Instead the congregation gave greater emphasis to the English word *priest.* It would seem that sacerdotal metaphors, wanting in the Latin text, are to be imposed on an English translation.

But in terms of this paper what is important to note is the change made in the prayer for the ordination of presbyters. Not only is it much longer, the prayer details the ministry of this office.

---

[53] Note also that the *Veni creator* is not appointed to be sung at this point, as in the former rite.

First of all, it is clearly stated that the ministry of presbyter is not for itself. Rather, "By the power of the Holy Spirit you provide within the Church of Christ your Son various forms of ministry to shape your priestly people."[54] In terms of sacerdotal metaphors, then, the People of God come first in relationship to the priesthood of Jesus. The prayer goes on to refer to the various offices of ministry found in Old Testament times, as we have already seen, offices which are but type to the Christian antitypes.

After asking for helpers the bishop goes on to pray that they may receive the dignity of the presbyterate and, as did the former prayer, the "Spirit of holiness." The description of ministerial duties begins with preaching; then only follows the presiding over sacramental rites—"stewards of your mysteries"—including baptism, Eucharist, reconciliation, and anointing of the sick. They are to impetrate God's mercy for the people whom they pastor so that all nations, gathered in Christ, become "one holy people."[55]

Unlike the previous ordination rite the post–Vatican II rite balances both ministerial and sacerdotal metaphors, tending toward the former, especially in the ordination prayer. The most important sacerdotal formulae and actions are now so revised that besides becoming "explanatory rites," the language, for example, of the *porrectio instrumentorum* no longer carries the notes of giving sacerdotal power to the candidate to confect the Eucharist. Instead, the latter is seen as the great mystery belonging to the whole Church over which the minister has the privilege to preside.

Episcopal Ordination: The Ordination Prayer

With the recognition that episcopacy is an order, not simply a consecration, it was necessary for the revisers of the ordination rites to make some radical changes, especially in the ordination prayer. And in so doing the meaning of episcopacy was thrown into greater light. The pre–Vatican II prayer for the ordination of bishops is found in the Leonine and later Roman sacramentaries. The controlling metaphor is that of the "high priesthood," and, relative to the Old Testament, the ministry of Aaron is especially recalled. An inordinate amount of time is spent, however, on the meaning of his sacred vesture in contrast to the vesture of the Christian bishop. Finally, as noted before, the metaphoric image of

---

[54] The translation is from the ICEL version of *Rites of Ordination of Bishops, Presbyters, and Deacons* (Washington, D.C.: International Commission on English in the Liturgy, 1993) 81.

[55] Ibid., 82.

anointing—"Complete the fullness of your mystery in your priests, and equipped with all the adornments of glory, *hallow them with the dew of heavenly unction*" (emphasis mine)—seems to have influenced the development of an actual rite for anointing the episcopal candidate.

In the post–Vatican II rite of ordination of a bishop the crucial ordination prayer is drawn from an earlier source, the *Apostolic Tradition* (ca. 215 C.E.). In that document, in which we find the first evidence of prayers of ordination for bishop, presbtyers,[56] and deacons, the rite of ordination of a bishop is a liturgical continuum of election, handlaying with prayer, kiss of peace, and Eucharist.[57]

The prayer of ordination is drawn, therefore, from a rite that is early testimony to the role of the local church as well as neighboring churches in the ordination of a local leader. Elected by all members of the local church, ordained, however, by neighboring bishops, not by the local presbyterate, still the impetration of the Spirit (the *epiclesis*) is joined in by all.[58] Later developments will add the imposition of the book of Gospels on the head of the bishop, the anointing of the bishop's head as mentioned before, the investiture with ring, miter, and pastoral staff, and formal seating of the ordinand in his *cathedra.* But for all intents and purposes the episcopal ordination rite is complete in the *Apostolic Tradition.* One question that may be asked is: with the return to the prayer of the *Apostolic Tradition,* should not this bring with it those other elements which were seen as essential to ordination, that is, the role of the people in election and prayer?

Now to the prayer itself. The text first testifies to the belief that God calls the Church into being and guides it. In calling Abraham's descendants to be a "holy nation," God has chosen both rulers and "priests," so that the "sanctuary" will not remain empty. From this recollection we move to the epicletic portion of the prayer, in which God is asked to pour forth the governing spirit upon the candidate:

> So now pour out upon this chosen one the power which is from you, the governing Spirit whom you gave to your beloved Son, Jesus Christ, the Spirit given by him to the holy apostles, who founded the Church in every place to be your temple for the unceasing glory and praise of your name.

[56] Who are more elders or advisors than liturgical officials, it would seem.

[57] James F. Puglisi, *The Process of Admission to Ordained Ministry: A Comparative Study,* vol. I: *Epistemological Principles and Roman Catholic Rites,* trans. Michael S. Driscoll and Mary Misrahi (Collegeville: The Liturgical Press, 1996) 28.

[58] Cf. *Apostolic Tradition* 2:1: *"omnes autem silentium habeant orantes in corde propter discensionem spiritus"*; cf. Puglisi, *The Process of Admission,* 31–3.

After establishing that the particular charism of the episcopacy is that of governing, the prayer offers two further scriptural metaphors for the "office of bishop": shepherd and high priest. The bishop therefore is to be a pastor and to engage in sacred ministry. The latter includes the eucharistic offering, exercising through the Spirit forgiveness of sins, assignment of other ministers, and the loosing of bonds. In this second appeal for the Spirit (of high priesthood) "we reach the end of a process which qualified with Old Testament priesthood the ministry of the bishop, which the New Testament avoided doing."[59]

Finally, the prayer asks that the bishop realize in his own life what he exercises in public: "May he be pleasing to you by his gentleness and purity of heart."

It is important to recognize that the bishop does not receive two spirits, one of governing *(spiritus principalis)*, the other of sacerdotality *(spiritus primatus sacerdotii)*, but one Spirit, that of Christ.[60] Note also that the ordinand does not receive the priesthood, but the "priestly ministry because it is through the service of the bishop that the saving action of Christ is made present sacramentally." As a consequence, the purpose of the epiclesis is to prolong the work of Christ until the present and to preserve the place of Christ "as the author of salvation and as the only high priest."[61]

James Puglisi, after a thorough study of the ordination prayer from the *Apostolic Tradition,* concludes the following:

1. The prayer asks that the bishop receive a personal charism—the same grace as Jesus received for his mission and that he gave to his apostles.
2. As shepherd and high priest for his people, the ministry of bishop is essentially pastoral.
3. The bishop's pastoral ministry is qualified as "priestly," but only as manifesting the "unique priesthood of Christ," since only Christ has full title to "high priest."
4. The powers of the bishop are rooted in the action of the Holy Spirit. Although the bishop is seen as successor to the apostles, since the apostles received the Spirit as a college, the bishop cannot be successor to the apostles "except as he is included in the college which succeeded to the apostolic college."
5. Finally, the community prays that the bishop remain without fault and faithfully fulfill his duties.[62]

[59] Puglisi, *The Process of Admission,* 55.
[60] Ibid., 56.
[61] Ibid., 57–8.
[62] Ibid., 59–60.

Conclusion

Clear differences in meaning exist between the pre– and post–Vatican II rites of ordination. The abundance of sacerdotal images in the pre–Vatican II rites clearly focuses on the sacral quality of the ordained presbyter. Moreover, rather than continuing to speak with the power of metaphor—with the profound connection such metaphors have with the person of Jesus Christ and his body the Church—many of these sacerdotal images were taken literally. As a consequence, there was little relationship to the mission and ministry of Christ.

With this focus on the meaning of the presbyterate, the bishop not being considered an order, the understanding of the presbyterate as a ministry suffered greatly. For example, the French liturgist Pierre-Marie Gy reminds us that the majority of medieval priests did not exercise the ministry of the word and were actually incapable of doing so. Furthermore, he states, they seemed to have little awareness of any responsibility to evangelize. As a consequence, there was not only a disjunction between the minister of the sacraments and the minister of preaching, but a conclusion that despite the need for the ordained to preach, preaching was not part of the sacrament, regardless of the fact that the presbyteral ordination prayer continued to take account of preaching.[63]

The reorganization of the ordination rites, now including bishop and presbyter, achieves a better balance of pastoral and sacred images. And, especially with regard to the ordination of the bishop, the relation to Jesus Christ is once more secure. Jesus is the unique shepherd as well as the unique priest. His ministers exercise oversight of the baptized and leadership at the table. And so they realize Christ's shepherding and priesthood. But these latter metaphors are broken. Oversight is not domination but servanthood; leadership in worship is not for the baptized but with the baptized. For the images of Christ as priest and ruler, as well as prophet, take us directly to the cross, from which he rules with pierced hands and on which, with hands outstretched, he exercises his "high-priesthood."

---

[63] Pierre-Marie Gy, "Évangélisation et sacrements au moyen âge," *La Liturgie dans l'Histoire* (Paris: Cerf, 1990) 163.

3

The Ministry of Presbyters and the Many Ministries in the Church

THOMAS F. O'MEARA, O.P.

For a few decades there has been not one priesthood but the orders of bishop, presbyter, and deacon, and in that time around the world other ministries have appeared. The community faces the challenges of being a local church through a commitment to varied ministries, some part-time, some full-time, some drawn from baptism, some from ordination. The following pages present some observations on how the priest-presbyter serves within this new (in fact, old) ecclesiology.

How the Priesthood Changed After Vatican II

Very rapidly in the years after the council, ministry in the Roman Catholic Church, both in the United States and around the world, changed. It changed by the priesthood returning to the distinct orders of bishop, presbyter, and deacon; it changed by the baptized entering ministries of theological education, liturgy, and social justice; it changed by a dramatic increase in numbers and by professionalization and education, for instance, in campus ministry and health care ministry; it changed by sisters expanding the number and immediacy of their ministries. The increase in parish forms led to the development of diocesan offices directing ministry. If we consider the basic place of ministry, the parish, from 1965 to 1975 parishes changed in terms of which ministries were done and in terms of who did them. The parish was no longer a place of rapid Masses in Latin with baptisms and marriages or with an occasional golf tournament and parish dance. The liturgical roles of deacons, lectors, cantors, and Communion bearers illustrated the expansion of ministry outside Sunday morning, for the Church now understood that community liturgy existed to nourish the Church's external, evangelistic ministries of social justice, of ministries to families, to the aging, or to the young. Indeed, the very model of ministry had changed; parishes and dioceses had changed in their theological, ecclesiological, and professional patterns.

I was ordained a priest in the Dominican Order in June 1962, three months before Vatican II began. In those times, in the summer of 1962, newly ordained Dominicans spent the summer helping out on weekends at parishes in Illinois, Iowa, and Wisconsin; the rite we used was that of the Dominican Order in place by 1260. The parish offered Masses and sacraments in Latin and little more. Converts were quickly instructed; marriages needed brief, mainly legal, preparations; baptisms, except for the gingerly pouring of water, were not intelligible; Communion was brought to the sick monthly. No one not ordained entered the sanctuary (the pre-pubescent altar boys were more angelic than human), and—in terms of a parish—no ministry, that is, no ministry formally and publicly connected to the Church's life (as education, liturgy, and the RCIA are), took place outside of the sanctuary (collecting canned goods or coaching basketball teams are not what St. Paul had in mind with *diakonia*). In fact, the parish of 1962 was little different from a parish in 962 when the Norman Vikings were settling down in northern France seven hundred years before the Puritans founded towns in New England. The concrete form of the parish of 1962, or of 962, however, does not, by and large, resemble the parish today in most of the United States existing since 1972 in a post-conciliar style.

A second reflection on the changing model of ministry touches the books of the New Testament. In the years just before the council, the American parish was full of repressed vitality, but Sunday morning had little connection with the descriptions of Church and ministry that were read at Mass in the letters of the New Testament. What did it mean to say that all Christians were to be active in the body of Christ, when they sat passively facing forward in church pews and dared not disturb the pastor or school principal? Why read a list of ministries in Paul's letters to the Romans and Corinthians, when there was only one activity in a church, that of the priest? What did the mention of ministries of "evangelist" or "deacon" mean when little formal outreach in American society took place (beyond the extensive and successful schools and hospitals conducted by religious), and deacons existed only briefly in seminaries? The word *ministry* was a Protestant term not used by Catholics, and *charism* was something that years later made a dangerous figure like Catherine of Siena or Dorothy Day respectable. But one can apply easily those passages on charisms and ministries to the Church we know now. Any parish where the liturgy is done well and where that liturgy is continued in the ministry of education, care, and social service does not consist exclusively of a pastor and one or two assistants, with sisters nearby running a grade school. The new model involves a staff of full-time ministers, a community of ministers (led by the pastor) with their education, expertise, natural gifts, and commission. The contemporary parish resembles theologically the church of Paul or Origen.

These changes in ministry, theological and epoch-making, took place under the impetus of the council, for its documents set in motion for the subsequent years much more than they expressed. The work of Vatican II was to "translate," to "accommodate," to bring up to date *(aggiornamento)*. In terms of ministry such a translation brought to life the ideal of early Christianity and worked to serve large parishes filled with educated and active people. It was certainly a momentous shift, occurring rapidly and enthusiastically in the United States, drawing on American characteristics like the delight in belonging to groups, the tradition of helping and service, and a natural activism. But the spirit of the council determined that new theological themes (which were often in fact venerable traditions or early theologies) would gain an influential freedom: the People of God over against hierarchy alone; grace as empowerment rather than insurance policy; liturgy as the ritual for ministry; a theology of charism flowing into ministry. A restored theology of baptism called people to a life whose ministries and charisms were there to be used, and a theology of baptism into a called people (church) meant belonging to a local church that found that there were opportunities for ministry all around.[1]

Change in the form of parish and diocesan offices did not come from bishops or from plans drawn up by chancery officials; nor did it

---

[1] See John E. Linnan, "Ministry since Vatican II: A Time of Change and Growth," *New Theology Review* 3 (1990) 33–44. Many have found my definition of ministry helpful (often simply because it is the only definition offered), but few have fully agreed with it: "Christian ministry is the public activity of a baptized follower of Jesus Christ flowing from the Spirit's charism and the individual personality on behalf of a Christian community to witness to, serve and realize the kingdom of God." Thomas F. O'Meara, *Theology of Ministry* (Mahwah, N.J.: Paulist Press, 1999) 167.

come from the methodologies of theologians, sociological surveys of the Catholic Church, or academic observers of American religion. It did not come about because of a decline in priests: that was not to become evident until the late 1960s, although a decline in vocations to the diocesan priesthood and to religious orders of men and women had begun before the council and was likely tied to changing aspirations of Catholics who were no longer of an immigrant world. The new model of the parish came from the stimulus of Vatican II; however, it was providentially in place to supply for the decline in the quantity and quality of priests. Healthy and grand theological movements also came from the grass-roots, as Christians began to see and live differently. Change is not an instant revolution or a chain of successes. In old and huge organizations like the Catholic Church change is a complex phenomenon. The past never fully disappears; old forms are not fully replaced; the new must be both incarnational and traditional. It seems unavoidable to conclude that these changes came from a deep encounter between the Spirit of the risen Jesus and the People of God. Apparently the Holy Spirit wanted to alter, to broaden the way the Church's members understood themselves and understand the Church's mission.

Did the expansion of the ministry, far from endangering the presbyterate, contribute to its preservation? The priest prior to Vatican II was caught in a routine of automatic words and actions. Probably that ethos of apostolic frustration furthered widespread alcoholism. Priests and sisters lived passively in a network of powerful male and female ecclesiastical autocrats making solitary, often poor decisions. The absorption and then imprisonment of ministry in the immigrant parish could not have survived much longer.

Theological Metamorphoses of Early Church Ministry and of the Modern Priest

The above has been an empirical sketch of the changing model of parish. We want to look briefly at two valuable reflections on the passage of ministry through history. Alexandre Faivre is well known for his study on clergy and laity in the early centuries of the Church, a book translated into English. Since then he has published *Ordonner la fraternité. Pouvoir d'innover et retour à l'Église ancienne,*[2] which treats in great detail the emergence of words and functions for ministry in the first three centuries of

---

[2] Alexandre Faivre, "Conclusion: Le pouvoir d'innover," *Ordonner la fraternité. Pouvoir d'innover et retour à l'Église ancienne* (Paris: Cerf, 1992) 435–50; the book includes a fifty-page annotated bibliography.

the Church and places this "innovation" in the context of more Christian writers of each century. To conclude he speaks of three processes in which he finds deep structural-theological issues. The first is the power to begin something new and the limits of innovation. The second is the relationship and tension between "the foundational originality" and a "continuing originality." Finally, there is the movement from a newness that is seminal and rather radical in establishing the Christian community as a "temple" with immediate presence of the Spirit in each individual called to ministry on to that newness enclosed, for subsequent times, in the writings of the New Testament. Faivre is prompting us to wonder at the freedom the first Christians felt in Church life, to be rather surprised that they viewed their pneumatic life as creative of the names and arrangements of ministries. We should notice that in Faivre's perspective what follows the first century is not simply Church history or the history of theology and exegesis, nor is it a tradition of past documents. Instead it is a primal originality, a birth continuing in a variety of social forms—ministerial, liturgical, and theological—suitable to various cultures ranging from Ethiopian to Celtic. "One has passed from a theological discourse to a symbolism legitimizing a power, from a community discipline consented to out of love one passes to an authority that makes forms legitimate."[3] This is why Christians, "co-heirs with Christ according to the Spirit" (Rom 8:16), must always test the institutions they have received in light of the original event and the continuing originality given by the Spirit.

A second text looks at the changes in the symbol-role of the priest between the preceding centuries (from Trent through French spirituality to American immigrant church) and Vatican II. A few years after the council, for the volumes of *Unam Sanctam* being edited by Yves Congar as commentaries on the documents of the council, Henri Denis wrote of five basic theological (liturgical and ecclesial) changes that a new council brought to Trent.[4]

First, the point of departure for subsequent changes was expanding the understanding of the mission of the Church from the priest's celebration of the Eucharist (joined to the congregation at the time of Communion) to a fuller mission of the Church. Second, Denis thinks that the recent council sees the institution of the priesthood not to be found solely at the Last Supper but in Jesus' institution of apostles and disciples, apostolate and ministry. Third, the specificity of the presbyter is

---

[3] Ibid., 450.
[4] Henri Denis, "La Théologie du presbyterat de Trente à Vatican II," *Les Prêtres* (Paris: Cerf, 1968) 193–201.

not solely in the power to consecrate bread and wine but to act in various ways in the power of the risen Christ, precisely for and in Christ as the head of his body. Fourth, the priesthood is essentially ministerial: it is not solely cultic but flows from the ministry of the apostles and active ministers announcing the Gospel and founding churches. Finally, the relationship of the presbyter to God does not occur in celebratory isolation during the words of consecration, but that action and all that he does is bound to God's grace in the life and context of a fuller ministry of the pastor.

The Priest and Community in the Midst of History

The priesthood, the ministry, and the community do not exist apart in a world of books or bureaucracies, but are inevitably part of culture and history, part of a historical period beginning in the last third of the twentieth century. The priesthood for centuries before 1962 was partly of the age of Ambrose, of the fourteenth century, of the French school of spirituality, and of the United States where the priest was to immigrants pastor and companion.[5] Five historical trajectories of Christian motifs and forms are intersecting now and they explain the recent expansion of ministry in the Catholic Church: (1) the Pauline theology of the body of Christ with varied activities; (2) the social distinction between clergy and laity; (3) the ministry of women; (4) passing beyond the recent past; (5) the reemergence of circles of ministry.

Living within the Body of Christ

Today more and more Christians work in direct Church ministry. There are many parishioners, young and old, who wish to work not simply in planning a picnic but in educating converts or bringing Communion to the sick. Most pastors are assisted by several full-time ministers and by many part-time ones. Paul welcomed all ecclesial gifts, refusing to be embarrassed by or hostile to whatever was useful to the ministry of the Church. He minimized sensational gifts and accented those which were public services to the Gospel. Charism is the contact between the life of the Spirit and an individual personality, and, in my view, charisms lead into the life of the Church and are the foundation for the ministries building up the community (1 Cor 12:7; 3:7, 16; Rom 12:4). There can be many charisms ranging from momentary inspirations to life-long decisions; at times in a Christian's life, we suspect, invitations will be given to serve the Church. Paul gave harmony to the

---

[5] See Thomas F. O'Meara, "The Metamorphoses of Ministry," *Theology of Ministry* (Mahwah, N.J.: Paulist Press, 1999).

diversity of important ministries, to communal services, by the metaphor of the human body with its many activities. The "body of Christ" presents a sociology of cooperation among ministries and actions in the Church; it presumes a living organism, with no inactive group and no spiritual elite. The lists of diaconal charisms in Romans, Corinthians, and Ephesians are not intended to exhaust or control ministry. The ministry of leadership is mentioned by several names in the New Testament, and is inevitably present in a community; leadership, however, is not the only ministry, nor are other ministries derived from it (1 Cor 16:15). The wider community of New Testament ideas now available through the liturgy and education has influenced the expansion of ministry. In an unsettling way the dynamic parish of 1999 resembles a Pauline community in 55 C.E. perhaps more than it resembles a parish in 1959.

Beyond the Distinction of Clergy and Laity

For a long time the terms clergy and laity, based on the presence or absence of the rites of ordination (or tonsure), have divided the Church in two. By the time of the *Apostolic Tradition* of Hippolytus (ca. 220 C.E.) the word *clergy* was used for an ecclesiastical state (not a ministry) to which bishop, presbyters, and deacons (in Eastern churches, deaconesses?) belonged. There is, however, another New Testament meaning for *kleros*. In Acts, Colossians, and Ephesians, the word is used for the share that all Christians, all members of a church, have in the word and reality of Christ, "the inheritance of the saints in light" (Col 1:12). This is not simply a fortunate "lot" but a "good thing" prepared for the believer by God. A sharing in the Lord comes precisely not just to the clergy (the later *klerikoi*) but to the whole People of God. And that breadth of the Spirit is the originality of Christianity (Rom 8:1ff.).

During the third century the focus of the community began to shift from evangelization to solemn liturgy and orthodox teaching, although the external mission of the Church was considerable. The separation of clergy from the people may have been nourished by the tendency of the churches to want to resemble the Jewish people of the inspired Pentateuch and to have similarities with their pagan neighbors' cults. Yves Congar has written: "To look for a 'spirituality of lay people' in the Scriptures makes no sense. There is no mention of laity. Certainly the word exists, but it exists outside the Christian vocabulary."[6] In American usage "lay person" means someone who is ignorant of the area under discussion, who is out of the field of action. Most meanings of the word are not positive, and ecclesial usage cannot escape their overtones.

[6] Yves Congar, "Laic et Laicat," *Dictionnaire de Spiritualité* 9 (Paris: Desclée, 1976) 79.

The fullness of baptism, the universal access to God, the avoidance of dualism, the basic equality of men and women in the kingdom of God—these biblical themes supersede subsequent divisions. One cannot make sense of today's parish in light of the clergy/laity distinction interpreted in a strict dualism. When the magisterium defends that distinction, it is defending not the words, not a dualism, and not a graced division in the Church between those solely active and those largely passive; it is legitimately defending the distinction between ministries. That the ministry of pastor is central and more important than that of reader is obvious, but the ministry of reader is not nothing, not a tolerated usurpation of clerical activity. Ministries differ in importance and distinctions among ministries (and ministers) remain, but they are, according to the New Testament, grounded upon a common faith and baptismal commissioning.

Women in Ministry

There have always been women in ministry, but only in recent decades have they been readmitted to ministries formally linked to the liturgy; they have always been in education in terms of schools but only recently readmitted to ecclesial education. The growing presence of women in ministry has flowed not from that of the *apostle* (Junias) or *deaconess* of the first centuries, but after 1970, upon the work of religious women, whose history began in the twelfth century. In the seventeenth century by combining cloistered forms with some active ministry women religious were permitted to work in education and health care, and after a century or more this led to active religious congregations (often begun as assemblies of celibate women in a private association for some work). The United States with a thousand and more schools, hospitals, and other institutions has been the modern display ground of the congregations of active religious women. Religious women did not hesitate to establish in the most difficult circumstances all kinds of institutions, most of whose works correspond to Pauline ministries. If we consider health care, religious education, the care of the poor, and retreat houses to be ministries, then one must conclude that over 60 or 70 percent of Catholic ministry in America during the twentieth century has been done by women. The time of these large, expanding, ministering congregations is coming to an end, but their trajectory leads on to something beyond. By the early 1970s women not belonging to religious congregations were entering ministry, and for decades they have been prominent in so many areas of ministry, including that of seminary education and directing parishes.

Passing beyond the Recent Past

The Baroque, reaching from 1580 to 1720, was an epochal period. That time of cultural renewal and of religious expansion was more than the Tridentine Counter-Reformation: it was a major Catholic restoration and renewal. The Baroque is the most recent major era in Roman Catholic life. With variations it reappeared and continued from 1820 to 1960. With Vatican II world-wide Catholicism began to leave the Baroque (the transitions of the priesthood given by Denis is one illustration).

The Baroque spirit brought to the Church new theologies, spiritualities, and arts, and these usually manifested interplays between personality and grace (e.g., as articulated by Ignatius Loyola, Philip Neri, or Teresa of Avila). A universality begun by Columbus' exploration and Galileo's astronomy offered to the Catholic mind a new world view. God was experienced in a vastness, freedom, and goodness flowing through a world of diversity, movement, and order, while Christ appeared in a more human way, filled with a personal love, redemptive and empowering. This was a time of great missionary work and great interior conversations with the divine. Actual grace is the central theological theme of the Baroque: a transient force influencing adolescent vocations, validly received sacraments, or death-bed decisions; grace was a power for life, a force to aid each individual in following God's will, a force contacting the will and emotions more than the intellect. The Baroque furthered methods of prayer and meditation, as ornate statues told emotional stories and crowds passively attended liturgies like folk missions, novenas to saints, or rites surrounding the Blessed Sacrament. The Baroque went underground during the Enlightenment and then reemerged, albeit with some new emphases, as Romanticism moved beyond the Enlightenment. The nineteenth century had its originality (it added a neo-medieval restoration), but that age more often than not composed variations on the Baroque. That time from 1830 to 1960 is the period just before Vatican II, and it has its theology of priestly, consecrated, and ministerial life and activity.

Ministry from the Baroque to Vatican II was done by parish priests, very much located within sacraments and sacramentals somewhat mechanically performed; it was an activist ministry strengthened by a theology of actual graces brought by sacraments and by personal prayer. The baptized were kept from the real, public ministry just as they were kept from the sanctuary. Seminary education gave the impression that ministry was largely about the methods of spirituality, canon law, and the rubrics of liturgy, that the fallen world could receive only so much redemption, and that all not in orders or vows existed in a secular sphere capable not of ministry but of a vague witness.[7]

The understanding of ministries flowing out of baptism and expanding around the leadership of pastor and bishop, a rejection of the strict separation of secular and sacred, grace no longer viewed within the context of a waterworks of laws and definitions, a view that there were ministries that existed outside of liturgy, the involvement of the baptized in liturgy itself, the joining of meditation with liturgy and public action—these themes of Vatican II and of Pope Paul VI have drawn the Baroque trajectory into something new.[8]

---

[7] Yves Congar, "Not a hierarchology," *Ministères et communion écclésiale* (Paris: Cerf, 1971) 10. Congar described the institutionalized ecclesiology that had lasted almost four centuries.

> We can note the ecclesiological aspect of Roman centralization, which is linked to a further important aspect. Trent had affirmed in the face of Protestantism that Christ is not solely a redeemer but that he is also a law-giver. In this line, even in its work at sustaining and demanding a kind of bishop who was truly pastoral, it favored the construction of a hierarchical order: not one arranged around the Eucharist but one around the "regime" of which Rome occupies the center and summit. Despite the admirable expansion of Christian life and pastoral ministry, an era of legalism began, replacing a somewhat theoretical ecclesiology. Finally an orthodoxy, not only of faith but of theology, is fixed by a kind of canonization of the conceptual and verbal system come down from scholasticism which from then to our own times has incorporated itself into Catholicism.

L'Église de saint Augustin à l'époque moderne (Paris: Cerf, 1970) 368. The ecclesiology of the Neo-Scholastic manuals can be found in *Tractatus de ecclesia Christi ad mentem S. Thomae Aquinatis* (Malta: Muscat, 1949), a textbook by Gerard Paris widely used in the *studia* of the Dominican Order. This text presented the four causes of the Church in Aristotelian language: the formal cause was the bishops; the efficient cause was Jesus, the Holy Spirit, and the bishops; the final cause was heaven; the material cause, like clay for a statue, was everyone who was not a bishop, provincial, or pastor.

[8] As a bridge between the end of the Baroque and developments after Vatican II of women and men in ministries, we note an important historical-sociological study. It is important because of the decline in the numbers of members of religious orders that along with the decline in the diocesan priesthood presents an uncomfortable situation, but perhaps one indicating a new direction. Raymond Hostie, a Belgian sociologist, searched the histories of *all* religious orders in the Western church and found in them a similar life-cycle. He delineated stages of foundation, solidification of identity, flourishing, decline, and demise. The cycle lasts about 130 years. All orders have gone and go through this cycle—but most go through it only once. The Benedictines, the Franciscans, the Dominicans, and the Jesuits have gone through it several times. Today we see the demise of some religious orders of men and of many religious orders of women. In light of Hostie's study, this is not surprising: we find ourselves at the end of a cycle begun when many, many religious orders came into

The Re-Appearance of Baptismal Ministry

Rapidly in the years after 1965, as the ministry changed, Catholic men and women began in great numbers to study theology and to study for various ministries (if in 1960 there was only one or two places where a non-cleric could study theology, after 1975 it took the *National Catholic Reporter* several issues to list them). This remarkable phenomenon, the dual expansion of theological education and ministry, had had its preparation. Various organizations were founded in the century or so after 1830 that drew individual Christians into active groups; these ranged from third orders and confraternities to Catholic Action, the Vincent de Paul and Holy Name Societies, Jocists, urban houses of Christian witness. But they were qualitatively different from today's expansion of ministry. Taking for granted the distinction of sacral and sacred worlds, they did not pass beyond witness and material assistance into the essential ministries of the Church. In the 1970s parishioners' activities underwent a pneumatic metamorphosis as men and women (and permanent deacons) became active in liturgical ministries during and outside of Mass, as well as in services of education, liturgy, peace and justice, music, ministry to the sick and dying.[9] In the United States the expansion of

---

existence after the French Revolution and during the romantic restoration after 1830. The many congregations of religious women in this century in America are largely the gift of this recent period. This ministerial time has brought their great ministerial accomplishments, but its characteristic of great numbers is ending.

We might conclude that ahead will be new religious orders—and that might be, but they will not be the small, unhealthy, restorationist groups imitating 1920 or 1950 that have been encouraged by the pontificate of John Paul II. Will there be a fourth form of religious life ranking with monks, friars, and active orders? It is possible, however, that such a future is not the plan of the Holy Spirit. It may be that for the numbers and need of ministries even tens of thousands of vowed men and women are not adequate (although they remain important). More ministers are needed to work among the great number of believers and non-believers: for ministering to their graced lives with some individuality, for meeting heightened levels of education in America and cultural diversity in the world, and for engaging the great works of mercy and evangelization that a large global population needs. The end of this recent cycle of religious life is indeed leading ahead, but it may be leading into broader modes and kinds of ministry: in short, into a Church of ministers, many with the same education as priests and religious. These are the people who have entered education and ministry in the past three decades. See Hostie, *Vie et mort des ordres religieux. Approches psychosociologiques* (Paris: Desclée, 1972); for a summary see R. Fitz and L. Cada, "The Recovery of Religious Life," *Review for Religious* 34 (1975) 690–9.

[9] One often finds what seems to be a new idea in unlikely sources. Not long after 1500, Thomas de Vio, Cardinal Cajetan, wrote:

ministry and the expansion of theological education were intertwined from the beginning and influenced each other.

The trajectories just sketched are stimulated by history and culture at work among Catholics today. Each trajectory brings us to our present situation and suggests that this new situation is neither utterly new nor unexpected. The theology of the body of Christ indicates that ministry for the baptized should be ordinary; history indicates that the ministries of women have existed; the present age has brought a model that goes beyond the sole performance of whatever was being done by clergy or by religious and priests.

Two Facets of a Contemporary Theology of the Priest Amid a Community of Ministers

In my reflections on ministry, stimulated not by academic require-ments or research but by observing and experiencing the shift in the model of the parish, two theological aspects, ultimately not new or novel, have appeared as important: (1) the recent reversal in the relation-ship of liturgy to ministry, and (2) the model of concentric circles for ministry that allows for plurality and qualitative differences.

Liturgy as Nourishing Sacrament of Wider Ministry

The reversal of liturgy and extra-liturgical ministry means that ministry is as basic as liturgy, and that liturgy exists to serve and nourish ministry. This reversal is one of direction and inclusion, not of upheaval: it is a move from symbol to reality, from solitary priest to community, from liturgy to services. Service to the kingdom of God flows from litur-gical enactment into real, public, social actions.

Liturgy is intended to confirm and nourish ministries in the world. Before World War II the parish had often been a social center, but until Vatican II parishioners saw few traces of Church ministry outside of Sunday morning. Since Catholics easily viewed the priest solely as litur-gist, they presumed other ministers must remain inside Sunday Mass.

The faithful, because they are moved by the Holy Spirit to the works of their spir-itual life . . . , act as parts of one totality. . . . Each faithful believes he or she is a member of the church, and as a member of the church believes, hopes, ministers the sacraments, receives, teaches, learns, etc., and does them on behalf of the church as a part of the whole to whom they [the activities] all belong.

Commentaria Cardinalis Caietani on *Summa theologiae* II–II, q. 39, a. 1, in Sancti Thomae Aquinatis, *Opera Omnia,* Leonis XIII, P. M., edita, vol. 8 (Rome: Typographia Polyglotta, 1895) 307.

Christians do not enter the world as ministers because they have been consecrated as liturgists. Just the opposite is true: offices and roles in the liturgy are justified by public service. Liturgy reflects real ministry.[10] A deacon has a liturgical role because of an external social ministry. To turn briefly to the deacons, although their identity and origin seem pluriform, the dominant work that characterized them in the ages of the martyrs and of the Constantinian establishment was extensive programs for the urban poor or the Christian needy. Whatever liturgical role deacons had was derived from this. This reversal by which action in the world grounds liturgical symbol is a central facet of a realistic theology of ministry.

The sharpest example of this is the leader of the community. The leader presides among the ministries of a church in their public services. Hence, this coordinator is thereby the normal minister to preside at that special aspect of the community's life, the paschal liturgy of Sunday. Hervé Legrand, O.P., observes that most Christians believe their eucharistic assembly is possible because it is enacted by a priest whose personally possessed and unique power fashions this. In fact, the bishop and then the presbyter preside at the Eucharist because their ministry is one of leadership and spiritual discernment in nourishing and building up the community. "Thus presidency of the Eucharistic assembly is seen as including the liturgical, prophetic and ministerial dimensions in the pastoral charge of building up the church, a charge conferred in ordination."[11] Legrand finds in a variety of patristic and liturgical documents from the first five centuries of the Church that reversal by which not sacral priesthood but leadership in charism, liturgy, and public life is the foundation of bishop and later presbyter, of eucharistic leader.

The presbyter and bishop, correctly defined, are not the same as educator and deacon: not because their role as community leader sets them apart from extra-liturgical ministry (indeed they are the center and

---

[10] "The principal roles in the Christian celebration manifest the very structure of the church. The functions in the assembly have two sides: on the one hand, they are (liturgical) functions; on the other hand, they reveal that which the 'ecclesia' is, reveal its structure." P. Gy, "Ordres et fonctions dans l'assemblé liturgique," *Bulletin du comité des études* 52 (1968) 185.

[11] Hervé Legrand, "The Presidency of the Eucharist according to the Ancient Tradition," *Worship* 53 (1979) 430. Congar agrees:

> It is by being a local church that a community enacts a liturgical prayer. . . . This (church) must verify in itself the essential aspects of church (convocation, institution, communion). . . . But if the church is realized to a high degree in liturgical action, it is nonetheless not reduced to it. The church is also mission, kerygma, teaching, service, political critique and action.

Y. Congar, "Reflexions sur l'assemblé liturgique," *La Maison-Dieu* 115 (1973) 8–15.

enabler of all ministries and not just liturgical ones), but because the role of the leader of the community is not the same as the community's social advocate. With an expanded ministry, with new ministries realizing the old services of prophet, teacher, evangelist, and deacon in the public sector—and they would have at times liturgical roles—the community's vocation and breadth is evident.

Liturgy serves the spirit of the Christian by word and symbol, by silence and sacrament, by sounds and colors. There is a way in which liturgy remains secondary (for even sacrament is not full reality), for the symbolic and verbal nourishment of the Christian has some further goal beyond the church building, rites, and Sunday morning. Thomas Aquinas concluded that there was a diversity of ministers in the body of Christ, because there existed a diversity of actions "necessary for the church."[12] If the ecclesial source and effect of liturgy is ministry, nonetheless, a parish has to do not only with a priest attracting attendance at Sunday Mass but with assembling a people whose being as the body of Christ requires sacraments and expects ministries.

The Model of Ministries as Concentric Circles

The theological line reaching from Johann Adam Möhler to (in two different branches) Yves Congar and Karl Rahner understands the Church as the body of Christ, that is, as an organic collective self of various charism-inspired ministries. This ecclesial model also finds support (as it did for Möhler and Congar) in the Greek theologians of the third century. The Spirit is the soul or transcendental ground of the community, an underlying permeating (transcendental) presence of grace and its realization in charism. This theology suggested to me, as it did to others, a new pattern of considering ministry: namely as circles of ministries around the leader of the community (who could be Christ or his Spirit, or the pastor or bishop). The communal leader stands not over against or in competition with other ministries, but as a leader who enables (as we saw, the static debilitating line of clergy and laity is unrealistic and inadequate). The other ministries themselves are not all the same, but they are all truly ministry: the ordained and those working full-time in a church along with all kinds of part-time ministers, volunteers, and assistants in the parish. It is best not to try to find their identity fully in the linguistic division into "lay" and "ordained." We live in a time when simple linear divisions into two groups are not adequate, and all Christians are basically enabled for ministry through baptism.[13] Rather,

---

[12] *Summa Theologiae* II–II, q. 183, a. 2 (citing Rom 12:4).
[13] See Gerard Austin, "Baptism as the Matrix of Ministry," *Louvain Studies* 23 (1998) 101–13.

the ecclesiology and practice make it clear which ministries are more or less central, more or less full-time, and designated to begin by an ordination or a commissioning (no ministry should begin only by being hired).

The model of concentric circles stands in contrast to the line that divides this group from that, a model unable to recognize degrees of ministry, to recognize ministries as such, and to let there be degrees (some very different from the others) of ministers. Here all ministries are based upon the underlying animating force of the Spirit in the community and unfold from charism and personality vitalized by baptism and drawn to ministry. Circles of ministry indicate a similarity in ministry, but there is a difference and distinction between degrees of ministry ranging from leadership to occasional services. The distinctions and differences are initiated by baptism, commissioning, and ordination but are ultimately based upon the goal of the ministry.

Karl Rahner finds the primal gift of ministry preserved within the historically manifest forms. The relationship between the Church and its individual structure, between forms in the New Testament and in the teaching of Jesus before Easter, and in today's Church "is an important and difficult question . . . , for within the time of the New Testament itself there is a history and a becoming of the constitution of the church."[14] Ministry is not a sacral officialdom from which all prophets, innovators, and charismatics have fled. The Church, far from hoping for a time without forms, is itself the place of the concrete presentation and realization of invisible grace. The Church listens to revelation and the call of the age in the same moment, receiving in a new way that which from the beginning was entrusted to it.[15] The Church, distinguishing between a single potentiality ("one pastoral ministry") and its "degrees," should be interested not in quantitative control but in fullness and quality.[16]

---

[14] Karl Rahner, *Das Amt in der Kirche* (Freiburg: Herder, 1966) 11; see J. T. Farmer, *Ministry in Community: Rahner's Vision of Ministry* (Louvain: Peters [Eerdmans], 1993).

[15] Karl Rahner, "On the Theology of Revolution," *Theological Investigations* 14 (New York: Seabury Press, 1976) 324.

[16] Karl Rahner, "Meaning of Ecclesiastical Office," *Servants of the Lord* (New York: Herder & Herder, 1968) 21–8. "Office has a functional character in the church as a society, even though this society with its functions (proclamation of the word, sacrament, leadership of the church's life as society) constitutes a sign of the reality of the church—the free Spirit, faith, hope and love" (Karl Rahner, *The Shape of the Church to Come* [New York: Seabury Press, 1974] 56). One can today discern "the Spirit pressing the church to give practical effect to this new awareness." The ecclesial source of the new vitality is baptism: "by sacramental consecration every Christian in the church has been authorised and empowered for the task of actively co-operating in the work

Such a Church existing in history for human beings cannot be a closed system; revelation and even theology are never exhausted by this or that form.[17]

> Each member of the church is an active co-bearer of the self-construction of the church, and precisely as this self-construction of the church means concretely the mediation of salvation to the individual. But this fact does not mean that the function through which the individual Christian is co-bearer of the self-construction of the church is the same for all individuals.[18]

The priest, for Rahner, is "based in a community and commissioned by the church to be the full and official preacher of the Word of God so that the sacramentally highest level of intensity of this word is entrusted to him."[19] The personal center of incarnational life is closely joined to preaching the word and celebrating the Eucharist. If the priest-pastor is at the center of the life of the Church, still that ministry no longer exhausts all ministry. In the Church before Vatican II there was really only one ministry; now, there are others. Even if the Church does not give a service a title or an ordination ceremony, it might still exist.[20] Here a Rahnerian theology of degrees of implicit and explicit grace finds its variation in Church life. Just as Christ is the definitive center of a world of religions with some revelation and grace, so Christ, but also the bishop and pastor, are centers of varying degrees of ministry, some indispensable, others important. Grace and ministry, drawn from the event of Christ but not all explicitly recognized in history as such, work within vastly different times and peoples. In Church life the center is retained, but not at the expense of the condemnation or diminishment of those who exist in other degrees.

---

of the church both interiorly and exteriorly" (Karl Rahner, "The Role of the Layman in the Church," *Theological Investigations* 8 [New York: Herder & Herder, 1971] 53–7).

[17] "The hierarchy of orders is not identical with a 'hierarchy' of free charisms in the church which also belong to the essence of the church; nor is nearness to God a privilege of the clerical states which is also not simply the sole bearer of the realization of being the church" (Rahner, *Das Amt in der Kirche,* 33).

[18] Karl Rahner, *Selbstvollzug der Kirche, Sämtliche Werke* 19 (Freiburg: Herder, 1995) 83.

[19] Karl Rahner, "Der theologische Ansatzpunkt für die Bestimmung des Wesens des Amtspriestertums," *Concilium* 5 (1969) 196.

[20] Rahner often referred to the empirical reality of ministry, noting that the baptized were doing ministry habitually and professionally without having received any sacramental commissioning, commissioning that existed in the Church precisely to assist them in ministry. See Rahner, "Vatican II and the Diaconate," *Theological Investigations* 10 (New York: Herder & Herder, 1973) 227–31.

Looking back on his years of work in Church structure, Yves Congar also found a linear model inadequate. He proposed a return to a deeper tradition in which Christ's Spirit underlay a community with various circles of ministries within it.[21]

> The church of God is not built up solely by the actions of the official presbyteral ministry but by a multitude of diverse modes of service, more or less stable or occasional, more or less spontaneous or recognized, and when the occasion arises consecrated, while falling short of sacramental ordination. . . . It would then be necessary to substitute for the linear scheme a scheme where the community appears as the enveloping reality *within which* the ministries, eventually the instituted sacramental ministries, are placed as *modes of service* of what the community is called to be and do.[22]

This is very different from the Church in the 1950s when a few thousand out of millions shared in an ecclesially (but not always socially) insignificant "apostolate" gingerly bestowed by bishops. That model changed. "It is worth noticing that the decisive coupling is not 'priesthood/laity,' as I used it in *Jalons,* but rather 'ministries/modes of community service.'"[23] Congar himself gave a sketch of the model that would replace the bipolar division of clergy and laity. It is a circle with Christ and Spirit as ground or animating power upon ministries in community. "It would then be necessary to substitute for the linear scheme a scheme where the community appears as the enveloping reality *within which* the ministries, eventually the instituted sacramental ministries, are placed as *modes of service* of what the community is called to be and do."[24]

---

[21] Yves Congar, "My Path-Findings in the Theology of Laity and Ministries," *The Jurist* 32 (1972) 178. Congar wrote shortly after the council ended:
A certain number of new emphases keep reappearing. There is, first of all, the insistence on community of life and on dignity in the order of Christian existence; then there is the correlative and profound theme of hierarchy as service; the acknowledgement of the existence of charisms among all the faithful, and for the priest [there is] the duty of taking them into consideration. All this affords a rather new pneumatological view of the church.
"The Laity," *Vatican II: A Reappraisal,* ed. Theodore Hesburgh (Notre Dame, Ind.: University of Notre Dame Press, 1968) 247.

[22] Congar, "My Path-Findings," 178, 181. Congar spoke of the basic equality of the baptized and of a diversity of services and offices that involves some inequality— at times he put "laity" in quotation marks—in "Vision de l'église comme peuple de Dieu," *Le Concile de Vatican II* (Paris: Beauchesne, 1984) 114.

[23] Congar, "My Path-Findings," 176.

[24] Ibid., 181.

The People of God and the animating Spirit of the Church are open to and restless for the rush of diversity in unity.[25]

If ultimately Christ and his Spirit are the ground, the center, and the goal of the circles of ministry to people, the pastor—the presbyteral leader and coordinator—exists empirically and ecclesially at the center of the circles. The priest's ministry is not an administrator or group enabler; to call him derisively "an orchestra leader" is to misunderstand his proper ministry. Issues in ecclesiology have appeared because the presbyter moved from the one who did everything in the parish (services that ecclesiastical life curtailed) to a ministry that is not particular but finds its traditional and contemporary particularity from leadership. This leadership is grounded in preaching and presiding.

★ ★ ★

What these pages have described, a leaving and a beginning, is a difficult passage, but it is the unavoidable present time, a time that Pope Paul VI, opening the second session of Vatican II, said had come to free "the noble and destiny-filled name of 'church'" from "forms full of

---

[25] Offering an example of the pre-conciliar mentality where ecclesiology was absorbed by law or spirituality is Hans Urs von Balthasar. His ecclesiology can only avoid difficult issues since most of it was written before the council or in some hostility to it. Ecclesiology is not helped by describing the Church mainly as a "mystery," and by describing roles in the Church as pious imitations of New Testament figures. Repeatedly the laity is not permitted to leave its constraints, for fear that the clerical state will be qualified.

> It should not be forgotten, however, that the lives of the laity will always be directed towards goals proper to themselves and that any attempt to burden them with an ecclesial ministry . . . in imitation of the apostolate of those in the states of election will soon prove to be impossible not only because of the practical difficulties involved, but also because of the realistic boundaries that separate the lay state from the states of election. Lay persons are obliged to practice Christian love of God and neighbor as perfectly as possible. . . . The popular attempts being made in France and elsewhere to remove the distinction between laity and clergy by a continual interchange of services, ministries, and even "offices" and "functions" . . . seem to me to be . . . unbiblical.

Han Urs von Balthasar, *The Christian State of Life* (*Der christliche Stand,* 1977) (San Francisco: Ignatius, 1983) 16, 383. This is not an ecclesiology or systematic theology but a spirituality, never escaping its Neo-Platonic and German idealist ethos and Barthian sympathy; inevitably, freedom and growth, life beyond post-Baroque spiritualities, within a wider range of grace, sacrament, and ministry bring its devotees anxiety. See Dermot Power, *A Spiritual Theology of the Priesthood: The Mystery of Christ and the Mission of the Priest* (Washington, D.C.: Catholic University of America Press, 1998).

holes" and from "being close to collapse."[26] To reflect upon the expansion of ecclesial ministry in the past few decades is to conclude that the Spirit is determined to bestow on more people more ministries, and to disclose to the world Church how much there remains to be done.

[26] Paul VI, "Allocutio Secunda SS. Concilii Periodo Ineunte," *Acta Apostolicae Sedis* (Sept. 29, 1963) 55 (1963) 895. When we look at the future we see a single factor attracting our attention: the decline of the numbers of diocesan and religious priests. There are three other movements equally important: the end, as we have known them in the United States, of active religious orders of religious women; the expansion of approved or semi-approved ministries in parish and diocese by baptized Christians; the presumption by baptized Catholics that they would be active in their parishes and dioceses. It appears that bishops have given up the perspective which is that of a single ministerial structure, that of the 1950s and of a return to it through a fantasized increase in vocations (the more serious issue of the decline in the quality of vocations is avoided).

As the ministry enters its fourth decade of expansion there are new issues: the multiplication of certificate programs in ministry and the positive and negative relationship of that widespread movement to the necessary level of theological education and to the previously usual summer M.A. programs; the preparation for the lack of priests by expanding the education of permanent deacons; the acceptance of candidates for the ministry of presbyter who are incapable of sustained work among adults; the decision in France and Germany that full-time baptized ministers are hired not by the parish but by the diocese (which is the local church); a large number of religious and laity heading parishes without priests.

4

The Place of Preaching in the Ministry and Life of Priests

STEPHEN VINCENT DeLEERS

Arguably, one of the best-received teachings of the Second Vatican Council was its restoration of the biblical, liturgical homily to the celebration of the Eucharist and other sacraments. The People of God today have embraced that restoration, and they hunger for effective preaching. What the council stated as doctrine is now fully enfleshed in the baptized: "The People of God is formed into one in the first place by the Word of the living God, which is quite rightly sought from the mouths of priests."[1]

In this chapter, I will examine the place of preaching, first in the Church's own doctrinal self-understanding, and then in the ministry and life of priests.[2] The primacy of preaching for the Church and its priests will emerge, as will the implications of that primacy.

The Church's Self-Understanding: The Doctrinal Place of Preaching

The Second Vatican Council paid a great deal of attention to the place of preaching in the life of the Church. Forms of the word *praedicare*

---

*Scripture quotations in this chapter are taken from the New Revised Standard Version Bible, Catholic edition, © 1989 by the Division of Christian Education of the National Council of Churches of Christ in the USA. Used by permission. All rights reserved.

[1] *Presbyterorum ordinis* (hereafter PO) 4. Citations from the Second Vatican Council are taken from Austin Flannery, *Documents of Vatican II* (Grand Rapids, Mich.: Eerdmans, 1975).

[2] I will use the term *priest* to refer to both bishops and presbyters (cf. Latin *sacerdos*), and the term *presbyter* to refer solely to those ordained to the presbyteral order (cf. Latin *presbyter*).

occur 125 times. Taken together, these references paint a clear picture of the place of preaching in the Church and in the ministry of bishops and of presbyters.

The Primum Officium

The decree On the Ministry and Life of Presbyters *(Presbyterorum ordinis)* begins its consideration of the ministry of presbyters with this clear statement: "It is the first task of priests as co-workers of the bishops to preach the Gospel of God to all . . . ."[3] Having in the sentence before stated that "the People of God is formed into one in the first place [*primum*] by the Word of the living God," the council fathers then proclaim the "first task" [*primum officium*] of presbyters to be that of proclaiming the gospel. What is the warrant for this claim?

The text itself and its accompanying note make clear the proximate basis for the claim of presbyters' *primum officium:* the *primum officium* of bishops. Presbyters are *"cooperatores"* with the bishops, so what was posited of the episcopal ministry in *Lumen gentium* could be extended to the ministry of presbyters: "Among the more important duties of bishops that of preaching the Gospel has pride of place."[4] As the document notes, this teaching comes from the Council of Trent. The primacy of preaching applies both to bishops and to their co-workers, the presbyters.

However, a wider reading of the council documents makes clear that this priestly *primum officium* has an even deeper foundation: preaching is also the first task of the Church.

According to the Second Vatican Council, who preaches the gospel? The short answer is: the Church. "Church" occurs as the explicit subject of the verb "to preach" twice as often as any other subject, and alone accounts for more than a quarter of the explicit references to an agent of preaching. It is the Church that preaches the gospel. Preaching is fundamentally ecclesial, for preaching is the Church's duty, the Church's foundation, and a source of the Church's growth and unity.

In the council documents, to attend to the various agents of the Church's preaching is to read a sort of theological history of preaching. The first preacher is Jesus Christ, who in the Vulgate translation of the synagogue scene in Luke 4 says that he was sent to preach freedom to captives, and sight to the blind (*"praedicare captivis remissionem, et caecis visum,"* Luke 4:18), a passage cited in *Ad gentes.*[5] Jesus is described as

---

[3] PO 4. Flannery here translates *"Evangelium Dei omnium evangelizandi"* as "preach the Gospel of God to all."

[4] *Lumen gentium* (hereafter LG) 25.

[5] *Ad gentes* (hereafter AG) 3.

preaching in seven other places across several other documents.[6] Jesus both preached and fulfilled the gospel.[7]

The next preachers were the apostles, commanded by Christ to continue his work.[8] This command to the apostles was also meant for their successors, the bishops,[9] and for their collaborators, the presbyters,[10] both of whose primary duty is to preach the gospel.[11]

But Christ's command to preach was intended for the whole Church.[12]

> The Church has received this solemn command of Christ from the apostles, and she must fulfill it to the very ends of the earth (cf. Acts 1:8). Therefore, she makes the words of the apostle her own, "Woe to me if I do not preach the Gospel" (I Cor. 9:16). . . . Each disciple of Christ has the obligation of spreading the faith to the best of his ability.[13]

Though this particular text speaks of "spreading the faith" *(fidei disseminandae)*, other texts speak explicitly of the Christian obligation to preach. For instance, "The disciple of Christ has a grave obligation to Christ . . . to be faithful in announcing [the truth learned from Christ]. . . . He must also take into account his duties toward Christ, the life-giving Word whom he must preach."[14] The council also speaks of the following as "preaching": the faithful,[15] deacons,[16] laity,[17] missionaries,[18] travelers,[19]

---

[6] AG 3, *Dignitatis humanae* (hereafter DH) 11; *Gaudium et spes* (hereafter GS) 32; LG 5, 21, 40, 58.

[7] See AG 3 and *Dei Verbum* (hereafter DV) 7.

[8] AG 5 (twice).

[9] AG 1.

[10] LG 28.

[11] LG 25, PO 4 (the footnote to which gives extensive documentation of the traditional insistence on preaching as the first duty of bishops and presbyters). Cf. AG 38, *Christus Dominus* (hereafter CD) 12, 13.

[12] Cf. AG 6, 39; DH 13; *Nostra aetate* (hereafter NA) 4; *Orientalium ecclesiarum* (hereafter OE) 3.

[13] LG 17, 25 ("preach the Gospel" here renders the Latin word *"evangelizavero"*; cf. *Sacrosanctum concilium* [hereafter SC] 2).

[14] DH 14 alt. Flannery has omitted the reference to preaching by translating *"quod praedicandum est"* as "whom he must proclaim."

[15] SC 2.

[16] AG 16.

[17] LG 35, using the same phrase *"fidei praecones"* (heralds or preachers of faith) it uses to refer to the primacy of preaching for bishops, 25.

[18] AG 23.

[19] *Apostolicam Actuositatem* (hereafter AA) 14.

parents,[20] and religious.[21] It is the Church—the People of God, the *Christifideles*—who preaches. Of course, even more fundamentally it is Jesus Christ, the first preacher, who continues in and through his Church to "preach the word of God to all peoples."[22]

The ecclesial character of preaching is further manifest in preaching's role in gathering and up-building the Church. First, preaching "gathers" people into the Church.[23] God revealed himself in Christ, and by the Holy Spirit empowered the apostles "that they might preach the Gospel, stir up faith in Jesus Christ and the Lord, and bring together the Church."[24] "The principal instrument of this work of implanting the Church is the preaching of the Gospel."[25]

Because preaching has the effect of gathering people into the Church, it is foundational. Preaching founds the Church, which in turn continues the preaching task. "The mystery of the Holy Church is already brought to light in the way it was founded. For the Lord Jesus inaugurated his Church by preaching the Good News, that is, the coming kingdom of God."[26]

> The apostles, on whom the Church was founded, following the footsteps of Christ "preached the word of truth and begot churches." It is the duty of their successors to carry on this work so that "the word of God may run and be glorified" (2 Thess. 3:1) and the kingdom of God proclaimed and renewed throughout the whole world.[27]

Preaching not only gathers the Church, in the beginning and now, but it also up-builds the Church already gathered. This up-building is quantitative and qualitative. "It is through the faithful preaching of the Gospel by the Apostles and their successors . . . through their administering the sacraments, and through their governing in love, that Jesus Christ wishes his people to increase, under the action of the Holy Spirit."[28] Priests must "preach the word of God to all the faithful so that they, being firmly rooted in faith, hope and charity, may grow in Christ,

---

[20] AA 11; LG 11, where parents are pictured as the preachers of the domestic church (again using the term *"praecones"* as had been used of bishops).

[21] *Perfectae caritatis* (hereafter PC) 20; cf. CD 35.

[22] LG 21; cf. AG 8.

[23] LG 26; cf. PO 4 on preaching's intrinsic role in "setting up and increasing the People of God."

[24] DV 17; cf. LG 19.

[25] AG 6.

[26] LG 5.

[27] AG 1. The first quotation is footnoted in the document: Augustine, *Enarr. in Ps.* 44, 23.

[28] *Unitatis redintegratio* (hereafter UR) 2; cf. AG 20.

and the Christian community may give that witness to charity which the Lord commended."[29] "Their task as heralds of the Gospel . . . is the attainment of the spiritual growth of the Body of Christ."[30]

Finally, the ecclesial character of preaching is clearly reinforced in the council's concern about the divisions in the Church. "The division of Christians is injurious to the holy work of preaching the Gospel to every creature, and deprives many people of access to the faith."[31] *Ad gentes* here cites the even stronger statement in *Unitatis redintegratio:* "Certainly, such division [of Christians] openly contradicts the will of Christ, scandalizes the world, and damages that most holy cause, the preaching of the Gospel to every creature."[32] On a more positive note, however, preaching's important place in the life of the Church means that its renewal is an aid to ecumenism. "Church renewal therefore has notable ecumenical importance. Already this renewal is taking place in various spheres of the Church's life: the biblical and liturgical movements, the preaching of the Word of God. . . . All these should be considered as promises and guarantees for the future of ecumenism."[33]

Preaching, then, is profoundly ecclesial: it is a defining task of the Church, and it founds, gathers, up-builds, and calls to unity the Church.

The council has much more to say about preaching, but this brief overview of preaching as the Church's first task provides the context for and sheds light upon the *primum officium* of the priest. Both *Presbyterorum ordinis* 4 and the wider documents suggest that the primacy of preaching is a dual primacy.

On the one hand, preaching has a chronological primacy in the activity of the Church and her ministers. As was just seen, it is the proclamation of the word that founds the Church. It is the proclamation of the word that begins the process of conversion leading to baptism. In each celebration of the sacraments, it is the proclamation of the word that precedes and grounds the sacramental act. Ecclesially, individually, liturgically: the preaching of the gospel has a chronological primacy.

On the other hand, though, preaching is not an activity that passes away after its moment in the sun. Beyond its chronological primacy, preaching also enjoys a ministerial primacy, taking pride of place in the ongoing efforts of the Church and her ministers. *Presbyterorum ordinis* 4 makes clear the thoroughgoing ministerial place of preaching with

[29] CD 30; cf. GS 52.
[30] PO 6; cf. 2, 4.
[31] AG 6.
[32] UR 1.
[33] UR 6.

several evocative image pairs. Preachers *"set up* and *increase* the People of God. For by the saving Word of God faith is *aroused* in the heart of unbelievers and is *nourished* in the heart of believers. By this faith then the congregation of the faithful *begins* and *grows"* (emphasis added). Indeed, the paragraph continues, the "preaching of the Word is required for the sacramental ministry itself, since the sacraments are sacraments of faith, drawing their *origin* and *nourishment* from the Word." Preaching chronologically precedes the sacraments, but it also provides their ongoing sustenance.

To say, then, that preaching is the *primum officium* of priests is to claim a dual primacy for preaching. Preaching is chronologically the first task of priests, since it founds churches, calls to baptism, and precedes sacramental acts. But preaching is also ministerially the first task of priests: the "preaching of the Word is required for the sacramental ministry itself." If a priest's ministry of sacrament and leadership is to bear fruit, his preaching must take precedence.

One might ask whether the council contradicts itself by claiming both that preaching is *primum officium* of priests and that "the liturgy is the summit toward which the activity of the Church is directed; it is also the fount from which all her powers flow."[34] Which has the priority, preaching or the sacramental life? *Sacrosanctum concilium* makes clear that to pose that question is to pose the classic "chicken-and-egg" dilemma, so organically linked are word and sacrament. Thus,

> just as Christ was sent by the Father so also he sent the apostles, filled with the Holy Spirit. This he did so that they might preach the Gospel to every creature. . . . But he also willed that the work of salvation which they preached should be set in train through the sacrifice and sacraments, around which the entire liturgical life revolves.[35]

Lest there be any confusion, the council goes on to plainly state:

> The sacred liturgy does not exhaust the entire activity of the Church. Before men can come to the liturgy they must be called to faith and conversion. ". . . And how are they to hear without a preacher? . . ." To believers also the Church must ever preach faith and penance; she must prepare them for the sacraments.[36]

The dual primacy of preaching makes possible the centrality of the liturgy in the life of the Church. There is no contradiction here.

---

[34] SC 10.
[35] SC 6.
[36] SC 9.

The Nature of the Church's Preaching

According to Karl Rahner, the Church ordains ministers that its necessary and constituent tasks may be accomplished.[37] This implies that those who order the Church should have the Church's priorities as their own. In the case of preaching, then, a priest must not only embrace preaching as his first duty,[38] but also strive to preach in the manner intended by the Church. Council documents reveal the twofold nature of the Church's preaching.

"Traditioning" Nature

The preaching of the Church, and thus of its ordained, is an ongoing act of tradition. In the Dogmatic Constitution on Divine Revelation *(Dei verbum),* the council explicates the Catholic understanding of "tradition." Briefly but profoundly:

> What was handed on [*traditum est*] by the apostles comprises everything that serves to make the People of God live their lives in holiness and increase their faith. In this way the Church, in her doctrine, life and worship, perpetuates and transmits to every generation all that she herself is, all that she believes.[39]

Preaching serves an essential role in this "traditioning" dimension of the Church, both in the handing on of tradition and in its development.

First, preaching serves tradition because it hands over what has been received:

> Christ the Lord, in whom the entire Revelation of the most high God is summed up . . . commanded the apostles to preach the Gospel . . . which he fulfilled in his own person and promulgated with his own lips. . . .

---

[37] "The really fundamental offices in the Church are the most indispensable constituents of the Church herself. She only exists by possessing and transmitting the functions given her by Christ, and the powers bound up with and serving them. By the transmission of office, especially when this gives power to exercise the fundamental functions of the Church, to bear witness to Christ's message, to celebrate the eucharist, and, we must add, conversely, to hand on these powers which are constitutive of the Church, the Church in one important respect keeps on re-constituting herself anew." Karl Rahner, *The Church and the Sacraments* (New York: Herder & Herder, 1963) 97–8.

[38] Those who order the Church also order preaching. The embrace of preaching as *primum officium* implies not only the priest's personal preaching, but also his service as "moderator of the entire ministry of the word" (cf. Code of Canon Law, c. 756 [regarding bishops for their dioceses] and c. 767.4 [regarding pastors for their parishes]).

[39] DV 8.

This was faithfully done: it was done by the apostles who handed on, by the spoken word of their preaching, by the example they gave, by the institutions they established, what they themselves had received.[40]

This same "traditioning" function continues down to this day: tradition transmits the entirety of the word of God "to the successors to the apostles so that, enlightened by the Spirit of truth, they may faithfully preserve, expound and spread it abroad by their preaching."[41]

However, the Church's preaching not only transmits tradition, but also enables its ongoing development and our further insight. "The Tradition that comes from the apostles makes progress in the Church, with the help of the Holy Spirit. There is a growth in insight into the realities and words that are being passed on."[42] The council notes that this progress and growth in insight occurs in several ways, preaching among them. This progress and growth "comes from the preaching of those who received, along with their right of succession in the episcopate, the sure charism of truth."[43] It also comes about through the contemplation, study, and experience of believers. "Thus, as the centuries go by, the Church is always advancing towards the plenitude of divine truth, until eventually the words of God are fulfilled in her."[44] Preaching, then, has a traditioning nature, not only handing on what has been received, but also enabling tradition to progress toward the fullness of truth.

Interpretative Nature

The second fundamental aspect of the preaching of the Church and her ministers is its interpretative nature. In one sense, the purpose of the Second Vatican Council itself made clear the nature of the Church's preaching: "At all times the Church carries the responsibility of reading the signs of the times and interpreting them in the light of the Gospel if it is to carry out its task."[45] The Church's preaching is not removed from everyday life, but emerges from the midst of it: "The joy and hope, the grief and anguish of the men of our time, especially those who are poor or afflicted in any way, are the joy and hope, the grief and anguish of the followers of Christ as well."[46]

[40] DV 7.

[41] DV 9. The text here is *"praeconio suo fideliter."*

[42] DV 8. The text footnotes Vatican I, Dogm. Const. on the Catholic Faith, c. 4 (on Faith and Reason): Denz. 1800 (3020).

[43] DV 8.

[44] DV 8.

[45] GS 4.

[46] GS 1.

As the Church, so its bishops and presbyters "are to preach the message of Christ in such a way that the light of the Gospel will shine on all the activities of the faithful."[47]

> Moreover, the priest's preaching, often very difficult in present-day conditions, if it is to become more effective in moving the minds of his hearers, must expound the Word of God not merely in a general and abstract way but by an application of the eternal truth of the Gospel to the concrete circumstances of life.[48]

The council makes it clear that preaching is not merely self-referential; it rather seeks to interpret all of human life in the light of the gospel.

This interpretative quality of preaching also emerges in its engagement with the Scriptures. This engagement could be described as "adaptation." Three aspects of this adaptation are significant.

First, the council highlights the reciprocal relationship of Scripture and preaching. On the one hand, "apostolic preaching . . . is expressed in a special way in the inspired books";[49] "the writings of the New Testament stand as perpetual and divine witness to" the preaching of the apostles and gathering of the Church.[50] On the other hand, the Church utilizes all possible resources "in its preaching to spread and explain the message of Christ, to examine and understand it more deeply, and to express it more perfectly."[51] This "more perfect expression" implies not mere repetition, but adaptation. Scripture records preaching, preaching expounds Scripture.

Second, however, to ensure fidelity to the gospel being adapted, preaching must be grounded in Scripture. "It follows that all the preaching of the Church, as indeed the entire Christian religion, should be nourished and ruled by sacred Scripture."[52] A necessary precondition of this grounding is that preachers "immerse themselves in the Scriptures by constant sacred reading and diligent study. For it must not happen

---

[47] GS 43; cf. GS 76 (twice).

[48] PO 4.

[49] DV 8.

[50] DV 17; cf. DV 18, 19 (twice), 20.

[51] GS 58. In this connection note must be made of the reciprocal authority of Scripture and the Church's magisterium. "The task of giving an authentic interpretation of the Word of God . . . has been entrusted to the living teaching office of the Church alone. . . . Yet this Magisterium is not superior to the Word of God, but is its servant." DV 10. Cf. UR 21: "For in the Church, according to Catholic belief, its authentic teaching office has a special place in expounding and preaching the written Word of God."

[52] DV 21.

that anyone becomes 'an empty preacher of the Word of God to others, not being a hearer of the Word in his own heart'"[53] (the council here quoting St. Augustine).

Finally, though, this grounding of preaching in Scripture does not alter the fact that the gospel must be adapted to the hearers of each age.

> The Church learned early in its history to express the Christian message in the concepts and language of different peoples and tried to clarify it in the light of the wisdom of their philosophers: it was an attempt to adapt the Gospel to the understanding of all and the requirements of the learned, insofar as this could be done. Indeed, this kind of adapted preaching of the revealed Word must ever be the law of evangelization.[54]

This adaptive stance is grounded in the incarnation itself. "Indeed the words of God, expressed in the words of men, are in every way like human language, just as the Word of the eternal Father, when he took upon himself the flesh of human weakness, became like men."[55] "In his self-revelation to his people culminating in the fullness of manifestation in his incarnate Son, God spoke according to the culture proper to each age. Similarly the Church has existed through the centuries in varying circumstances and has utilized the resources of different cultures in its preaching."[56] These cultural resources important to preaching include science and the academy, art and literature; by acknowledging the arts and using them, "the knowledge of God will be made better known; the preaching of the Gospel will be rendered more intelligible to man's mind and will appear more relevant to his situation."[57]

Preaching, then, has an interpretative character which manifests itself in its reading of each age and culture in the light of the gospel and its adaptation of the gospel with language understandable by the people of each age and culture.

In sum, the Church's own self-understanding places preaching at the forefront of the Church's activities. In light of this, it is no surprise that those who order the Church—bishops and presbyters—should have as their first duty the task of preaching the gospel, handing it on in its fullness and interpreting it for today.

[53] DV 25; cf. AG 24, 26.

[54] GS 44 alt. Flannery has "this kind of adaptation and preaching," which weakens the Latin: *"accommodata praedicatio lex omnis permanere debet."*

[55] DV 13. Just before, the council quotes Chrysostom on "God's loving kindness . . . in adapting his language with thoughtful concern for our nature."

[56] GS 58.

[57] GS 62; cf. AG 41.

Priestly Ministry and Life: The Practical Place of Preaching

Having established the doctrinal primacy of preaching in the life of the Church and its ministers, I now turn my attention to the priest himself. What place does preaching hold in the ministry and life of priests? In exploring this question, three areas seem fruitful: the first two involve unpacking the implications of the traditioning and the interpretative nature of priests' preaching, and the third involves examining the homily, the most typical kind of preaching engaged in by priests in the United States.

A Priest's Preaching Is Traditioning

As was seen above, according to the Second Vatican Council preaching is an act by which the tradition of the Church is handed over to and developed for the people of each time and place. The words of St. Paul to the Church in Corinth become each priest's own: "For I received from the Lord what I also handed on to you" (1 Cor 11:23). The priest as preacher is a man of the tradition, charged with its faithful handing on. As such, the priest is necessarily a lifelong student of all the Church is, and all that she believes. The primacy of preaching in a priest's ministry and life therefore implies a life of study. The more deeply priests come to know the Church's Scripture, its doctrine, and its practices, the more fully they achieve the Church's primary task.

Especially in our day, however, the paradox of the priests' call to study could not be clearer: never before in the history of the Church have there been as many resources for study and as little time, or even motivation. The periodicals, the books, the regional and national workshops on all dimensions of our tradition are ever before us; sources for theological study are no more than a computer click away. And yet, as the demands upon priests grow—not only because of the shortage, but also because the People of God have grown in the appreciation of all that the Church is called to—the time priests claim for study is reduced. I'm sure that many parish councils would endorse a priest's desire to spend one afternoon a week in study, but how many make such a commitment? Indeed, how many even want to make such a commitment? The immediate gratification of hands-on ministry often trumps the long-term rewards of study. At any rate, there can be no doubt that the primacy of preaching, which by nature is a traditioning task, demands that priests grow in their knowledge and appreciation of tradition.

The council also boldly noted that ordained preachers not only hand on tradition, but also serve its ongoing development and progress in the Church. As priests preach, "there is growth and insight into the realities and words being passed on."[58] The traditioning nature of preaching, then, also implies a heightened ecclesial identity on the part of the priest. In priests' preaching the tradition develops, so priests must take care that what they propose is in fact legitimate development. Now, this does not mean that one never takes chances; some of the most effective preaching and teaching happens at the edges.[59] However, it does mean that priests are aware that their preaching proposes a "we" that is the Church. Our preaching plays a role in the Church's self-understanding, particularly as manifest in a certain congregation. And so priests are aware of themselves as men of the Church, men of tradition, as they verbally paint the picture of "we the Church."

A Priest's Preaching Is Interpretative

As was noted above, the Second Vatican Council proposed that the Church's preaching was not only a handing on of tradition, but also an act of interpretation. The preacher does not merely restate the Scriptures, but adapts them to the needs of the people in a given time and place. All that is of genuinely human concern is the Church's concern, and its preaching reflects that, as the light of the gospel is cast upon and interprets the signs of our times.

If such interpretative preaching holds pride of place in a priest's ministry and life, what would be the implications? First, the interpretative preacher must know both the Scriptures (and wider tradition) and the world in which we live. Karl Barth's image of the preacher as one with a Bible in one hand and a newspaper in the other provides nice shorthand for the range of knowledge the interpretative preacher must have. However, Barth's view of those two sources was a "Christ against culture" stance: the newspaper gave examples of our failure under the law, the Scriptures gave the good news of our salvation. A more Catholic approach recognizes the priority and presence of God's grace, from the beginning of time to the present moment. The Bible is the privileged witness of that grace at work in the past as well as the lens through which we recognize grace at work here and now (the newspaper). For the priest as interpretative preacher, Bible and newspaper represent the range of knowledge necessary to interpret today's world in the light of the Scriptures, and the Scripture in terms of today's world.

---

[58] DV 8.

[59] "The risk of error does not constitute a valid objection against performing what is a necessary task: that of bringing the message of the Bible to the ears and hearts of people of our own time." Pontifical Biblical Commission, *The Interpretation of the Bible in the Church* (Boston: St. Paul Books, 1993) 121.

Second, the priest who embraces the "law of evangelization"—
"adapted preaching of the revealed Word"[60]—recognizes his own deeply
personal stake in the preaching enterprise. Where the traditioning function calls the priest to be a man of the tradition, the interpretative function calls the priest to be a man of personal faith. When a priest preaches,
he is speaking in his own words the word of the Lord. What *Dei verbum*
notes about the Scriptures is equally true about the preacher's adaptation
of the Scriptures: "Indeed the words of God, expressed in the words of
men, are in every way like human language, just as the Word of the eternal Father, when he took upon himself the flesh of human weakness, became like men."[61] The scandal of preaching is the scandal of the
incarnation: humans bearing the presence of God. The priest as a man of
personal faith trusts that God can work in and through the priest's own
life and words. At the same time, the priest recognizes that he himself
has chosen what to say in preaching; the preacher is not God's ventrilo-
quist. As the traditioning nature of preaching leads the priest to be faithful to the "we," so the interpretative nature of preaching leads the priest
to embrace the "I": I preach what I feel to be important and life-giving
for the people entrusted to me, and I take full responsibility for my mutual interpretation of Scripture and the signs of the times.

A Priest's Preaching Is Homiletic

The primacy of preaching is a dual primacy: chronological and
ministerial. For most priests serving in the United States, it is the ongoing, ministerial primacy of preaching that is the most common. Priests
here are less involved in founding churches than in up-building existing
communities. Primary evangelization is much less common than
preaching to those who already believe, and the most common form of
such preaching is the homily. Indeed, the Second Vatican Council said
that "the liturgical homily should hold pride of place" within "the ministry of the word."[62] To understand what the Church asks of the homiletic
preacher, then, can greatly develop the priest's own understanding of the
implications of the primacy of preaching.

In another place, I have extensively presented the teaching of the
Church regarding the nature of the homily.[63] From the Second Vatican
Council through post-conciliar documents and up to 1995, a fivefold

---

[60] GS 44.
[61] DV 13.
[62] DV 24.
[63] Stephen V. DeLeers, *A Process for the Assessment of Liturgical Preaching Reflecting Official Roman Catholic Understanding of the Homily* (Ann Arbor, Mich.: UMI, 1996) 3–73.

description of homiletic preaching has emerged. A Catholic homily is at once personal, liturgical, inculturated, clarifying, and actualizing. Each of these descriptors suggests stances and behaviors for the priest as homilist.

The Homily Is Personal

The homily is the only part of the liturgy in which the priest is required to speak in his own words. This personal dimension of preaching suggests several things. Priests must continue to develop their oral communication skills; certain techniques and approaches serve the personal "conversation" that is the homily, and others do not. In his preaching, a priest must manifest genuineness that is served by sincerity and transparency. We come across as sincere when our words, gestures, and affect are congruent; we are transparent when the "I" emerges as a person of faith. The homily is not a preaching of self, but it is a preaching by a self. The use of the first person singular suggests that a priest is speaking from his own faith and taking responsibility for what he is saying. Finally, the personal preacher manifests empathy for his listeners, and even more, love for them. The priest who strives to know his people well will be a more effective preacher, but the priest who loves his people will be most effective of all. Priests show that love by preaching in a way that respects people's dignity and freedom, that shows care for the people, that communicates acceptance and positive regard.

The Homily Is Liturgical

The Second Vatican Council taught us that the homily is a part of the liturgy itself.[64] The liturgical nature of much of a priest's preaching suggests a number of things. First, the priest must be immersed in the liturgy to be an effective preacher. Priests must know and respect the rites and texts entrusted to them. As the liturgy itself, so the homily reinforces the assembly's identity as Church. Further, the priest identifies with the rest of the assembly and speaks on their behalf; "we" emerge. The use of the first person plural in the homily echoes its use throughout the rest of the liturgy and accomplishes the same thing: a proclamation of our communal identity in Christ through baptism. Finally, a priest who preaches homiletically connects word, ritual, and assembly. The priest-presider as preacher has the unique opportunity not only of preaching in a way that echoes the actions and prayers of the rest of the liturgy, but also of choosing prayer texts that will echo the homily. The unity of word and sacrament, which the homily serves, is symbolized in the person of the priest, preacher, and presider over the Eucharist.

[64] SC 52.

The Homily Is Inculturated

It has already been noted that the Church's preaching has an interpretative function, and the homily is no exception: it correlates and interprets Scripture and human experience. For the priest as preacher, the task of inculturation implies a heightened awareness of language, symbols, customs, and events of the time in which he lives and the community in which he preaches. God's word, if it is to be effective, emerges through the homily clothed in the language and images of the assembly's culture. The priest as preacher uses language easily understood by and relevant for his people, and uses the symbols familiar to them. It is frightening to imagine, then, a priest who did not read a newspaper or books, who did not know what was popular in film and television, who had not experienced the cultural mirror that is talk radio. If preaching is primary in a priest's ministry, then his life is the life of his people. As the council noted, priests are "disciples of the Lord along with the faithful . . . , brothers among brothers as members of the same Body of Christ."[65] Priests' preaching reflects this immersion in the life of the rest of the faithful; the priest preaches "the Word of God not merely in a general and abstract way but by an application of the eternal truth of the Gospel to the concrete circumstances of life."[66]

The Homily Is Clarifying

The Church's traditioning function in preaching has already been noted, and the homily is a clear example of that function. The priest as preacher is called to speak clearly and insightfully about the tradition. To do this in an effective oral manner implies that, in each homily, he will make one central point clearly, indeed a point that is worth making, theologically and pastorally. With only ten or so minutes with which to work, there is no time for multiple points, and there is no time for the fringe, the arcane, the bottom rungs of the hierarchy of truth. The priest who clearly hands on the tradition knows the fullness of that tradition, and utilizes the tools of exegesis and theological reflection to communicate and even develop what he himself has received.

The Homily Is Actualizing

The priest as preacher is called to speak a word at once personal and liturgical, a word that inculturates and clarifies. In the last analysis, though, all of this is in service of actualizing the Scriptures that have been proclaimed,[67] so that "written text thus becomes living word."[68]

---

[65] PO 9.

[66] PO 4.

[67] See *The Interpretation of the Bible in the Church,* IV A, B, 117–24.

[68] Ibid., 124.

Such a thing is God's work, the work of the Holy Spirit; the priest as preacher strives to remove as many roadblocks as possible to let the Spirit work. And so the priest communicates a sense of importance in what he is saying: a "ho-hum, same stuff-different day" demeanor is a major roadblock. The priest expects that God will act through his preaching, and manifests his own wonder at the myriad ways that God is at work. The priest communicates lived truth, not mere book knowledge. And when the day is done, the priest as preacher communicates good news and evokes the reality of our salvation in Christ. Given this, moralizing is not only a sign of poor preparation,[69] but also a betrayal of the preaching task itself, which exists that the scriptural word of salvation might manifest its power in the lives of our people today.

In all these ways and many more, the Church's understanding of the homily can assist the priest in claiming and living out the primacy of preaching in his ministry and life.

I return to *Presbyterorum ordinis* for a concluding thought. That document on the ministry and life of presbyters invited recognition that "priests will acquire holiness in their own distinctive way by exercising their functions sincerely and tirelessly in the Spirit of Christ."[70] Taken with its early words about the primacy of preaching among a priest's functions, the council fathers have suggested that a primary means to holiness is the priest's dedication to preaching—a suggestion many priests have experienced as true. To preach is to grow in knowledge of the God of the Scriptures and the people whom we serve. To preach is to grow in appreciation of the Church in all that she is and believes, for a good preacher knows Scripture, liturgy, our doctrinal and moral tradition, and our practices. But above all, to preach is to grow in love of God and our neighbor. Pope Paul VI recognized this fact and wrote about it with grace; his words both summarize and provide a final benediction for the place of preaching in the ministry and life of priests:

> The work of evangelization presupposes in the evangelizer an ever-increasing love for those whom he is evangelizing. That model evangelizer, the Apostle Paul, wrote these words to the Thessalonians, and they are a program for us all: "With such yearning love we chose to impart to you not only the gospel of God but our very selves, so dear had you become to us" (1 Thess. 2:8). What is this love? It is much more than that of a teacher; it is the love of a father; and again, it is the love of

---

[69] Ibid., 129.
[70] PO 13.

a mother. It is this love that the Lord expects from every preacher of the Gospel.[71]

---

[71] Paul VI, On Evangelization in the Modern World *(Evangelii nuntiandi)* (Boston: Daughters of St. Paul, 1975) 79. On the "mother love" of the preacher, Paul VI cites 1 Thess 2:7-11; 1 Cor 4:15; Gal 4:19.

Crisis in priesthood
shortage → force
toward pastorally

5

Priesthood in the Context of Apostolic Religious Life[1]

THOMAS P. RAUSCH, S.J.

In the history of the Church, priesthood has taken on various forms. What is today known as the diocesan or "secular" priesthood developed from the ministry of local community leadership, fully expressed in the ministry of the bishop. Parish priests or pastors exercise a ministry of word, sacrament, and pastoral leadership within a local church community, whether on the parish or the diocesan level.

With the clericalizing of the monastic life, originally a lay movement, a monastic priesthood developed. Exercised under the jurisdiction of an abbot, monastic priesthood is focused on the *opus Dei* or liturgy. It offers an example of a priesthood that is less clerical, more communitarian, and characterized by a monastic restraint in liturgical celebration.[2]

"Religious" priesthood, exercised by those who constitute the "regular" as opposed to the "secular" clergy, developed from the apostolic religious orders that began to emerge with the founding of the Franciscan and Dominican orders in the early thirteenth century. In this chapter I would like to explore priesthood in the context of apostolic religious life.

---

*Scripture quotations in this chapter are taken from the New American Bible, © 1991, 1986, 1970 by the Confraternity of Christian Doctrine, 3211 Fourth Street N.E., Washington, D.C. 20017-1194 and are used by permission of the © holder. All rights reserved.

[1] The present chapter is a revised and updated version of a chapter in my *Priesthood Today: An Appraisal* (New York: Paulist Press, 1992).

[2] See Kevin W. Irwin, "On Monastic Priesthood," *American Benedictine Review* 41 (1990) 225–62.

We will consider, first, the charism of priesthood in apostolic religious communities. Then we will look at a loss of focus on that particular charism in the post-Tridentine church. Finally, we will attempt to outline some characteristics of apostolic religious priesthood for the future.

The Charism of Apostolic Religious Priesthood

According to Karl Rahner, priesthood in the Catholic Church combines in one office the distinctive roles of prophet and priest.[3] Priests preside over the ritual expression of a community's worship; their role is cultic, leading the community in addressing itself to God. The prophet, however, addresses the community in God's name, speaking God's word.

In the Christian tradition, from the time of prophets and teachers of the New Testament (1 Cor 12:28; Acts 13:2) and the wandering charismatic prophets and teachers of the Didache (10:7), the cultic has been rooted in the prophetic. Those who came to be called priests *(sacerdotes)* preside at the Eucharist because they have instructed the community though the word and exercised a role of pastoral leadership within it. In terms of Catholic theology, ordination enables the priest to exercise a ministry of word and sacrament in the name of the Church and thus *in persona Christi*. The Church's pastoral office should never be reduced to a purely cultic function.

If Christian priesthood has always had both a cultic and a prophetic dimension, the way it is lived out in the Church has often emphasized one dimension more than the other. In an article originally written for Jesuit scholastics preparing for ordination, Michael J. Buckley distinguished between a primarily cultic priesthood and one more prophetic in orientation.[4] A cultic priesthood is characterized by an emphasis on sacramental ministry or by the liturgical prayer of the choral office. It describes the ministry of a parish priest or pastor who presides over the liturgical and sacramental life of a local congregation, the cathedral canon who serves the sacramental life of a major church, or the ordained monk who devotes himself to the *opus Dei*.

A prophetic priesthood is a priesthood given to the ministry of the word in its fullest sense. It is primarily kerygmatic rather than liturgical, though it does not exclude the liturgical. What distinguishes a priest exercising a prophetic priesthood from one whose ministry is focused on

---

[3] Karl Rahner, "Priestly Existence," *Theological Investigations* 3 (Baltimore: Helicon Press, 1967) 243–4.

[4] Michael J. Buckley, "Jesuit Priesthood: Its Meaning and Commitments," *Studies in the Spirituality of Jesuits* 8 (1976).

the leadership of a stable local community is availability for mission. This is how Buckley describes it:

> A prophetic priesthood, one which was concerned to speak out the word of God in any way that it could be heard, assimilated, and incarnated within the social life of human beings, a priesthood which spoke with the religious experience of human beings and—as did the prophets of the Old Testament—coupled this care for authentic belief with a concern for those in social misery: the ministry of the word, the ministries of interiority, the ministry to social misery.[5]

For Buckley, the Society of Jesus is characterized by such a prophetic priesthood. As a clerical order, the Jesuits represented a new form of the ancient presbyterium; they were a group of priests with a primarily prophetic mission. But so were the Franciscans and the Dominicans, as John W. O'Malley showed in an article on religious priesthood published twelve years later. O'Malley did not use Buckley's distinction between a cultic and a prophetic priesthood, but he made basically the same argument, contrasting the "division of labor" between diocesan and regular clergy: "The former relates more easily to 'priest'—celebrant for the community and its public servant; the latter more easily to 'prophet'—spokesperson and agent for a special point of view."[6] In a later article on priesthood, O'Malley argues the need "to move the discussion beyond the vagueness of spirituality and charism" to the more concrete ground of ministerial need that has so shaped religious priesthood in the life of the Church.[7]

The Franciscans, Dominicans, and Jesuits were not the only religious communities to exercise a priesthood more prophetic in orientation. There were other mendicant communities in the late Middle Ages, Carmelites, Augustinians, and Servites, while the sixteenth century saw the establishment of a number of communities—Barnabites, Theatines, Capuchins, and Vincentians—dedicated to the apostolic life, based on the various ministries of the word. Nor should the present restriction of preaching at the Eucharist to the ordained be understood as the only expression of the prophetic charism. But in order to understand more clearly the charism of religious priesthood, we will consider the Franciscans, Dominicans, and Jesuits more carefully.

[5] Ibid., 150.

[6] John W. O'Malley, "Priesthood, Ministry, and Religious Life: Some Historical and Historiographical Considerations," *Theological Studies* 49 (1988) 256.

[7] John W. O'Malley, "One Priesthood: Two Traditions," *A Concert of Charisms: Ordained Ministry in Religious Life,* ed. Paul K. Hennessy (New York: Paulist Press, 1997) 14.

Franciscans and Dominicans

Both Francis of Assisi and Dominic de Guzman were influenced by the *vita apostolica,* the great evangelical awakening that swept through Europe in the twelfth century.[8] The communities they established sought to embody the values of this apostolic way of life, living in poverty and simplicity, preaching the gospel in the towns and cities, free to go where there was need.

Though the movement begun by Francis was originally lay in orientation, preaching was basic to his apostolic vision from the beginning. He began preaching in Assisi in 1209, the day after he heard Matt 10:7-9, where Jesus sends his disciples out to preach, cure the sick, and live in simplicity, proclaimed on the saint's feast. Others joined him, wandering the countryside, preaching in the towns and villages. In the early days his companions were sometimes mistaken for members of other evangelical fraternities—particularly the Waldensians, whose orthodoxy was suspect. At the same time, lacking education and without episcopal supervision, they were in danger of falling into heterodoxy themselves.

A great part of Francis' achievement was his success in keeping his movement within the Church. He sought and received papal recognition when Honorius III in 1223 approved his "Second Rule" or *Regula Bullata,* giving his community the status of a religious order. But as the movement grew the "lesser brothers" became more structured, necessitated by the requirements of their preaching mission. The community began to place an increasing emphasis on religious formation as well as formal education, and Francis himself is thought to have been ordained a deacon. Thus the community underwent a "clericalization."

The Dominican first order was clerical from the beginning. Dominic was a priest, a cathedral canon who became involved with his bishop in an itinerant ministry against the Albigensians in southern France. The order grew out of those who joined Dominic. They lived an itinerant life, owning only what they could carry and supporting themselves by begging, all for the sake of the proclamation of the gospel.

In identifying his largely clerical community as an "order of preachers," Dominic was giving expression to a new kind of priesthood. The ministry of his followers was not to be modeled on that of the regular clergy who had authority over local communities as well as financial claims upon them. Furthermore, preaching in the thirteenth century was not seen as the ordinary role of priests; they carried out a sacramental minis-

[8] M.-D. Chenu, *Nature, Man, and Society in the Twelfth Century* (Chicago and London: University of Chicago Press) 242–3.

try in local churches, but the bishop was the official preacher. Priests were primarily cultic ministers. But Dominic intended a specifically active or apostolic form of clerical religious life, focused on a preaching ministry.

Dominican structures and manner of life, including their emphasis on poverty, developed from the pragmatic task of preaching the gospel. Everything was subordinated to this. The nuns and lay brothers, present from the beginning, apparently shared in this task by providing a material and spiritual base for the preachers. Dominic sent his followers far and wide, to preach and later to study. Because of the community's apostolic orientation, regular observance of the rule was always secondary. The constitutions were understood as human law, not binding under pain of sin. Superiors could give dispensations from traditional monastic observances, including choir, which interfered with preaching or study. Though the order had to struggle in its early days to defend its preaching ministry, separated from the responsibility of pastoring local communities, it won the right to be acknowledged as an order of preachers. The mission for preaching given the order by Honorius III in 1217 was unprecedented, derived from the exempt character of the order's priests as evangelical assistants to the bishops and the pope, rather than from the responsibility of bishops and pastors to preach or to see that sermons were preached in their churches. Four years later the pope added a general mission of hearing confessions.

Thus the Franciscan and Dominican movements resulted not just in a new kind of religious order, but also in a new kind of priesthood. As O'Malley has pointed out, the mendicant priests differed from the local clergy in a number of significant respects. First, influenced by the *vita apostolica* and committed to poverty, very early the friars combined spirituality and ministry into an apostolic lifestyle. Second, because of their emphasis on preaching, they began a systematic program for the education of their new members. Third, their ministry, geared to respond to needs that transcended local boundaries and jurisdictions, required them to move about "like the apostles." Their ministry was itinerant, characterized by mobility. This meant a break with existing Church structures of government.

Finally, this unique ministry was recognized from the beginning by papal exemptions from episcopal supervision. The monastic orders also enjoyed an independence from episcopal control, but unlike Cluny, Cîteaux, and other monastic communities, the mendicants required exemption, not just for their own governance, but precisely for the sake of their wide ranging ministry.[9] This development "created in effect a church

---

[9] O'Malley, "Priesthood, Ministry, and Religious Life," 233–7.

order (or several church orders) within the great church order, and it did this for the reality to which church order primarily looks—ministry."[10] What emerged was a new kind of priesthood, freed from the confines of local congregational ministry, episcopal jurisdiction, or monastic enclosure, precisely for the sake of the word, thus, a prophetic or kerygmatic priesthood. When the Dominicans revised their constitutions after Vatican II, they described themselves as "cooperators of the episcopal order through priestly ordination," with the "prophetic office" as their special function.[11]

The Jesuits

The Jesuits, founded in the sixteenth century, represented another group of priests with a similar pastoral mission. On September 27, 1540, Pope Paul III canonically established the Society of Jesus with his decree *Regimini militantis Ecclesiae.* The decree recognized the first ten Jesuits as a single apostolic "body" or presbyterium, grouped not around a bishop as head of a diocese, but around the pope for the service of the universal Church. The Formula of the Institute describes the Jesuit vocation as a willingness to go wherever they were sent, under special obedience to the pope:

> In addition to that ordinary bond of the three vows, we are to be obliged by a special vow to carry out whatever the present and future Roman pontiffs may order which pertains to the progress of souls and the propagation of the faith; and to go without subterfuge or excuse, as far as in us lies, to whatsoever provinces they may choose to send us—whether . . . among the Turks or any other infidels, even those who live in the region called the Indies, or among any heretics whatever, or schismatics, or any of the faithful.[12]

From the beginning the Jesuits were travelers. Francis Xavier departed for India in 1540, the year the society was officially approved as a new religious order. By 1556, the year Ignatius died, there were Jesuits working in India, Japan, Brazil, and Africa. Jerome Nadal, Ignatius' secretary, described the Society of Jesus as most itself when on the move, so that "the whole world becomes its house."[13]

[10] Ibid., 236.

[11] "Cooperatores ordinis episcopalis per sacerdotalem ordinationem effecti, ut proprium officium habemus munus propheticum," *Liber Constitutionum et Ordinationum Ordinis Fratrum Praedicatorum* (Rome: Curia Generalitia, 1986) Fundamental Constitution V:18.

[12] Ignatius, *Constitutions,* 4; George Ganss, *The Constitutions of the Society of Jesus* (St. Louis, Mo.: Institute of Jesuit Sources, 1970) 68.

[13] Cited by John O'Malley, "To Travel to Any Part of the World: Jeromino Nadel and the Jesuit Vocation," *Studies in the Spirituality of Jesuits* 16 (1984) 7.

There were significant differences between the mendicants and the Jesuits. Dominican priestly life was to be rooted in liturgy and contemplation. But as the traditional form of such a communal life in the thirteenth century, even for canons, was essentially monastic, there was a monastic dimension to Dominican life from the beginning, though mitigated by Dominic's emphasis on the priority of preaching. Similarly, the Franciscans took on some monastic practices as they developed.

Ignatius' community was unique for its time because it was established without a distinctive habit, prescribed fasts and penances, or the obligation of the choral office. The omission of choir was to cause some problems for Ignatius and the early Society. Those in Rome appointed to examine the Institute as Ignatius presented it could not conceive of a religious order whose members did not gather regularly for the office. But Ignatius wanted his priests to be mobile.

Thus Jesuit priesthood was not primarily cultic. In addressing the society's mission, *Regimini militantis Ecclesiae* mentions preaching the gospel, both to believers and to unbelievers (what we would call today evangelization) and the sacrament of reconciliation. It did not mention the Eucharist, even if the mission of a priestly order includes the celebration of the Eucharist. Though his own spirituality was profoundly eucharistic, Ignatius did not insist that each Jesuit celebrate daily, nor did he always do so himself. But Jesuits were to attend daily. In the Jesuit tradition (at least until concelebration became common), a Jesuit on the day of his final vows generally did not say Mass, but attended and received Communion from the one receiving his vows.

The Jesuit mission was focused on preaching and evangelization. The ministry of the word dominates the early Jesuit sources. In the Formula of the Institute, preaching is the first ministry mentioned and the *Constitutions* "rank preaching and lecturing as, generally speaking, more important than hearing confessions and giving the *Spiritual Exercises.*"[14]

O'Malley shows how Jesuits were preachers, not just at Mass, but in the Church outside of the liturgy as well as in the streets and hospitals. They wrote books to aid preachers with examples from classical literature and the Fathers of the Church. They gave sacred lectures and taught catechism to children. They went on "missions," both foreign and domestic, reclaiming a sense of "journey" or "pilgrimage" for the word "mission," which had been previously confined almost exclusively to trinitarian theology. They gave retreats and were involved in spiritual direction. They

---

[14] John W. O'Malley, *The First Jesuits* (Cambridge, Mass.: Harvard University Press, 1993) 91; see his description of the various "Ministries of the Word of God" undertaken by the early Jesuits, 91–133.

established a network of schools to carry out their religious mission. And they were active in what we now call "social" ministries, working with the poor and the sick and establishing houses for reformed prostitutes.[15]

The Jesuits were not the only religious priests to exercise this kind of prophetic priesthood. The sixteenth century saw the establishment of a number of communities dedicated to an apostolic life, based on the ministries of the word.

Loss of a Prophetic Focus

In the centuries following the Council of Trent, a number of factors had the effect of changing the prophetic or kerygmatic understanding of apostolic religious priesthood into a more traditional cultic one. Some communities underwent a process of monastification. The Dominicans took on a more monastic character in the several generations that followed Dominic's. Their liturgical rite, developed under the administration of Humbert, the fifth master general of the order, reflected monastic usages. Its maintenance as a rite distinct from the Roman ritual until after the Second Vatican Council contributed to a more cultic understanding of priesthood within their community. So did their increasing responsibility for staffing large churches and pastoring local communities.

The theology of priesthood that emerged from Trent also contributed to a more cultic understanding of priesthood. Behind it stands the figure of St. Thomas Aquinas. Like other medieval theologians, Thomas defined priesthood in terms of sacramental power, a *sacra potestas* that stressed the priest's cultic role in the celebration of the Eucharist rather than his relation to a particular community: "The power of orders is established for the dispensation of the sacraments . . . [and] is principally ordered to consecrating the body of Christ and dispensing it to the faithful, and to cleansing the faithful from their sins."[16] Thomas did not ignore the ministry of preaching; he treats it along with confession and study in his article on religious life in the *Summa Theologiae*.[17] He assumed that preaching was the responsibility of religious orders like his own, though subject to the authority of the pope and respectful of the bishop's authority in his diocese.

But Thomas' failure to mention preaching in the context of the priesthood was to have unfortunate consequences in the subsequent history of Catholic theology. His theology of the priesthood was confirmed by the

---

[15] O'Malley, "Priesthood, Ministry, and Religious Life," 239–41.

[16] *Summa contra Gentiles,* Bk. 4, chs. 74, 75 (New York: Image Books, 1957) 287, 289.

[17] *Summa Theologiae* II–II, q. 188, a. 4–5.

Council of Trent and was passed down through the subsequent manualist tradition to our own time. Those preparing for the priesthood prior to the Second Vatican Council learned their theology from those manuals. Unlike the Reformation traditions, which focused on the pastoral office as a preaching office (Predigtamt) or ministry (Dienst), Roman Catholic theology continued to focus on the priesthood in terms of the sacred power the priest possesses, which enabled him to consecrate or "confect" the Eucharist. Such an approach reduced the priesthood theologically to a cultic function.[18]

But perhaps nowhere is the cultic concept of the priesthood more clearly seen than in the tradition of the so-called private Mass, or more accurately, the solitary Mass, the practice of celebrating the Mass without either congregation or the presence of another member of the faithful. Church law has sought to prevent the solitary Mass since the ninth century. However, after the Second Vatican Council, the general Instruction of the 1969 Missal (no. 211) and the 1983 Code of Canon Law (c. 906) mitigated somewhat the prohibition of solitary celebrations.[19] For many religious priests, formed in a sacerdotal spirituality that saw the primary meaning of priesthood in "offering the holy sacrifice of the mass," the solitary Mass has become their most frequent experience of Eucharist; they find their own priesthood most clearly expressed in those quiet moments. This is a personal matter and should be respected. But from a theological perspective, the private Mass and ultimately the triumph of the solitary Mass have played an enormous role in changing the primarily prophetic priesthood of many active religious communities into one much more cultically conceived and experienced.

A Prophetic Priesthood Today

An apostolic religious priesthood is one exercised primarily "outside the sanctuary." It represents a move away from an overly clerical understanding of ordained ministry and from the "sacral model" of priesthood that developed in the Middle Ages and dominated the Roman Catholic understanding of priesthood down to the Second Vatican Council. If the council shifted to an understanding of priesthood as ministry, its documents assume that all priests are ministering to the faithful, in parishes, in hierarchical union with the bishops, authorized by ordination.[20] But if

[18] In my early years in the Society of Jesus (1960–65) we never had a homily at Mass, not even on Sundays.

[19] Cf. Thomas P. Rausch, "Is the Private Mass Traditional?" *Worship* 64 (1990) 237–42.

[20] O'Malley, "One Priesthood," 11–13.

there is an increasing emphasis today on the ordained minister as the liturgical leader of a local community, there remains a need in the Church for a priesthood more prophetic than cultic in orientation.

How might such a prophetic priesthood be conceived? It would be an evangelical or kerygmatic priesthood. Rather than serving a local community, it would be at the service of the universal Church. It would be free enough to imagine new ways of being church.[21] It would be directed toward "the ministry of the word, the ministries of interiority, the ministry to social misery."[22] Its ministry of the word would address both believers and non-believers. Structured by the requirements of preaching the word in all its dimensions, a prophetic priesthood might involve the following.

Mobility

Preaching the gospel wherever Christ needs to be proclaimed requires mobility. The early Franciscans and Dominicans were wandering preachers. Dominic intended his community to be a highly mobile group; they were not to be tied down to traditional ministries. Thus he "left his Order, at least at first, with a definite instinct against the official care of souls."[23] Dominic succeeded in realizing for the first time "a way in which the itinerant, non-territorial, priestly apostolate could be institutionalized."[24] Much the same could be said for Francis, though for his community the struggle to institutionalize his charism was a long and divisive one.

The early Jesuits understood themselves as reformed priests, free to go wherever they were missioned, with the availability symbolized by the fourth vow of special obedience to the pope. For this reason, certain ministries were originally excluded. In the words of the *Constitutions:*

> Because the members of the Society ought to be ready at any hour to go to some or other part of the world where they may be sent by the sovereign pontiff or their own superiors, they ought not to take a curacy of souls, and still less ought they to take charge of religious women or any other women whatever to be their confessors regularly or to direct them.[25]

Today many apostolic orders have lost much of their mobility because of their commitments to established works. Their founders did not intend

---

[21] Cf. David N. Power, "Theologies of Religious Life and Priesthood," *A Concert of Charisms,* 91.

[22] Buckley, "Jesuit Priesthood," 150.

[23] Simon Tugwell, *The Way of the Preacher* (London: Darton, Longman & Todd) 23.

[24] Ibid., 82–3.

[25] Ignatius, *Constitutions,* 588; Ganss, *The Constitutions of the Society of Jesus,* 262–3.

them to be tied to places, institutions, dioceses, or countries. Even less should they be wedded to a particular social class or culture. A prophetic priesthood needs to be free to go wherever there is need.

Evangelization

A priesthood structured by a commitment to the word of God is essentially evangelical. Many apostolic religious communities or missionary societies of priests have a strong commitment to evangelization. But too often the Catholic Church today has given up the work of evangelization to Protestant evangelicals. In the United States, the Catholic Church has hardly begun to address the challenge of evangelization in an affluent and secular culture. What Mary Catherine Hilkert has said about the direction that preaching the gospel should take for Dominicans today applies equally to other apostolic religious communities: "The growing strength of fundamentalism, the political power being exerted by the new right in religion, and the vast areas of this country which are classified as 'unchurched' all call for a response on the part of an order founded specifically for the proclamation of the gospel."[26]

Social Justice

The Church in the late twentieth century has become increasingly aware of the social dimension of the proclamation of the gospel. The 1971 Synod of Bishops stated explicitly: "Action on behalf of justice and participation in the transformation of the world fully appear to us as a constitutive dimension of preaching the gospel."[27] In the renewal of religious life that followed the Second Vatican Council, a considerable number of religious communities have sought to make a commitment to justice and solidarity with the poor an intrinsic part of their mission. That commitment should also characterize a community whose priesthood is prophetic in orientation. Furthermore, working for justice is one particularly significant way that non-ordained members of a community can share with the ordained in expressing in their own ministries the community's evangelical charism or its prophetic priesthood.

The Intellectual Life

In spite of the fact that neither Dominic nor Ignatius foresaw the commitment to the intellectual life that would come to characterize their communities, both orders became involved in higher education

---

[26] Mary Catherine Hilkert, "The Dominican Charism: A Living Tradition of Grace," *Spirituality Today* 38 (1986) 155.
[27] "Justice in the World," 1971 Synod of Bishops, no. 6.

and scholarship even within their founders' lifetimes. Franciscans also began teaching in universities early in their history. In each case, this involvement was a direct result of their efforts to provide a quality education for their own junior members. The mendicants stressed education precisely because of their preaching mission. Their members were soon studying and teaching at the great universities of Europe. Ignatius set up houses or "colleges" at the better universities of his day for his scholastics. Soon the lectures these colleges provided drew other students who sought admission.

Both the Dominican and Jesuit constitutions reflect the high value their founders placed on solid intellectual formation. Dominic provided dispensations from community observances for the sake of study as well as preaching. Part IV of the Constitutions of the Society of Jesus is devoted entirely to Jesuit colleges and universities. Ignatius saw the development of any human talent or gift as useful for the sake of the order's mission. Because of this, his order became synonymous with a lengthy intellectual formation. By the time of his death in 1556, the number of Jesuit colleges had grown to forty-six. By the early seventeenth century, the Jesuits were staffing more than four hundred educational institutions.

A religious community whose priesthood is prophetic in orientation can neglect the intellectual life only at the expense of its ministry of the word. Teaching belongs to the mission of the priest. If the gospel is to penetrate and illumine a complex, technological culture such as our own or be able to challenge the pervasive secularism of contemporary Western societies, it will take minds that are not just highly trained, but insightful and cultivated. This demands an emphasis on higher education and a commitment to the intellectual life.

Conclusions

The Church's priesthood can admit of various forms of expression. Given the shortage of priests today and the growing need for local community leaders able to celebrate the Eucharist, the Church of the future will probably see more forms of priesthood, rather than fewer.

The religious orders, both monastic and apostolic, with their own forms of priesthood, have and will continue to enrich the Church with their witness and their ministries. It would be a tragic mistake to attempt to force a redefinition of their priesthood in order to address the current shortage of ordained pastors. Pope John Paul II has repeatedly called the Church to a new evangelization. The gospel must be proclaimed and interpreted, not just in the context of parishes and local communities, but to the Church itself, to the complex cultures in which it lives, to the millions who are unevangelized or unchurched today, and to those on society's margins.

The dawning of the third millennium brings with it the hope for the realization of a global community. This means that the reconciliation of the Christian churches and dialogue with the great religions of the world will become even more a basic part of the Church's evangelical mission, and so, of the mission of apostolic religious orders. For example, in reflecting on the Jesuit mission at the end of the twentieth century, the Thirty-Fourth General Congregation (GC) reaffirmed that the "ministries of the Word—the ministries named before all others in the formula of our Institute—have always been of primary importance for Jesuit priestly ministry."[28] The congregation expanded the "service of faith and the promotion of justice" language of GC 32: "In the light of Decree 4 and our present experience, we can now say explicitly that our mission of the service of faith and the promotion of justice must be broadened to include as integral dimensions proclamation of the Gospel, dialogue, and the evangelization of cultures."[29] Other documents dealt with ecumenism (Decree 12) and interreligious dialogue (Decree 5).

Thus there is and will continue to be a need for a more prophetic priesthood, evangelical in orientation, free to respond to new situations, skilled at bringing the word of God to bear in all its many dimensions—preaching, teaching, carrying out the spiritual ministries of interiority and the prophetic ministries of social justice. This kerygmatic or prophetic priesthood describes how the priesthood of many apostolic religious communities should be understood.

[28] Decree 6: "Ministerial Priesthood and Jesuit Identity," no. 21, *Documents of the Thirty-Fourth General Congregation of the Society of Jesus* (St. Louis, Mo.: Institute of Jesuit Sources, 1995) 93.

[29] Ibid., Decree 2: "Servants of Christ's Mission," no. 20, 38.

6

The Minister: Lay and Ordained

JACK RISLEY, O.P.

One of the more vexing problems that faces the Church today is the relationship between the priesthood of those who are ordained and the baptismal priesthood of all the faithful. This question has numerous roots. In the United States and elsewhere, the Church now embraces a large number of laity who are highly educated and highly competent. This phenomenon is highlighted by an increasing number of laity and a decreasing number of ordained priests. Furthermore, the American spirit of equality stresses similarities among people rather than differences.

The issue, however, does not arise solely from the situation of the Church in the United States. During the 1940s and 1950s, and culminating in the Second Vatican Council, the liturgical movement emphasized the active role of all the faithful in the celebration of the Eucharist and in the general liturgical life of the Church. Even before this, there are scriptural references to the role of both specially deputed ministers and the whole body of the People of God in the fostering of worship. Pope Pius XII, in his encyclical letter *Mediator Dei,* emphasizes the role of the laity in sacramental celebrations, but he is also clear about the two different ways of sharing in the priesthood of Christ: "The fact, however, that the faithful participate in the Eucharistic Sacrifice does not mean that they also are endowed with priestly power."[1] The Second Vatican Council understood this to mean that the common priesthood of the faithful and the ministerial or hierarchical priesthood, as they are called, "differ essentially and not only in degree."[2]

---

[1] Pope Pius XII, *Mediator Dei* 82, N.C.W.C. Edition, 1947.

[2] *Lumen gentium* 10. Conciliar and post-conciliar documents are quoted from Austin Flannery, ed., *Vatican II: The Conciliar and Post Conciliar Documents* (Collegeville: The Liturgical Press, 1975).

Both Vatican II and post-Vatican documents emphasize that the priesthood of the laity and the priesthood of the ordained are "ordered to one another (since) each in its own proper way shares in the one priesthood of Christ."[3] But the Vatican has felt in recent times that this common sharing in Christ's priesthood has led some in the Church to misunderstand it; so in a document entitled Some Questions Regarding Collaboration of Nonordained Faithful in Priests' Sacred Ministry issued on November 13, 1997, it attempts to make clearer their essential diversity:

> This diversity exists at the mode of participation in the priesthood of Christ and is essential in the sense that "while the common priesthood of the faithful is exercised by the unfolding of baptismal grace—a life of faith, hope and charity, a life according to the Spirit—the ministerial priesthood is at the service of the common priesthood . . . and is directed at the unfolding of the baptismal grace of all Christians." Consequently, the ministerial priesthood "differs in essence from the common priesthood of the faithful because it confers a sacred power for the service of the faithful."[4]

So this sets up the problem that I believe necessitates further theological reflection on the issue of priesthood in the Catholic Church. In spite of positive developments, the relationship of the priesthood of the laity to the ordained priesthood still raises many questions. For example, it is always difficult to state precisely how a difference in kind is distinct from a difference in degree. There is the danger of making them so unlike each other that the one disappears in favor of the other. One may so separate the ordained priest from the faithful that the role of the latter is diminished. This would mean that the difference is one of subordination rather than coordination. Both ministerial priesthood and the common priesthood of the faithful are essential to the nature of the Church. If either is diminished the whole Church suffers. Furthermore, in the official pronouncements of the Church there is still a suspicion that expanding the role of the laity will necessarily lead to a diminution of the ordained priesthood.

In what follows I would like to move toward a new way of conceiving the relationship between the common priesthood of the faithful and the ministerial priesthood of the ordained. I will explain that they are diverse ways of sharing in Christ's priesthood but that this does not mean that one (the ordained) is *separate* from or *superior* to the other.

---

[3] Ibid.
[4] "Theological Principles, 1. Common Priesthood of the Faithful and the Ministerial Priesthood," *Origins* 27:24 (November 27, 1997) 400–1.

Ontological Foundation

Before I go on I would like to add one more item from the Church's official magisterial theology of the priesthood by way of Pope John Paul II, because I think it opens the way to this new approach. John Paul II, both in talking about the priesthood of the laity in *Christifideles laici* and about the formation of priests in *Pastores dabo vobis* speaks of the whole priestly people as having "a real ontological share in [Christ's] one eternal priesthood."[5] And that is because we are all "baptized into priesthood," to take a wonderful phrase from Fr. Aidan Kavanaugh. We have always tended to think of ordained priests as being intrinsically or "ontologically" priests by reason of ordination, and not just fulfilling a priestly role. The same can be said of all the baptized, according to John Paul II. Discipleship sealed by baptism gives all members of the Church a common ontological foundation of priesthood from which different ministries flow. Lay priesthood, as well as ordained priesthood, is more than a function conceded by "real" priests. It is part of their Christian being. Let us now see how the two are interrelated.

One Priesthood—Two Modes of Participation

The ministry of the ordained (bishops, priests, and deacons) and the ministry of the non-ordained (lay people) are not two streams within the ecclesiological landscape of the Church but part of the one stream of living water (John 7:38) that flows from baptism and opens up for all Christians a participation in the priesthood of Christ, as well as in his prophetic and kingly ministry. All Christian discipleship and all ministry flow from baptism and the gifts of the Holy Spirit. As Thomas O'Meara has written, "Christian ministry is the public activity of a baptized follower of Jesus Christ flowing from the Spirit's charism and an individual personality on behalf of a Christian community to witness to, serve and realize the kingdom of God."[6]

Thus the one stream of the common priesthood, which has its ground in Christ's priesthood and which ordained and laity share sacramentally (through sacraments of initiation) and equally (but distinctly), is the gift of Christ to the Church and to the world. But it embraces two modes of participation that exist and operate as different gifts. There is a pluralism based on different functions within the Church, but these two ways of sharing Christ's priesthood are intrinsically united and interdependent.

---

[5] Pope John Paul II, *Pastores dabo vobis,* ch. II, n. 13, *Origins* 21:45 (April 16, 1992) 724.

[6] Thomas O'Meara, *Theology of Ministry* (New York: Paulist Press, 1983) 142.

They need each other and support one another. If the ordained priest-hood is a ministry of leadership in the Church and is an *official* witness of Christ within the Church, then it needs those who receive that witness in faith, who offer their spiritual sacrifice to God in the liturgy, and who bring that witness into the world. As David Coffey says, "There is some-thing anomalous about an exercise of the ordained priesthood that does not directly involve the participation of the common priesthood." On the other hand, as Coffey goes on to say:

> He (the priest) represents Christ in that he sacramentally makes visible and active in the Church an invisible reality, Christ in his headship. This is not the case with his representation of the Church, for in a real sense the Church is visible already. But in this case he adds headship, apostolate, or leadership to the action of this group of believers, in order to constitute them as church in the full sense. Apart from his presence and ministry they are only a group of believers, unable of themselves to represent the church.[7]

The true Church, therefore, is an ecclesiological integration of gifts and ministries in which priests and people need and depend on each other for the realization of their respective vocation.

Priesthood and Power

How can we actually describe or portray their relationship? It has various aspects but I would like to focus on it as a power-relationship. The ordained or "hierarchical" priesthood is frequently talked about or thought of in terms of power; some people have a power not present to others in the church, power conferred by reason of ordination. It is be-cause of this that some (Coffey) think that "hierarchical priesthood" is no longer a suitable term because it conveys overtones of power-based domination. Others, most notably women in the Church, would say that you cannot talk about priestly power without talking about patriarchy, and that, indeed, the exercise of power in the Church by priests is an in-ference of a patriarchal system. Yet it is the thesis of this article that power does not have to be a divisive or discriminatory element within Church ministry, but rather one that integrates and connects in mutuality. If power is an element of priesthood, we have to begin with the common, shared power that comes from Jesus' priesthood. As one bishop says, speaking of the priest's role in the Church, "The issue of power is of great signifi-

[7] David Coffey, "Common and Ordained Priesthood," *Theological Studies* 58 (June 1997) 233–4.

cance. Power is the basic ability to bring about change. It is also the power to prevent things from happening."[8]

Both the ordained and the common priesthood are "powerful": the power to serve the redeemable world and to change it from a sinful world to the reign of God. Power or *dynamis* is everywhere in the New Testament, present within and flowing from the life of Jesus and that of the disciples. Primarily it is the power of God to salvation (Rom 1:16). But we know, as Jesus makes clear (Mark 10:41–45), the servant of God uses power not for self but for others. The disciples were not to seek the power and honors of the world, as the sons of Zebedee had asked for, but only the power of servanthood exemplified by Jesus: "The Son of man himself came not to be served but to serve, and to give his life as a ransom for many" (Mark 10:45 NJB).

Donald Goergen in his book *The Power of Love* says that to talk of the love of God you have to speak of the power of God. It is not the power of coercion, which is the "power" of sin—which actually is lacking in power—but the power of love that makes us free and that brings forth life. That is why the Holy Spirit is both love and power. They are two sides of the same coin. In the words of Goergen:

> The Holy Spirit is power. In fact, the Holy Spirit reveals to us the true and authentic character of power. The Lord himself in that sense is the supreme exemplification of power. Sin, then, is revealed as not being true power but false power. . . . Love in fact is a power more powerful than any coercive force might be. There is no power more powerful than the power of love. No other power has the courage to risk freedom. The power of love is sufficient to let go of control, the power to let the other be while at the same time it offers union.[9]

This is an important issue in our ecclesial existence because, as Goergen also notes,[10] it is around the positive reality of the power of love that the Christian life revolves and organizes itself.

Power as Relationship and Process

Relationship

It is necessary not to be naïve about power, and we must see it in the Church according to an image different from that which the world

[8] Bishop Robert Morneau, "Roles of the Presbyteral Leader," National Federation of Priests' Councils, April 21–24, 1997.

[9] Donald Goergen, *The Power of Love: Christian Spirituality and Theology* (Chicago: Thomas More Press, 1979) 252–53.

[10] Ibid., 245.

holds. James and Evelyn Whitehead in their book *The Emerging Laity* approach it wisely when they say, "Power is not something that leaders carry about with them; it is a process occurring within a group."[11] Within this concept, power is seen as a *relationship* rather than as an individual possession. It refers to *interactions* that go on among the people of a community, among those who lead and those who receive and are served by the ministry of leadership. There is an energy that flows both ways and that either creates and enhances community or threatens and obstructs community. In one case, it binds people into mutual commitment and service; in the other case, it manifests itself in unhealthy and destructive coercion and restraint.

When I think of priestly power in light of power as a relationship I am reminded of what John Paul II says about priesthood in *Pastores dabo vobis*. There he sees both the Church's and the priest's identity as based on the relationship within the Trinity.[12] The Church is the sacrament of the Trinitarian communion between Father, Son, and Holy Spirit. John Paul II speaks of the "fundamentally 'relational dimension' of priestly identity" whereby the priest is "sent forth by the Father through the mediatorship of Jesus Christ . . . in order to live and work by the power of the Holy Spirit in service of the church and for the salvation of the world."[13] And so the pope sees ministerial priesthood defined "through the multiple and rich interconnection of relationships which arise from the Blessed Trinity and are prolonged in the communion of the church."[14] Thus it seems to me that the leadership power of the ordained priest can be seen as a relationship with other powers and creative energies in the Church community, so that, as John Paul II says, there is a "rich interconnection of relationships" that form a true communion.

Process

The Whiteheads point out that this image of power as relationship is intimately related to another image of power that is growing in importance in the social sciences: power as a *social process*. It is the "flow of collaboration and resistance and debate through which the people (of a group) interact with one another."[15] Thus it is a social power that determines relationships as the members of the community interact and seek to fulfill

[11] James and Evelyn Whitehead, *The Emerging Laity: Returning Leadership to the Community of Faith* (Garden City, N.Y.: Doubleday, 1988) 36.

[12] See *Pastores dabo vobis*, n. 12.

[13] Ibid.

[14] Ibid.

[15] James and Evelyn Whitehead, *The Emerging Laity*, 39.

their goals and realize their hopes, using the strengths and gifts they have in accordance with their respective vocations. For the Church it is a question of tapping into the presence and power of the Holy Spirit that moves within the community of faith, and of discerning and distinguishing the power of the Spirit from other forms of power that often are destructive of community.

Priesthood and Order

Within this social process there is a process of role differentiation that we in the Church call a differentiation of gifts, ministries, and vocations. As in any human organization, these ecclesiological entities need social structures of exercise and interaction. It is important to recognize that these structures are historical and relative, that is, relative to cultural, political, and ecclesiological settings that shape structures. Kenan Osborne, in his exhaustive study on ministry *Ministry: Lay Ministry in the Roman Catholic Church,* comes to the conclusion that the key to understanding the development of ministerial structures in the Church is the Greco-Roman term *ordo,* which came to designate what priesthood is. I will use his study as background for my own thesis and refer the reader to his book for more details and substantiation of his points.

Osborne argues that just as there were "orders" within the Greco-Roman political and social world that determined positions of power and influence, so there came to be an established positioning within the Church as *ordo* was applied to Church structure. The "clerical" order was established through the *ordinatio* of Church leaders. "Lay people" *(laikoi)* as non-ordained had no "order" and therefore were "disestablished" or "depositioned" in terms of such a sociopolitical structuring within the Church. It is easy to understand how this came about in a religious Christian state after 300 C.E. in which government leaders and Church leaders were integral to each other's sphere.

This, says Osborne, was a change of departure from the New Testament and earlier Christian understanding of ministry. Its point of departure was the meaning of *discipleship.* But within the insertion of *ordo* into Church structures, as the Church increasingly modeled itself on an "ordered" Greco-Roman society, it was the hierarchical positioning and power-positioning of Church leadership that became the hermeneutical instrument to interpret Christian discipleship, rather than vice versa. Sociopolitical structures became ontologized ("This is the *nature* of the beast") and theologized ("This is what *God* ordained").

Osborne believes that we must get back to a gospel theology of discipleship in which the lay/cleric distinction is not found, even in terms of ministry and leadership. Believing that the true point of departure is the meaning of discipleship, Osborne examines it in each of the Gospels and throughout the New Testament. Within the Gospels he notes that the "ecclesial" dimension of Mark's Gospel is focused on the Jesus community of which Mark is a part, and not on a "hierarchical in-group." The disciple is simply what every follower of Jesus should and should not be, and not what is a good (or bad) "cleric" (or "lay" person). He points out that you cannot deduce from Luke that there are two ways of following Jesus: a general way for an undifferentiated group, and another way for an inner-circle of leadership. Luke does reveal in Acts that there is a leadership group in early Christianity, but there is no clear indication of how it arrived at its leadership or how it established it structurally. Osborne also argues that even with the specific emphasis in Matthew's Gospel on leadership in the Jesus community and the unique role of Peter, there is no indication that a leader has a different standard of measurement than that of any other disciple. In John's Gospel the only two criteria for discipleship are faith and love, and neither position, nor status, nor leadership, nor sex is the basis for discipleship. There are incipient structures of leadership in John, but it is not specified how they came to be.

Osborne sees in the documents of Vatican II the beginning of a theology in which the matrix of discipleship, which is common and equal to all members of the Church, is put before any distinction among them (i.e., cleric/lay). The People of God refers to all indiscriminately (*Lumen gentium* 9). So he affirms that the bishops of Vatican II did enhance the issue of gospel discipleship. "Nonetheless," he says, "when it comes to the issue of ordained ministry, too often gospel discipleship still does not serve as the fundamental hermeneutic to understand the ordained servant-leadership of the church."[16] It seems to me that what Osborne is saying is that the real power comes from discipleship and not first and foremost from ordination. The latter specifies the power that is there.

Power in the Church

We must always remember that the structures of ministry and leadership in the Church are in relation to the larger goal of the Church community, which is to be "a kind of sacrament" in the world (*Lumen gentium* 1). In fact, to follow this line of thinking we can, along with the Whiteheads,[17] say that "the sacraments are the basic power structure of a Chris-

---

[16] Kenan Osborne, *Ministry: Lay Ministry in the Roman Catholic Church, Its History and Theology* (New York: Paulist Press, 1993) 594–5.

[17] James and Evelyn Whitehead, *The Emerging Laity,* 46.

tian community," whereby its actions of celebration, reconciliation, and justice powerfully announce Christ's presence in the world.

What does this say then about the power that is to be distributed and exercised in the Church according to Christ's intentions? What is our criteria for evaluating ecclesiastical power? How can the power struggles we see in the Church be redirected by a reconciling notion of power itself? If power is seen as the ability to make something happen and achieve a goal, then power belongs to all members of the Church and to all its ministries, as we said previously. Both the psychologist Rollo May *(Power and Innocence)* and the theologian Henri Nouwen *(The Path of Power)* speak against a powerlessness that, on the one hand, is a "pseudoinnocence" that leads to violence (May), and, on the other hand, is a "theology of weakness" (i.e., "for weaklings") that makes us door-mats who allow the powers of darkness to dominate our lives (Nouwen). May puts it well with a quote from Martin Buber:

> We cannot avoid
> Using power,
> Cannot escape the compulsion
> To afflict the world,
> So let us, cautious in diction
> And mighty in contradiction,
> Love powerfully.[18]

This is what all authentic ministry in the Church is: to "love power-fully." As Nouwen points out and we noted previously, "God is powerful," and "Jesus docs not hesitate to speak about God's power."[19] Yet Nouwen also points out that when we talk about the power of the Church and its ministers, we are talking about "God's power," not our power. That's where Buber's "contradiction" comes in, what we call the "Gospel paradox." The coming into power and the exercise of power in discipleship is through human powerlessness. We can't claim the power. The power is given as gift and we are its stewards; it is to be used for God's purposes. It is the all-transforming power of love that Jesus claimed as the power to forgive sins and to heal and to call others to life. God wants to empower us in the way that he empowered Jesus, which is not to have and use the power of the world (the temptations), but to unmask the power games of the world (and of the Church) by entering human history and leaving human history in complete powerlessness (Bethlehem/Calvary).

[18] Rollo May, *Power and Innocence: A Search for the Sources of Violence* (New York: Norton, 1972) 242.

[19] Henri Nouwen, *The Path of Power* (New York: Crossroad, 1995) 34.

Thus, as Nouwen writes, there is a "theology of weakness (that) is a theology of divine empowering . . . , a theology for men and women who claim for themselves the power of love that frees them from fear and enables them to put their light on the lampstands and do the work of the Kingdom."[20] Baptized in powerlessness, and following Jesus in the beatitudes as poor, gentle, mourning, hungry and thirsty for justice, merciful, pure of heart, peacemakers and persecuted, and even while fearful and anxious and insecure themselves, they are not afraid to dare to take risks and bold initiatives in announcing the Good News and serving others.

Thus the contrast is striking between the two kinds of power. Worldly power is in direct proportion to its ability to dominate. Gospel power has an inverse proportion: the more you give up the need and desire to dominate or control, the more powerful you are. The latter is a power that unites instead of divides, not only those served but also those who serve, that is, the ministers in their differing roles. It heals the body of ministers instead of wounding them. It enables a community to grow as a community instead of paralyzing it. This relates to what Rollo May describes, on the one hand, as power that is exploitative, manipulative, and competitive—which helps define the gospel sense of "the power of the world"—and, on the other hand, what he calls "nutritive power," in other words, power "for the other," and "integrative power," that is, power "with the other person," which "abets my neighbor's power." He points out that this integrative power is also exercised by constructive criticism, what we might call "prophetic" ministry.

Certainly all of these powers are part of the reality of the Church, both on the plus side and on the minus side. But nutritive and integrative power can, I think, help us to come to a better understanding of the relationship between ordained and non-ordained ministry, as did the Whitehead's notion of power as a relationship and a process. For example, when the 1997 Vatican document mentioned above,[21] in distinguishing the common priesthood of the faithful from the ministerial priesthood, says that the latter "confers a sacred power for the service of the faithful," cannot that be to serve them in the complementary and integrative use of the faithful's own priestly power that serves the ordained ministry?

The Finality of Priestly Power

Now before we look at how the role of bishop/presbyter as leader is related to the ministry of the laity within this concept of nutritive, integrative, and interacting power that serves and brings about life—this power

---

[20] Ibid., 36.
[21] See above, fn. 4.

that is the God-given power of love—it would be helpful to see what specifically is this power directed toward in the exercise of priesthood. Priestly power for what? It is to look at priesthood from the point of view of its finality. This, rightly I believe, is the point of departure of Latin American liberation theologian Jon Sobrino in his book *The Principle of Mercy,* in the chapter entitled "Toward a Determination of the Nature of Priesthood."[22] He points out that the priesthood is not simply to be in function of historical and/or regional realities and problems, thus conditioning our theological imagination to current ecclesiastical structures and conceptualizations of priesthood.[23] It is in function of its finality which is discovered by departing from more fundamental theological and christological questions which "restore the question of priesthood to its comprehensive matrix."[24]

Now the finality of priesthood, Sobrino insists, whether it be Jesus' or our own, whether ordained or lay priesthood, is salvation. What my own Dominican Order says is the reason for everything Dominicans do is also the finality of the priestly character of the whole People of God: the salvation of people. And no matter where you look at priesthood in the religions of the world, past and present, it responds to a reality: humanity in need of salvation with the hope of attaining it. And that salvation is seen in reference to God. And the priesthood is seen as some kind of mediation between God and humanity to be saved.

For us Christians the whole question of salvation and mediation has reached a new state of being. Christ has changed the very way we think about it, as the letter to the Hebrews makes clear. Old Testament priesthood, like that of non-biblical religions, was a ritualistic solution to the problem of the distance between and separation of God and human beings, expressed as the reality of sin. How to bridge the gap, how to pacify and reach God, and thus find salvation? The answer is to exercise rites and rituals—sacrifice, expiation, purification, etc.—that allow us to approach and get nearer to God and be saved. It all makes up the world of the "sacred," and the priest is the key figure, because it is he (or she in some religions) who effects the mediation. And so, as Sobrino states, "the be-all and end-all of priesthood is to bring about that human beings be purified of their sin, reach God, and attain salvation. The nature of priestliness is 'mediatory' in this precise sense."[25]

---

[22] Jon Sobrino, *The Principle of Mercy* (Maryknoll, N.Y.: Orbis Books, 1994).

[23] We want a theology that emerges from Scripture and tradition and then tries to develop authentic practice from that, and not one that is used to try to justify untenable realities of authority, patriarchy, wealth, and power-over rather than power-with that have developed historically.

[24] Sobrino, *Principle of Mercy,* 108.

[25] Ibid., 112.

For the New Testament, the cultic solution of priesthood no longer holds because it is not necessary. Salvation is not mediated in the old sense because God is saving in and of God's self. It is God who comes near, or rather, reveals the divine nearness, the divine proximity. As Sobrino says, "That coming, that drawing near, belongs to God's reality,"[26] and that is what is revealed and uttered radically and irrevocably in the incarnation, in the person of Jesus Christ. As Paul would say so forcefully, it is salvation that is gained, not through priestly works but freely given by a gracious God. "It is an unconditional, irrevocable approach (of God), independent of the will of the human being."[27]

Thus the only mediation there is, is the mediation that is Christ in person (see 1 Tim 2:5), that is, both God in-the-coming and the human beings in-the-receiving and responding. It is the ontological link between the God who approaches in order to save and the human being who needs salvation and believes in it. And as Sobrino points out in his liberationist perspective, the mediatorial presence of Jesus manifests more than anything else the mercy of God, the God who comes preferentially near to the poor and weak and despised, so that "God's saving universalism [should] be understood in terms of God's saving partiality, and not the other way around."[28]

So where does priesthood stand now? It is simply Jesus, and "all that Jesus is is priestly."[29] "In order to draw near human beings salvifically, God has personally adopted an expression of this coming: Jesus."[30] And why does the Church need priests then? "It is necessary because God means to keep on approaching human beings and keeps on needing historical expressions of that salvific coming."[31] As Jesus did, the priest today exists as God's "salvific approach to human beings," doing whatever will help, in the Christian community and in the world around, to express and make real God's saving, loving nearness, or in Jesus' terms, what will help make people aware that "the reign of God is at hand."

And so priestly service is making people aware of and in touch with the goodness of God—unlimited, freely given goodness—and, at the same time, helping them to respond and correspond to God in the way Jesus did. Paul defines it as "faith expressing itself in love" (Gal 5:6 NAB). This service is done in activities that are liturgical, doctrinal, exhortatory,

---

[26] Ibid., 113.
[27] Ibid.
[28] Ibid., 114.
[29] Ibid., 115.
[30] Ibid.
[31] Ibid., 116.

admonitory, prophetic and justice-making, and pastoral. We communicate God's goodness, and to be effective what is required of us is that we be good as our heavenly Parent is good (Matt 5:48). And, as Sobrino is quick to point out, it is the Church, the community of faith, that is the "sacrament" (my word) of this goodness as a priestly body, not just certain individuals within the Church. "A priestly church is not the same as a church with priests."[32]

Now one can see from Sobrino's ongoing development of the theme that a priestly Church includes a priestly service that is distinctive and forms a priestly "college" in the narrower sense of the ministerial priesthood, as well as having the broad sense of an entirely priestly Church. This is because, although "the *locus* of priestly service is real history," and in all fields of human life, and not in a realm apart, "it may and must be religious and expressed in a *liturgy*" (emphasis added).[33] The liturgy makes it clear that the approaching "goodness" is *God's* goodness and not just any kind of goodness or any kind of salvation. And so the "concrete" good that is present and effected is religious in the sense that it is always "open to the 'more,'" and the One who is sacramentalized by it is always greater than the concrete "goodnesses" in which God approaches us.[34] And it is "liturgical" because the concrete good must be "accompanied by some word or deed calculated to express this openness," and by acts of "gratitude for and celebration of the approach of the good God."[35]

In Sobrino's schema, as I understand it, ordained priests or presbyters would be the ones who, in the liturgy (though not exclusively there), explain the word of the God who comes, "a word ever ancient and ever new"; and this is in terms of God's approach to the human being. In terms of the human being's response to God, the presbyter fosters a liturgical response, "with gladness when this coming has occurred, with repentance when it has been vitiated by human beings' fault, and with humility, asking that it come."[36]

Sobrino analyzes further the christological dimension, emphasizing again that "a priest is what Jesus is," and it is epitomized in Jesus as "the person of mercy,"[37] quoting what Albert Nolan, O.P., once said in *Jesus Before Christianity*.[38] Mercy is the criterion for priestly action, of media-

---

[32] Ibid., 118.
[33] Ibid., 122.
[34] Ibid., 122–3.
[35] Ibid., 123.
[36] Ibid., 123.
[37] Ibid., 127.
[38] Albert Nolan, *Jesus Before Christianity* (Maryknoll, N.Y.: Orbis Books, 1978) 113.

tion of the will of God, as well as that in which "Jesus renders God's coming real."[39] But it is also Jesus who brings in the priestly element of *sacrifice.* For Hebrews, priesthood means more than anything else "sacrificial offering" (Heb 5:1; 8:3). Jesus, then, in his very personhood is sacrificial offering; he is both priest and victim. As Sobrino expresses it, "Christ's sacrifice is the most historical element of his priesthood, and the most priestly element of his historical life."[40] Sacrifice is, of course, explained by love. And that's why we can say that Jesus' sacrifice is not a new and necessary mediation that brings an angry God near, but simply the wonderful way God chose to reveal God's limitless and unconditional approach to human beings. Jesus on the cross, as High Priest, is "but the consequence of a genuinely 'proexistential' priestly existence, an existence in behalf of human beings. To hold firm in sacrifice is nothing but to say in human fashion that one really loves human beings and seeks their salvation."[41]

Priestly Existence and Two Different Ways of Being Priestly

I think Sobrino's notion of "proexistential" priestly existence can help us understand both the difference between the two modes of participation in Christ's priesthood and their unity. It is two ways of being "proexistential," of existing on behalf of something beyond yourself. For both laity and ordained that is their Christian existence, that is what it means to follow Jesus Christ and fulfill the commandment of love. It is the good Samaritan, it is the father of the prodigal son, it is Jesus on the cross: real love for human beings to the point of sacrifice, an expression of God's own unconditional love. Both laity and ordained have a proexistential relationship with the world and with one another. The difference is how, within the Church, they exist the one for the other, the one on behalf of the other, united in their common existence on behalf of Christ and his body the Church. Let me try to articulate what this means, being inspired by some thoughts of Peter Fink, s.j., in his article "The Priesthood of Jesus Christ in the Ministry and Life of the Ordained."[42]

Fink says that "priesthood of the ordained is priesthood to the priesthood of the baptized and priesthood of the baptized is priesthood to the priesthood of the ordained."[43] It is a difference in relationship, just as—to

---

[39] Sobrino, *Principle of Mercy,* 133.

[40] Ibid., 136.

[41] Ibid., 137.

[42] In Robert J. Wister, ed., *Priests: Identity and Ministry* (Wilmington, Del.: Michael Glazier, 1990) 71–91.

[43] Ibid., 74.

use the comparison offered by Fink—there is an essential difference between husband and wife in the unity of marriage. But they are defined in relation to one another: "Husband is husband to wife; wife is wife to husband." The important thing here is that in the Church's priesthood, as well as in marriage, it is not a difference of exclusion or in degree of dignity and holiness, but of complementarity. Fink rightly points out that the difference should not suggest full or partial possession of Christ's priesthood—only Jesus Christ has the fullness—but rather "different modes of participation . . . within [the] sacramental identity of the whole church with the mystery of Christ."[44]

This also leads me to think that difference in "degree" is not the best word to use in comparing the priesthood of all the baptized and that of the ordained. It gives the impression that one mode is a higher or lower participation than the other. They are just different modes of participation according to different charisms and ministries in the Church. But perhaps we can, along with Fink, speak of different "degrees" of involvement in aspects of priestly ministry. He speaks of "Degree of closeness, degree of intensity, degree of personal investment in the Word, the sacrifice, and the pastoral care of Jesus Christ himself."[45] There are more demands on the presbyter: "It demands more of the person to preach than to listen, to lead prayer than be led in prayer, to govern and guide than be governed and guided."[46]

It seems to me that what Fink is talking about here is the mission and ministry of the bishop and presbyter *within* the Church according to their charism and role of leadership that defines their mode of participation in Christ's priesthood. Fink speaks of it in terms of their two primary ministries: "to call into unity the assembly of Christ and to lead that assembly in the prayer of Christ."[47] I suppose one can speak here of "closeness" to the historical Jesus in terms of preaching and investment in the word, and of pastoral care that was Jesus' whole life. It is the demands of the apostolic life, along with those of leadership, especially with regard to religious who are presbyters. We also might mention that the "proexistential" aspect of priestly existence is more highlighted or clearly manifested by bishops and presbyters who sacrifice worldly ambitions and opportunities in order to dedicate themselves to and stake their lives on the transcendent values of the gospel.

---

[44] Ibid., 76.
[45] Ibid., 77.
[46] Ibid., 76.
[47] Ibid., 81.

The laity, for their part, exercise their priesthood not only by their participation in the liturgical celebration and building up of the Christian community, but also by their "proexistential" existence in their mission in the world, and in their own families or communities, in which they sacrifice themselves for others in faith, hope, and love, being inspired, guided, and sustained by the Word, offering their bodies "as a living sacrifice, dedicated and acceptable to God" (Rom 12:1 NJB). They love and sacrifice themselves for their children as parents, for their communities as neighbors, for their countries as citizens, for world peace and justice as human beings, using the particular talents, skills, experience, and knowledge that they have as laypeople. And that is the core of their priesthood in imitation of Christ, into which they were baptized.

So we see two ways of participating in Christ's priesthood. Their difference, as Fink reiterates, is a complementarity that enables them to achieve a fullness that neither alone could achieve: "Each is essentially different from the other because each is ordered to and dependent on the other."[48]

The Ordained Minister's Powerful Ministry

So let us now look at how this power for salvation can be exercised in the priestly Church in which both ordained and non-ordained participate. As an ordained priest, and as one who believes that power in the Church is generally seen as a privilege of Church hierarchy or leadership, I will focus on the ordained minister's use of power as a service to a power-sharing community. What is the ordained priest's charism and function in relation to those of laypeople?

Presider/Coordinator

Perhaps the presbyter is best described as coordinator and overall presider in the sacramental life of the local church, coordinating the different roles or functions (charisms) within the community, and ordering them all to its common good. He also promotes and encourages the ministries of the laypeople, helping them to discover the charisms they are not aware of, urging them to trust them and use them in ministry, and advising them when their ministry is working against the larger community and threatening its unity. In this way he represents officially (i.e., as head or leader) the unique and eternal priesthood of Christ in which the whole community participates. He also "empowers" the laity in that through his leadership the power they already have from Christ in func-

[48] Ibid., 79.

tion of the Christian cult and of their Christian witness in the world truly becomes a united power of service flowing from a faithful ecclesial community. This "ordering" task of priestly leadership is meant to coordinate the mystical body's various powers in graceful and effective self-expression, so that there is a mutuality of powers that nurture one another.

As a liturgical presider the priest functions as a *symbol* in and for the community. Traditionally the content of this symbolism of the priest, as representative of Christ the Head, was "the Holy" and "leadership." What is this leadership in holiness? Mary Ann Jordan, clinical psychologist and adjunct professor in the Graduate School of Religion at Fordham University, states it this way:

> As human beings, we all have a need for an ordained presider—a "priest"— who can symbolize our common fund of beliefs and values, our common experience of a God who utterly transcends all our human limitations. . . . In short, we need someone who can symbolize a reality that transcends all time and all space.[49]

Rememberer

Another image I like refers to the role of keeping the community in touch with and in fidelity to the tradition of the Church: that of the ordained priest being a "remembering person." He presides at the remembering event itself, the sacrament of the Eucharist, in which we retell the story of Jesus (Liturgy of the Word) and reenact his dying and rising ("Do this in remembrance of me"). Every Eucharist is to remind us of what Jesus did for us and what we are to do for others. The sacrament of the ordained priesthood, holy orders, is another sacrament in function of memory because it raises up people in the Christian community who have the *ministry of memory.* Not that all Christians, ordained or non-ordained, are not to be "remembering persons" such that part of their ministry is to keep alive the memory of Jesus. But Jesus established in the Christian community people responsible for the memory, "keepers of the flame," as it were. So one of the ways ordained priests serve the life and ministry of laypeople is to be remembering persons who help them, lest their memory fails.

I think the presbyter, whether he is preaching from the pulpit, celebrating the sacraments, giving adult Christian education, giving a retreat or a mission, visiting the sick, or working for peace and social justice, is reminding people, through the Scriptures and tradition of the Church,

[49] Mary Ann Jordan, "Liturgical Presidency: Symbol in Crisis," *Assembly* 17:1 (November 1990) 503.

and through his and others' words and experiences, of what God has done and continues to do in people's lives; and he reminds them of their own experiences of faith and of God that would make the sacred memory of the Church alive and relevant to them. Thus they empower laypeople with the memory of Jesus and help them to be living reminders of Jesus. It is another form of leadership.

Artist

In a talk about the crisis of priestly identity to the Margaret Beaufort Institute for the Study of Theology in Cambridge, Vicky Cosstick, a good friend of mine and a woman theologian from London, offers the image of the priest as an artist. She says, "The priest should be a 'a poet of his people,' someone who sees the marvelous in ordinary people and things."[50] She quotes the Irish priest John O'Donoghue, who says:

> The intention of priesthood is not to bring people something which they lack and with which he has been exclusively gifted. Rather the priest attempts to kindle in them the recognition of who they are. Priesthood longs to awaken the *who* to its origin, presence, possibility and promise.
>
> A real artist is no functional fabricator of words, matter, colours or sounds. An artist is called: there is a necessity and inevitability about the artist vocation. Imagination and divinity are sisters. Consequently, explicit priesthood demands the awakening of the imagination as the way to bring our implicit priesthood home to the awareness of its eternal potential. A priest is an artist of the eternal.[51]

Pastor of Pastoring People

Finally, let me speak from my own experience. My own experience of the above has taken place especially in working with small, faith-sharing Christian communities (SCCs). Within the image of the local church or parish as a community of communities, the parish priest, especially the pastor, is the one who has to co-initiate, or at least affirm and integrate, the formation and promotion of the SCCs in the parish. He has to coordinate and integrate the small communities into the life and plan of the larger community, the parish, through the pastoral facilitators of the individual communities. Yet he knows that the SCCs depend, for their life and vitality and success, not on him but on their own members who are to use their gifts for their own SCC and for the whole parish. But he also needs to animate the facilitators and the members, making them aware

---

[50] Unpublished presentation given on May 9, 1998.

[51] John O'Donoghue, "The Priestliness of the Human Heart," *The Way,* in the *Supplement* 83 (Summer 1995).

of the importance of faith-sharing, aware of the gifts they have, and providing them with ways of using those gifts in ministries within the parish, as well as within their particular SCC. Only through the direction and coordination of the presbyter as leader/presider will the SCCs form a new image of Church within a parish and realize a new way of being Church. Without the presbyter's involvement and leadership, the SCCs will just remain a small movement within the parish, they will die, or they will never even get off the ground. The presbyter makes them truly an ecclesial experience and reality. But without the life that comes from the SCCs themselves, it goes nowhere.

Conclusion

The above reflection leads to the conclusion, I believe, that the ordained priest has a unique participation in the priesthood of Christ, but it is only that he might serve the priesthood of the faithful that belongs to every disciple. He is head so that he might better serve the body. As Pope John Paul II says in *Pastores dabo vobis:* "Priests are there to serve the faith, hope and charity of the laity."[52] The priest does this in three fundamental ways: by proclaiming the word, celebrating the sacraments, and building the community. He has all the power that love and the gospel, embodied in the Church, can give him. When he uses it well, the laity discover their own holy priesthood and power in Christ.

---

[52] Pope John Paul II, *Pastores dabo vobis,* ch. II, n. 17.

7

The Priesthood of Christ, the Baptized, and the Ordained

BENEDICT M. ASHLEY, O.P.

A Faith Answer to a Faith Question

Catechumens during their catechesis in the Rites of Christian Initiation are told that the sacrament of baptism they are preparing to receive will incorporate them into "a royal priesthood, a holy nation, God's own people" (1 Pet 2:9). They may well ask the priest who is instructing them, "Do you mean I will be a priest as you are?" Candidates preparing to receive the sacrament of holy orders, if they are to commit themselves honestly to its responsibilities, ought to ask, "What does that really mean today? How will this priesthood I will now receive be any different than the one I received in baptism?"

Such questions born of "faith seeking understanding" cannot be answered merely by reason but only by God himself, since they involve the mystery of the sacraments. We must look for God's answers in the divine word transmitted to us in Scripture and tradition and re-incarnated, so to speak, in the life of the Church today on its journey of faith.

Two important difficulties can be raised about a theological approach that emphasizes the primacy of faith in answering this question about priesthood. The first is that it seems to neglect the importance of the critical historical and developmental approach that has characterized

*Scripture quotations in this article are taken from the New American Bible, © 1991, 1986, 1970 by the Confraternity of Christian Doctrine, 3211 Fourth Street N.E., Washington, D.C. 20017-1194 and are used by permission of the © holder. All rights reserved.

post–Vatican II theology. To this I would respond that for over a hundred years scholars have striven to reconstruct the development of Church organization in the period prior to the letters of Ignatius of Antioch (ca. 107–117) and Irenaeus of Lyons (ca. 177) when the roles of bishop, presbyter, and deacon began to be generally fixed. The result, as anyone can verify from a survey of the literature, is a variety of theories, none of which can claim certitude on the basis of the scanty and scattered evidence available.[1]

Consequently, the results of critical historical research, though it helps the theologian to avoid naive anachronisms, cannot supply us with a definitive answer to the question of the meaning of holy orders.[2] A teaching claiming the certitude of faith cannot truly be such if contradicted by a certitude of reason. Yet a probability of reason—no matter how probable—cannot stand against a genuine certitude of faith. Reason says that the incarnation and resurrection are highly improbable, but faith says they are absolutely certain.

[1] While there seems to be a scholarly consensus that there was no one pattern of Church organization in this early period, even this consensus is questionable, as pointed out by David Albert Jones, "Was There a Bishop of Rome in the First Century?" *New Blackfriars* 60 (March 1999) 128–43, answering Eamon Duffy's *Saints and Sinners: A History of the Popes* (New Haven, Conn.: Yale University Press, 1997). Jones writes:

> Yet though sensitive historians like Chadwick can see the dangers of idealizing the apostolic order of ministry, they are consistently unaware how deeply this mindset has informed the interpretation of the evidence. The whole notion of the evolution, revolution, or supposed radical development in ministry in the first century is in fact a supposition *imported* by the observer. It is a classic case of theory distorting observation. There is a pervasive underlying mindset that idealizes early ministry as free, loose, inspired and lay, and sees the emergence of clerical forms as a fall from primitive innocence.

Can we assume that religious institutions must have a period of evolution? The Franciscan Order evolved because St. Francis took little interest in organization, but St. Dominic structured his order from its first two general chapters and today this structure survives essentially unchanged.

[2] The lack of decisive evidence on holy orders is hardly surprising considering how difficult it is to come to solid conclusions even about the historicity of many events in the passion narratives that the tradition was more concerned to transmit than the details of Church order. See Raymond E. Brown, *The Death of the Messiah,* Anchor Bible Reference Library, vol. 1 (New York: Doubleday, 1993) 13–22. For discussion on the relation of historical method to theology see Joseph A. Fitzmyer, *Scripture, the Soul of Theology* (New York: Paulist Press, 1994); and "Exegesis and Systematic Theology," in the Biblical Commission Document "The Interpretation of the Bible in the Church" (1995) 163–4; also K. Duffy, "Exegesis and Theologians," *Irish Theological Quarterly* 63 (1998) 219–31; and G. O'Collins and D. Kendall, *The Bible for Theology: Ten Principles for the Theological Use of Scripture* (New York: Paulist Press, 1977).

A second objection to the approach I am proposing concerns today's clergy shortage and the proliferation of lay ministries. Some think that we ought not to be seeking some abstract "essence of Christian priesthood." Rather we should ask, "What kind of ministers does the Church need today to carry out its mission effectively?" Nevertheless, there really is no way to answer that question without first listening to what sacred Scripture as interpreted by sacred tradition has to say about whether the Church will always have a priesthood and in what that office must consist. Of course, the Church must develop its doctrines and practices to meet the needs of time and place, but certain elements in its faith and life are permanent and irreplaceable. The primary question, therefore, is whether priesthood is one of these essentially permanent elements and why. It is to this question that I will attempt to supply a theological answer in what follows.

Why Every Human Community Needs a Priest

I very much agree with my colleague, Donald Goergen, who remarked at the conference (see chapter nine):

> We ought not take some pre-conceived understanding about priesthood and apply it to Christ, arguing that priests do this, therefore Christ did such and such, but rather the other way around: this is what Christ is; therefore this is who we as baptized or ordained should be. Christ is the model, the exemplar, the one from whom we learn what being priestly is all about.

Thus in what follows it must be understood that "priest" is an *analogical* term of which the priesthood of Christ is the *primum analogatum*. Yet it is also true that to contextualize the uniqueness of Christian priesthood we must compare it to the priesthoods of other religious cultures and show how they are alike, yet less alike than different. Hence it is helpful to recall that functions parallel to those of the Old Testament priesthood existed not only in all the pagan cultures surrounding Israel but universally in all known cultures, though in highly varied forms. Even in our secularized culture such priestly functions find certain disguised expressions. In a solemn ritual the U.S. president *in persona nationis* places a wreath before a monument of the war dead.

Very helpful to such a contextualization is a recent study in which Dale Cannon[3] identifies six functions common to almost all known

---

[3] Dale S. Cannon, *Six Ways of Being Religious: A Framework for Comparative Studies of Religion* (Belmont, Calif.: Wadsworth, 1996).

cultures that he calls the "ways" of dealing with "ultimate reality": (1) sacred rite, (2) right action, (3) devotion, (4) shamanic mediation, (5) mystical quest, and (6) reasoned inquiry. He then defines "priest" or "priestess" as "a duly authorized leader of sacred rites."[4]

A "sacred rite," according to Cannon, is an action that symbolizes some "ultimate reality" and connects those who perform it and those for whom they perform it with this ultimate reality.[5] One of these sacred rites of special importance is *sacrifice*. Similarly, Aquinas held that to offer sacrifice both by an interior act and an exterior rite pertains to the law of nature and defines it as follows: "Natural reason prescribes that we offer certain sensible things to God as a sign of our dependence on his generosity."[6] He also maintains that since sacrifice is the supreme act of worship and of the virtue of religion, it is the specifying act of priesthood.[7]

While this definition of priesthood as a universal human phenomenon shows that the Christian faith responds to deep human needs, it does not tell us what is specific to Christian priesthood, since it does not say what is sacrificed or how the priest is empowered to offer it. In the Old Testament, of course, it refers to the hereditary Aaronic priesthood that was empowered by a rite of anointment to offer sacrifices of animals and other food products, as well as incense. In the New Testament, as we shall see, the term *priest* (Greek *hiereus,* Hebrew *kohen,* Latin *sacerdos*)[8] is not used to refer directly to Church leaders. In fact, in the New Testa-

---

[4] Ibid., 54.

[5] The notion of the "shaman" adds to the notion of "priest" the element of *mediation.* Cannon notes (ibid., 60) this is the hardest religious concept for the modern mind to accept because it emphasizes, as I will show, that there is a wholly other spiritual world that certain human beings mediate to our worldly existence.

[6] *Summa Theologiae* II–II, q. 85, a. 1. On this natural universality of sacrificial worship see D. M. Knope's article in *The Perennial Dictionary of World Religions,* ed. Keith Crim (San Francisco: Harper, 1989) 637–40. The current tendency to speak of the Eucharist as a meal in preference to a sacrifice can minimize its reality as a mutual *gift* (the essence of sacrifice) *of persons to one another.* St. Paul in 1 Cor 10:18-21 compares the eucharistic meal to Jewish and pagan sacrifices.

[7] *Summa Theologiae* III, q. 82, a. 1; cf. Suppl., q. 37, a. 2, in which Aquinas argues that the order of priesthood is specified and thus distinguished from the diaconate by the power to offer the eucharistic sacrifice.

[8] For more details on accurate terminology see the chapter of Frank C. Quinn, "Ministry, Ordination Rites, and Language," in the present collection. See also A. Gelin, "The Priesthood of Christ in the Epistle to the Hebrews," *The Sacrament of Holy Orders* (London: Aquin Press, 1962) 37–8; H. W. Attridge, "Hebrews," *Anchor Bible Dictionary,* vol. 3 of 6, Anchor Bible Reference Library (New York: Doubleday, 1993); and Albert Vanhoye, *La structure litteraire de l'epitre aux Hebreux,* 2d ed. (Lyon: de Brouwer, 1976) v.

ment there seems to be no clearly defined terminology for such leadership roles. The most common term is "elder" *(presbyter)*, which R. Alistair Campbell[9] shows in a detailed study of the usage of the term in Jewish and Greek society might be applied to any honored member of a community. Thus it does not tell us what was the defining function of a Christian "presbyter," whether or not it was that of being a leader of sacred rites or included other functions.

At least one of the reasons that the documents of Vatican II[10] preferred the term *presbyter* to *priest* was that they also assigned to the presbyterate a participation in the threefold office *(munera)* of Christ as prophet, king, and priest.[11] In this way the council avoided the confusion produced by saying that a priest has the three offices of prophet, king, and priest, thus using priest equivocally, first as the name of a threefold office, and second as the name of only one of these offices. Yet in some later magisterial documents there has been a reversion to the term *priest* in the first inclusive sense. The term *priest* is much more familiar to Catholics than *presbyter* and, in the United States, the latter is associated with the Presbyterian Church.

[9] R. Alastair Campbell, *The Elders: Seniority within Earliest Christianity* (Edinburgh: T & T Clark, 1994). Campbell is a Protestant scholar who concludes that in the early Church milieu *elder* was a title of dignity appropriate for Church leaders before more specific terms had been established.

[10] For Vatican II's extensive teaching on the priesthood see *Lumen gentium, Christus Dominus, Presbyterorum ordinis, Optatus totius.* This teaching has been authoritatively systematized in *The Catechism of the Catholic Church,* #748–975 (on the Church) and #1536–400 (on the sacrament of holy orders). For theological analyses taking into account Vatican II teaching see David Power, *Ministers of Christ and His Church: The Theology of Priesthood* (London: Geoffrey Chapman, 1969); and Jean Galot, *Theology of the Priesthood* (San Francisco: Ignatius Press, 1984).

[11] See Peter J. Drilling, "The Priest, Prophet and King Trilogy: Elements of Its Meaning in *Lumen gentium* and for Today," *Eglise et Theologie* 19 (1988) 179–206, who warns that these are not "divided functions of ministry" but inseparable aspects of "service." That this concept had roots in Jewish Christianity is evident from the following passage in the Jewish Christian *Clementine Recognitions and Homilies, New Testament Apocrypha,* vol. 2, trans. Edgar Hennecke and Wilhelm Schneemelcher (Philadelphia: Westminister Press, 1965) 128–43:

> Now also if someone else was anointed with that oil, in the same way having received power from it he became either a king, a prophet or a high priest. If this temporal grace composed by humans was this powerful, then understand how great that ointment is that was taken by God from the tree of life, for the one that was made by humans confers such exceptional dignities among humans. For what in the present age is more glorious than a prophet, more celebrated than a high priest, more sublime than a king? (1.46.3–5).

Today the question commonly raised concerns which of these three functions best defines the presbyter.[12] Some argue that it is the role of shepherd (king) of the community who presides at the Eucharist only for that reason and hence the pastoral (kingly) role has preeminence. Others argue that since, as St. Paul says, "Faith comes through hearing" (Rom 10:17) by which the Christian community is called together in faith, preaching (prophecy) is preeminent. Others hold that the three offices are coequal. Others even question whether this is really the best way to describe Christian ministry.

To avoid taking a position on this question at the outset, I will use the term *presbyter* for the ordained minister who by ordination is empowered to lead the community in the celebration of the Eucharist but can also be its chief preacher and pastor. I also will not distinguish between the presbyter and the bishop, since Vatican II says that the latter has "fullness of the priesthood"[13] and it is priesthood that is here in question.

Was Jesus a Priest *(Hiereus, Sacerdos)*?

The Gospels make quite clear that the early Church considered Jesus a prophet. They all portray John the Baptist as a genuine prophet and then argue that Jesus was far greater than John. They also portray his ministry as one of preaching the coming of the kingdom of God witnessed by miracles just as had been the ministry of Elijah, type of all the Old Testament prophets. The early Church was also concerned to show that Jesus was a king, the Messiah (Greek *Christos,* the Anointed One), as is evident in the infancy narratives that trace his descent from David. He was to fulfill the Old Testament prophecies by being invested with the same divine authority conferred on David as king and on their successors by a ceremony of anointment. To avoid a political understanding of his mission, however, Jesus did not make this claim for himself publicly or permit the Twelve to do so. Yet privately he accepted Peter's profession of him as the Christ (Mark 8:27-30; Matt 16:13-20; Luke 9:18-21). According to the Synoptics, Jesus, even when asked by Pilate at his trial whether he was "the king of the Jews" (Luke 23:3), replied, "You have said it," and remained silent. Yet according to the Johannine tradition (John 18:8-40) Jesus further explained this by saying, "My kingdom is not of this world."

---

[12] For more detailed discussion see Jean Delorme, ed., *Le ministère et les ministères selon le Nouveau Testament* (Paris: Editions de Seuil, 1973).

[13] *Lumen gentium* 26.

There was question, however, whether Jesus was also a priest. Certainly Jesus was not a "priest," let alone a "High Priest,"[14] as Jews understood the term. His legal father, Joseph, was a member of the tribe of Judah, not of Levi from which the hereditary Jewish priesthood had to come (Matt 1:1-18; Luke 2:4-5; 3:1-38). Although his disciples and sometimes others addressed him as Rabbi, Master, or Teacher, he had no official approval as such by the scribes.[15] Was the lay status of Jesus a problem for early Christians? And if so why? Hebrews 7:14 certainly raises it: "It is clear that our Lord arose from Judah, and in regard to that tribe Moses said nothing about priests." There is evidence in the Dead Sea Scrolls that at least some Jews of Jesus' time expected both a "Messiah of David" and a "Messiah of Aaron," and perhaps thought of these titles as joined in one person.[16]

What really raised the question was the destruction of the Temple in 70 C.E., an event that the Gospels claim was predicted by Jesus himself, so it may have been dreaded by the Jewish Christians even before it occurred.[17] That destruction meant the end of Old Testament sacrificial worship. How then could the Christians, most of whom were still Jews, carry on an adequate worship? Of course, the Jews had worshiped in the Exile before the rebuilding of the Temple. They continued to do so in the Diaspora before its fall, and that worship has continued among Jews without the Temple. But for Orthodox Jews this synagogue worship was always relative to that of the Temple in actuality or promised restoration when the Messiah comes.

[14] The high priesthood of the Jews was "originally conferred for life, hereditary, and reserved to Zadokites." See U. Kellermann's article "Archiereus," *Exegetical Dictionary of the New Testament,* vol. 1, ed. H. Balz and G. Schneiderer (Grand Rapids, Mich.: Eerdmans, 1990) 164.

[15] "Rabbi" is from Hebrew *rab,* meaning great one, master, lord, with a suffix that means my lord, i.e., my master or my teacher. The disciples of Jesus addressed him in this way (Mark 9:5; Matthew 26–25; John 3:2, etc.) and Mary Magdalen (John 20:16) by the intensive "rabboni." Probably the Greek *didaskolos* (Matt 8:19; Luke 10:25; John 11:28) translated the same term. Jesus himself deplored the vanity of the rabbis flattered by their students and said: "You must not allow yourselves to be called Rabbi, since you have only one Master, and you are all brothers. . . . Neither be called Masters for you have only one Master the Christ" (Matt 23:8, 10). It is not certain when the rabbinate began to be recognized by a ceremony, but this "ordination" confers no sacred power. It is only a certification of the Talmudic erudition of the candidate by other rabbis who have themselves been so certified.

[16] See G. Vermez, *Jesus the Jew: A Historian's Reading of the Gospels* (Philadelphia: Fortress Press, 1973) 136–7.

[17] On Jesus' words about the destruction of the Temple see Brown, *The Death of the Messiah,* vol. 1, 429–60.

For the Jewish Christians, since they believed Jesus was the Messiah, this imperfect worship without priestly rites could not be an adequate answer. The urgency of this question may not be evident to us today because we are used to a separation of church and state. In the ancient world, however, the idea that a nation could exist without its gods and, therefore, without a priesthood to carry on their worship was unthinkable. It is to this precise question that the epistle to the Hebrews gives the only explicit and revealed answer that we will ever have and its answer is unambiguous.

Even from a literary point of view Hebrews is one of the most impressive books of the New Testament, although we are not sure who was its author.[18] In spite of its traditional name as an "epistle," it, like 1 Peter, was probably originally written as a homily. Because of its style many of the Church Fathers doubted that St. Paul was its author. Modern exegetes also note that it differs from Paul's authentic writings in its vocabulary, theology, the interweaving of doctrine and exhortation, the different manner of introducing citations, and its way of citing Scripture according to the Septuagint.[19] Nevertheless, it is an inspired, canonical work, and may have been written before the fall of Jerusalem in 70 C.E. since it seems to assume that the temple services were still continuing (Heb 10:1-3, etc.).

Some exegetes explain these references to temple worship as mere references to the Old Testament prescriptions for these services and note that Josephus some twenty years after the destruction of the Temple still speaks of its sacrifices in the present tense. Yet surely if the author wrote after the

---

[18] Possible authors are Apollos (Acts 18:24-28; 1 Cor 3:6), Clement of Rome (Phil 4:3; Origen's suggestion), or even Barnabas. The epistle, as contents and traditional title indicate, was probably sent to a predominantly Jewish-Christian community, and probably to one in Rome. First Clement, which has remarkable parallels to Hebrews following Eusebius, is commonly dated 95 C.E., but some now date it to ca. 70 C.E. See T. J. Herron, "The Most Probable Date of the First Epistle of Clement to the Corinthians," *Studia patristica* 21, ed. E. A. Livingstone (Leuven: Peeters Press, 1989) 106–21. As for the date of Hebrews, Paul Ellingworth, *The Epistle to the Hebrews: A Commentary on the Greek Text* (Grand Rapids, Mich.: Eerdmans, 1993) 31–3, holds that it was written to Rome before 70 C.E. and cites many authors of the same opinion, among these Barnabas Lindars, *The Theology of the Letter to the Hebrews,* New Testament Theology (Cambridge: Cambridge University Press, 1991) 19–21, who suggests 65–70 C.E. Also in a special study, Marie E. Isaacs, *Sacred Space: An Approach to the Theology of the Epistle to the Hebrews,* JSNT Supplement Series 73 (Sheffield, England: University of Sheffield Press, 1992), argues for just before or after 70 C.E.

[19] See Raymond E. Brown, *An Introduction to the New Testament* (New York: Doubleday-Anchor, 1997) 691–700.

destruction of the Temple, he would have mentioned the abolition of the temple sacrifices as a striking proof of his thesis that the services of the Old Law were only temporary, a mere shadow of the things to come.

It is obvious why Hebrews, in spite of the obscurity of its author, was thought by the early Church to be important enough to be included in the canon. It forcefully argues on the basis of many Old Testament references that (1) Jesus Christ is the Son of God superior to all creation; (2) yet he is also truly human, in all but sin like one of us; (3) therefore, as the Christ he is our mediator. He is the only true priest, and indeed the High Priest, who is able with us and for us to offer himself to God as a worthy sacrifice and thus bring us the gift of salvation from God, his Father.[20]

Hebrews not only establishes Jesus' right to the official dignity of a High Priest, since many of the high priests of recent memory had been less than worthy, but praises him as supremely fitted for that office. He is a High Priest who is faithful, sympathetic to his people, merciful, holy, blameless, in solidarity with human suffering, and his priesthood will endure forever (Heb 2:17; 5:5; 6:20; 7:16, 21-22). This permanence of Jesus' priesthood results from his resurrection and ascension to immortal life (Heb 7:23-24; 4:14). Thus he anticipates our own eternity with God and is its forerunner (Heb 12:2) or leader ("pioneer," Heb 2:10).

Might it be objected that since Hebrews alone in the New Testament calls Jesus a priest, that its teaching is marginal and not typical for the early Church as a whole? This doubt can be answered by noting that there are important passages elsewhere in the New Testament that, although less explicit and extensive than the thesis of Hebrews, support it. Thus, although the authentic epistles of St. Paul and the Synoptics never speak explicitly of Jesus as a priest, they carefully narrate his solemn words and action at the Last Supper. There he commands the Twelve to imitate him by continuing in perpetuity the performance of a sacred rite, the Eucharist. Moreover, this rite is sacrificial and hence specifically priestly since he says, "This is my body that is for you." "This cup is the covenant in my blood. Do this, as often as you drink it, in remembrance of me" (1 Cor 11:23-34; cf. 10:16-17; Mark 14:22-26; Matt 26:26-29; Luke 22:14-23). In 1 Cor 10:21 Paul also says, "You cannot partake of the table of the Lord and of the table of demons," and in the preceding verses uses the terms *thusia* (sacrifice) and *thusaterion* (altar of sacrifice) to make clear that he is comparing the Eucharist to pagan sacrifices. Certainly these many

[20] For analyses of the argument of Hebrews see Vanhoye, *La Structure litteraire de l'epitre aux Hebreux,* and Louis Dussaut, *Synopse Structurelle de l'Epitre aux Hebreux: Approche d'Analyse Structurelle* (Paris: Cerf, 1981).

references demonstrate that the early Church understood the Last Supper as a cultic, priestly act on Jesus' part to be continued as a central practice in the Christian community.

Moreover, in Paul's epistles, the word *leitourgos* and its cognates are usually used in a cultic sense and Paul seems to be thinking of his own ministry as a share in the sacrificial offering of Christ. Thus in Phil 2:17 he writes, "But even if I am poured as a libation [*leitourgia*] on the sacrifice [*thusia*] and service [*leitourgia*] of your faith, I rejoice and share my joy with you." Again he writes, "I urge you, therefore, by the mercies of God, to offer your bodies to God, your spiritual worship" (Rom 12:1; cf. 2 Cor 4:10). He also uses this language for an exchange of gifts with the Philippians (Phil 4:15-20) by which they have supported him financially because he had given them the gospel. He calls their gift "a fragrant aroma," "an acceptable sacrifice [*thusia*] pleasing to God." Paul again uses the term *leiturgia* for his collection of money as a ministry to the Jerusalem church in Rom 12:27 and 2 Cor 8:12. Similarly, Luke in Acts 12:2-3 uses a cognate to describe Christian worship in the church of Antioch: "While they were worshiping [*leitourgounton*] the Lord and fasting the Holy Spirit said, 'Set apart for me Barnabas and Saul for the work which I have called them.' Then completing their fasting and prayer, they laid hands on them and sent them off."

Perhaps even more significant is the use of the term *temple (hieron)* to refer to Christ himself. A principal accusation against Jesus at his trial was that he had declared he would destroy the Temple (Mark 14:58; cf. 15:29; Matt 26:61). Mark and Matthew call it a false accusation, but John 2:13-22 says that the disciples after the resurrection remember that he had in fact said this (v. 22) when he cleansed the Temple, "But he was speaking about the temple of his body" (v. 21). Furthermore, St. Paul and the Deutero-Pauline epistles speak of the Church as the body of Christ (1 Cor 6:15-29; Col 1:18; Eph 5:21-32). Hence God dwells in Christians as in a temple (1 Cor 3:16; 2 Cor 6:16; Eph 2:22-23). Thus it should be clear that Hebrews is not an isolated work in the New Testament but takes up and elaborates themes current in the apostolic Church that concur with its central argument that the death of Jesus is the one true sacrifice that can take away sin. Therefore, Hebrews elaborates a common New Testament theme when it declares that Jesus is the one and only true High Priest of whom the Levitical priests of the Old Testament were prophetic types.

Some Protestant exegetes who favor emphasis on preaching the Word as against Catholic emphasis on the priestly administration of the sacraments tend also to exaggerate the contrast between the prophetic and the

cultic or priestly traditions of the Old Testament.[21] It is true that the prophets often denounce those who obey the "cultic" prescriptions of the Law
while neglecting its moral commandments and exhortation to faith. "Obedience is better than sacrifice" (1 Sam 15:22). *Cult,* however, simply means
worship, and in the Bible *worship* and *priest* do not as such have negative
connotations, although of course the Bible has much to say about bad
priests and idolatrous worship. Quite the contrary, *priesthood* and *worship*
(whatever may be said of particular priests and their fidelity to their calling),
when they are in the service of the One God, are, for the Bible, always positive terms (Gen 14:18). That is why Hebrews is so concerned to show that
Jesus was not only a priest, but the High Priest, the Supreme Priest.

Some may still object that Hebrews so strongly emphasizes the priesthood of Jesus that a theology based primarily on it cannot do justice to
the prophetic and pastoral dimensions of the presbyterate. They think
that it was the reliance on Hebrews in medieval theology that led to a tri-
umphalist notion of priesthood. I would reply that even if Hebrews may
have sometimes been used to support clericalism, this was only by an
obtuse misreading. After Hebrews' defense of the divinity of Jesus in
chapters 1 and 2, it begins its discussion of Christ's priesthood with an
emphatic exhortation to the baptized:

> Therefore, holy brothers [and sisters], sharing in a heavenly calling, re-
> flect on Jesus, the apostle and high priest of our confession, who was faith-
> ful to the one who appointed him, just as Moses was "faithful in all his
> house." But he is worthy of more "glory" than Moses as the founder of a
> house has more "honor" than the house itself. Every house is founded by
> someone, but the founder of all is God. Moses was "faithful in all his house"
> as a servant to testify to what would be spoken, but Christ was faithful as a
> son put over his house. We are his house only if we hold fast to our boast
> and confidence in our hope (3:1-6).

Thus the dignity, honor, and glory of Christ as High Priest is in his
filial obedience to his Father in his mission of building the Church (the
house of God).[22] In what follows, no text of the New Testament surpasses

---

[21] On this see Bruce Vawter, "Introduction to Prophetic Literature," *New Jerome
Biblical Commentary,* ed. Brown, Fitzmyer, Murphy (Englewood Cliffs, N.J.: Prentice
Hall, 1990) 186–93. Some prophets were priests, and the notion of a fundamental
opposition between prophecy and cult promoted by some was based on the notion
that the Law was a late development in Israel.

[22] "Jesus the pre-existent (Heb 1:2) and exalted high priest (1:4; 5:5) chose to be-
come human (2:14) and a member of a specific *ekklesia* (2:12) and covenant people."
J. Scholer, *Proleptic Priests: Priesthood in the Epistle to the Hebrews* (Sheffield, England:
University of Sheffield Press, 1991) 89.

Hebrews in emphasizing that it is out of this sublime obedience that the Son of God has chosen to take on the role of the Suffering Servant. It tells us beautifully, "We do not have a high priest who is unable to sympathize with our weaknesses, but one who has been similarly tested in every way, yet without sin" (Heb 4:15). This is entirely consonant with Jesus' own words, "For the Son of Man did not come to be served, but to serve, and to give his life as a ransom for many" (Mark 10:45). Indeed, there could be no stronger remedy for clerical arrogance than to remind priests of the teaching, explicit only in Hebrews, that there is only one priest, the Suffering Servant, Jesus.

The Priesthood of the Baptized

Yet how are we to answer Protestant Christians who often ask, "If, as Hebrews so clearly teaches, Jesus is the only priest and his offering on the Cross was a wholly sufficient sacrifice for sins (Heb 10:11-18), how can priests be ordained to offer the Eucharist as a daily sacrifice? Is not the Christian minister ordained to be a preacher of the gospel not a cultic priest?" Hence most Protestants prefer for their ministers such titles as "Minister," "Pastor," "Elder" (presbyter), or "Preacher" for their appointed Church leaders. Yet at the same time they cannot pass over important biblical texts outside Hebrews. In the first epistle of St. Peter[23] we read, "You are a chosen race, a royal priesthood, a holy nation, a people of his [God's] own, so that you may announce the praises of him who called you out of darkness into his wonderful light. Once you were 'no people' but now you are God's people'" (1 Pet 2:9-10a).

This text, which quotes Exod 19:6 with reference to the chosen people, is also supported by the prophecy made to the Jews that in the Messianic age "you yourselves shall be named priests of the Lord, ministers of our God you shall be called" (Isa 61:6). The meaning of these texts is that God has chosen and consecrated Israel as his own people in a covenant by which they are bound to worship him only. This thought is carried further by two other texts of Trito-Isaiah:

> And the foreigners who join themselves to the Lord,
>   ministering to him,

---

[23] See William J. Dalton, *New Jerome Biblical Commentary,* 903ff., who holds that 1 Peter is Petrine (perhaps St. Peter through a secretary) and that "there is good reason for dating 1 Peter just before Peter's death, which took place probably in 65 A.D. It is probably of Roman origin since it has much in common with the Pauline literature of the same period." On the relation of 1 Peter to 2 Peter—probably the last book in the New Testament canon and pseudonymous—see Jerome H. Neyrey, *New Jerome Biblical Commentary,* 1017ff.

Loving the name of the Lord
    and becoming his servants
All who keep the sabbath free from profanation
    and hold to my covenant,
Them, I will bring to my holy mountain
    and make joyful in my house of prayer.
Their holocausts and sacrifices
    will be acceptable on my altar,
For my house shall be called a house of prayer
    for all peoples (Isa 56:6-7).

I come to gather nations of every language;
they shall come and see my glory. . . .
Some of these I will take as priests and Levites,
says the Lord (Isa 66:18-21).

Thus the Jewish people are called to be the mediator by which the True God will become known to all nations. Through them the Gentiles, too, will come to worship God in the Jerusalem Temple and from these non-Jews, too, some will be chosen to be priests. Hence these prophecies in their Christian fulfillment are not primarily made to individuals, but to the Church as a corporate body and hence to its members who by baptism have become parts of that corporate whole. "We," says St. Paul, "are one body in Christ, and individually parts of one another" (Rom 12:5). The Christian community, the Church, is a chosen race or nation, who are God's people, his very own consecrated by Christ as a holy and royal kingdom. The Church is priestly because it is called to announce God's praises "in a worthy way through Christ as God has himself willed." That this worship is sacrificial is clear from the following text: "He [Christ] is the living stone, rejected by men but chosen by God and precious to him; set yourselves close to him so that you too, the holy priesthood that offers the spiritual sacrifices which Jesus Christ has made acceptable to God, may be living stones making a spiritual house" (1 Pet 2:4-5, JB).

Thus the Church as the body of Christ is the temple in which sacrifices are offered, and hence it is priestly by sharing in the sacrifice of its head, Christ the High Priest. Some theologians of the Radical Reformation have sometimes used texts of this sort to oppose the "sacramentalism" of the Roman Catholic and Orthodox traditions. They have argued that what is in question here is a purely "spiritual" and therefore interior worship in faith having expression only in verbal prayers and preaching or at most hymn singing. That a cultic rite can "announce the praise of God" (1 Peter 9), however, is clear from the fact that the New Testament commends the external actions of baptism (Heb 10:22) and Eucharist (1 Cor 10:15-16) if performed in faith. One may also recall the text of Heb 13:15, "Through him then let us continually offer up a sacrifice of praise to God, that is, the fruit of lips that acknowledge his name."

The book of Revelation confirms this teaching of First Peter when it speaks of Christ, "who has made us into a kingdom, priests for his God and Father, to him be glory and power forever. Amen" (Rev 2:6). "You made them a kingdom and priests for our God, and they will reign on earth" (Rev 5:9). "The second death has no power over these; they will be priests of God and Christ, and they will reign with him for the thousand years" (Rev 20:6). This is the universal priesthood of all the baptized, recognized by the Second Vatican Council. It is symbolically effected in the chrismatic anointing of the sacrament of confirmation that follows baptism. Vatican II in its Dogmatic Constitution on the Church says:

> [The] faithful are by baptism made one body with Christ and are established among the People of God. They are in their own way made sharers in the priestly, prophetic, and kingly functions of Christ. They carry out their own part in the mission of the whole Christian people with respect to the Church and the world (n. 31).

We can conclude that the term *priest (hiereus, sacerdos)* can and indeed must be applied to all Christians, not indeed univocally but by analogy to the perfect priesthood of Christ. In this analogy the name is etymologically the proper analogue, since it is ordinary human priests, Jewish, Christian, Hindu, etc., that are known to us experientially, but Hebrews rightly argues on the basis of revelation that ontologically the *primum analogatum* is Christ. His priesthood is a *mystery* utterly other and more holy than we ever experience and hence is the object of faith not of reason. Other priesthoods as they pertain to the order of natural law, even the divinely established Levitical priesthood of the Jewish Temple, can only be types (in current terms "icons," "symbols," "metaphors") of Christ's one, true priesthood.

Hence all priesthood other than Christ's own can only be some form of participation[24] in his from which it must derive its whole meaning and

---

[24] "Participation" is a concept of Platonic origin, and this Platonic influence is notable throughout Hebrews. See S. L. Harris, *New Testament Introduction* (n.p.: Mayfield Publishing, 1995) 28. "Some New Testament writers, such as the author of Hebrews, use Platonic concepts to illustrate parallels and correspondences between the spiritual and physical worlds (Heb 1:1-4; 9:1-14). Hebrew's famous definition of faith is primarily a confession of belief in the reality of the invisible realm (Heb 11:1-2)." See also M. Bourke, "Epistle," *NJBC,* 921.

power. When Jesus said, "Call no one on earth your father, you have one Father in heaven" (Matt 23:9), he was not, of course, denying that we have fathers and mothers whom we are commanded by God the Father to honor (Matt 15:4). Rather, he was teaching that human fatherhood is only a share in that of the Supreme Father and Creator, the one perfect father. If it becomes more it is idolatry. Similarly, although Christ is the one priest, all those baptized as members of Christ's body and who through him worship the Father in the Holy Spirit truly share in his priesthood. Thus to say that Jesus was a layman not a priest was true only in the eyes of his unbelieving contemporaries. In actual fact, Christ is the only priest, and we baptized Christians are priests only in and for him as we are the Church. The Church is Christ's holy body nourished on his eucharistic body and blood offered for the world once and for all time on the cross.

The Ordained Priest

The teaching of Hebrews that Christ is the only priest implies a certain ecclesiology. As Moses was the mediator of the imperfect former covenant sealed in the blood of animal sacrifices, so Christ is the mediator of the perfect new and final covenant sealed in his own sacrificial blood, shed as proof of the divine love for humanity.

Since the first covenant was not made merely with individuals but with the chosen people, Israel, so the new covenant is made with the new Israel, the Christian community, the Church. Since, for Hebrews, the Church owes its very existence as a priestly people to its head, Jesus Christ the High Priest, it must also be a *hierarchical* organization.[25] The

[25] St. Paul greets the bishops and deacons at Philippi (Phil 1:1). In the Pastoral Epistles, dated (Brown) in the late first century, we read of bishops, deacons, and widows. In 1 Clement (ca. 70–95 C.E.) no mention is made of a bishop at Rome, but the letter concerns rebellion against presbyters at Corinth. By the time of St. Ignatius of Antioch (d. 107–117 C.E.) there is a monarchical bishop in Jerusalem and the churches of Asia Minor, along with a presbyterate and deacons. In the Didache (ca. 100 C.E.) we read of bishops, deacons, and itinerant prophets. By the time of St. Irenaeus (fl. 177 C.E.), who knew St. Polycarp who knew St. John and St. Ignatius, the three-fold hierarchy and the Bishop of Rome are all established. Our data, however, is scanty. Hence various reconstructions of the data are possible, but the essential points are (1) the Church was never just a "Jesus Movement" but an organized community of communities; (2) though the whole community participated in selecting leaders, apostolic authority was required for valid Church office. Edward Schillebeeckx tried to question this in *Ministry* (New York: Crossroad, 1981) and *The Church with a Human Face* (New York: Crossroad, 1985), but has been well answered by Pierre Grelot, *Église et ministères: pour un dialogue critique avec Edward Schillebeeckx* (Paris: Cerf, 1983); Albert Vanhoye and Henri Crouzel, "The Ministry in the

term *hierarchy,* although it was used by Vatican II in *Lumen gentium* without apology, today is an anathema to some for whom it seems to mean an oppressive power. In fact it is derived from the Greek *hieros,* sacred, and *arche,* a principle of order, and hence simply means "sacred order."

Order in any plurality, such as a community of persons, implies some principle of unity, whether this be majority vote, a governing group of leaders, a single presiding governor, or some mixture of these. Thus its constitution must provide for an assignment of authority and lawful obedience, and this is a "hierarchy," although various forms of hierarchical order are possible. The only alternative to hierarchical order is "anarchy" (*an- arche,* non-order), a society whose decisions for common action are made only by consensus of all the members.

It is true that today some Christians are of the opinion that the Gospel emphasis on human equality before God means that the Church should adopt anarchism as its polity. Nevertheless, such a concept is entirely utopian from a sociological or political science perspective, since historically anarchic societies have never long survived or, what is worse, turned into disastrous tyrannies. In those matters that exceed human reason, such as matters of faith, no argument is convincing to everyone, even to those well informed and of good will. Nor can one leave it to the Holy Spirit to produce a consensus in the Church if the organic structures that the Spirit has provided for the Church are ignored.

From a theological perspective there is absolutely nothing in the New Testament that shows an egalitarian anarchy to have been the ideal of either Jesus or the first Christians, who recognized not only the authority of God but also of both legitimate religious and secular rulers and the responsibility of obedience to them. The Church therefore is no mere "spirituality" for individuals or "movement," but a well structured, dynamically acting community whose organization is determined by its spiritual mission.

The actual unity of the Church in its human diversity, according to Vatican I, is "a moral miracle" that obliges those who recognize it as such to believe its teachings as those who witnessed Jesus' miracles were obliged to believe him.[26] Its mystery is especially brought out by two biblical

---

Church: Reflections on a Recent Publication," *The Clergy Review* 5:68 (May 1983) 156–74; and Walter Kasper, "Ministry in the Church: Taking Issue with Edward Schillebeeckx," *Communio* (Summer 1983) 185–95.

[26] "The church itself, with her marvelous propagation, eminent holiness, and inexhaustible fruitfulness in everything good, her catholicity and invincible stability, is a great perpetual motive for credibility and an irrefutable witness of her divine mission" (Vatican I, *Dei filius* 3; See also DS 3013).

metaphors. As we have already seen, 1 Pet 2:4-8 compares Christians to "living stones" to be "built into a spiritual house to be a holy priesthood to offer spiritual sacrifices acceptable to God through Jesus Christ." Of this edifice Christ is himself also a "living stone," the very "corner stone." The second metaphor, elaborated by St. Paul in the twelfth chapter of First Corinthians, compares the Church to a living body with its differentiated organs among which Christ is the head. By this analogy Paul could not have been thinking simply of Christ as the invisible head of the Church, but of the Corinthian presbyters who were its head in Christ's place, since in 12:27-31 he enumerates "'apostles, prophets, and teachers" among those with charisms of leadership.

The present negative connotation of the term *hierarchy* can be traced to the ecclesiology of Pseudo-Dionysius (fl. ca. 450), who first made the term influential. Philosophically a Neo-Platonist, he conceived this hierarchical order as strictly linear, so that each member contains the *totality* of the perfections of its subordinates. Hence no member has any perfections not received from its superior. Such a metaphysics resulted in an ecclesiology in which *all* grace descends from God to the bishops and is transmitted through the presbyters and deacons to the laity.

When this Dionysian notion of linear hierarchy is replaced by that proper to the metaphysics of Aristotle and Aquinas for whom cosmic order is *generically* but not *specifically* hierarchical, a very different ecclesiology results. In an ecclesiology based on their metaphysics, human beings do indeed contain the generic perfections of mineral, plant, and animal, but not their specific ones; for example, a man cannot fly like a bird or swim like a fish. Only God creates and hence contains all the perfections of his subordinates, and each creature reflects some divine perfection absent from all others.

Similarly in both secular and ecclesial government there is an order of authority for the common good of the community, yet each member of the society makes or should make a unique contribution to that common good. Hence in the Christian community, as St. Paul makes very clear in 1 Corinthians 12 by his analogy of the Church to a human body, there are many different gifts. Yet all are united by the governance of the head who rules not for his own interests but for the common good. Hence the honorable head serves, not oppresses "the less honorable members." Thus each individual is directly and uniquely related to God and the recipient of graces that depend on Christ alone, as well as the graces received through the ministers of the Church.

Paul's teaching is no other than that of Jesus himself who "came to serve not to be served," yet consistently insisted on the authority given him by his Father and the duty of his disciples to obey him. He also established the apostles as authorities in his place after his ascension.

Thus the analogy of the human body used by Paul makes clear that the Church is hierarchical, that is, has a sacred order in which Christ as High Priest is the hierarch, the principle of that organic order of mutual service. Since the Church is Christ's body by which he remains visibly present and active in mission in the world, its leaders must also sacramentally signify that priestly presence *within* the Church. This sacramental signification is more necessary than their own personal gifts and activities, though, of course, these ought to be appropriately faithful and fruitful.

To say, as do some Protestant theologians, that Christ's presence is sufficiently manifested in the preaching of his word minimizes the incarnation. Christ is indeed present through the preacher, but also through the sacraments, and above all through the communal offering of the Eucharist. All three offices of Christ—pastoring, preaching, and sanctifying—are inseparably related in Christ as head of the Church and therefore also in his sacramental representative within the community.[27] Precisely because the ordained priest represents Christ, his role cannot be that of oppressive domination but, like Christ's, is that of a servant. Did not Jesus say of himself, "The Son of Man did not come to be served but to serve and to give his life as a ransom for many" (Matt 20:28)?

What other participants in this conference have well brought out is that Vatican II strove to restore a more active participation of all members of the Church in its life and mission. Past tendencies for the laity to be mere passive recipients of the ministry of the clergy rather than use the graces of their confirmation in which this active aspect of baptismal initiation is symbolized and perfected must be overcome. Ordained priesthood exists to serve and assist the general priesthood of the whole Church in its full activation.

Hebrews itself does not, like the Gospels and St. Paul, speak of Jesus as "head of the body, the Church" or as "servant." Yet it conveys the same truth by emphasizing Christ's priestly role as a mediator. Unless Christ was both "head of his body, the Church" (Eph 5:23) and also its servant,

---

[27] As a Dominican, I call attention to the way this is put for members of the Order of Preachers in our *Fundamental Constitution,* n. V:

Since by priestly [*sacerdotalem*] ordination, we are co-workers with the episcopacy, we have as our special charge the prophetical function by which—with due regard for the changing conditions of men, times, and places—the Gospel of Jesus Christ is announced by word and deed throughout the world, so that divine faith is aroused or more profoundly penetrates the whole of the Christian life and builds up the body of Christ—which work is completed in the sacraments of faith.

he could not mediate between God and the people. As supreme head of his people, the Church, he is their representative before God.[28] Yet as Son of God he is also God's representative to the people. Probably one of the earliest Christian creedal formulas, patterned on the Jewish creed, the *Shema,* reads:

> For there is one God.
> There is also one mediator between God
>   and the human race,
> Christ Jesus, himself human,
> Who gave himself
>   as a ransom for all (1 Tim 2:5-6).

Yet Jesus' servanthood did not contradict his leadership role as priest, nor does it reduce the calling of the baptized to passivity. According to the Fourth Gospel at the Last Supper, after washing the feet of the Twelve he said:

> You call me "teacher" and "master," *and rightly so* [*kai kalos legete,* emphasis added], for indeed I am. If I, therefore, the master and teacher have washed your feet, you ought to wash one another's feet. I have given you a model to follow, so that as I have done for you, you should also do (John 13:13-15).

Certainly Jesus did not hesitate to teach with an authority far more confident than that of the scribes and Pharisees with their legalistic quibbling (Matt 7:29). Yet he did not claim this authority to teach and to judge (John 6:27) as his own right but based it on the mission he had from his Father, a mission not of condemnation but of salvation (John 3:26-21).[29] Hence ordained ministers are called to cooperate in that mission and to serve all the baptized in their cooperation in that same mission.

---

[28] For a thorough recent treatment of the various opinions on this issue see Melvin Michalski, *The Relationship between the Universal Priesthood of the Baptized and the Ministerial Priesthood of the Ordained in Vatican II and in Subsequent Theology* (Lewiston, Canada: Mellen University Press, 1996).

[29] In my *Justice in the Church: Gender and Participation* (Washington, D.C.: Catholic University of America Press, 1996) Appendix 1, 169–88, I discuss recent opinions that, influenced by democratic egalitarianism, exaggerate the *in persona Ecclesiae* aspect of priesthood at the expense of its *in persona Christi* aspect. As in christology, neither the divinity nor humanity of Christ can be neglected, so it must be remembered that the sacrament of holy orders is a divine action elevating the priest's humanity and thus authorizing his representation of the community. Some dislike to speak of it as an "ontological transformation," yet this is also true for baptism and confirmation since they, too, "seal" with a "character" or permanent active quality of empowerment.

I have elsewhere discussed at some length the thorny issue of the terms *in persona Christi capitis* as representing Christ the head of the Church and *in persona Ecclesiae* as representing the Church or Christian community in their application to the ordained priesthood.[30] These are complementary not contradictory terms, and their relation is explained in Hebrews by saying that Christ as High Priest is the one "Mediator" between God and his people. As the incarnate Word he is the Mediator who speaks for the people to God and for God to the people. Hence the ordained priest, in participating in Christ's priesthood, participates in his mediatorship. St. Paul explains his ministry as an apostle thus: "Regard us as servants of Christ and stewards of the mysteries of God" (1 Cor 4:1), and goes on to say that therefore he is responsible to no human tribunal, in other words, the judgment of the community. He is no doubt speaking of his preaching rather than the administration of the sacraments, since he has just remarked that he does not baptize, yet he clearly presents himself as speaking for God to the community. The ordained priest must preach the Gospel in the name of Christ without compromising with the "popular opinions" of his flock.

On the other hand, it is Hebrews itself in 5:1 that says, "Every high priest is taken from among men and made their representative before God, to offer gifts and sacrifices for sins." In principle, it has always been admitted as shown in the ordination rites that bishop, priest, and deacon are chosen from the Christian community and with its consent. Yet the sacrament of holy orders can be conferred only by the bishop who must have the final decision about the nominee. While all too often the consent of the community has been merely nominal, the principle remains valid, although its effective application in various periods of Church history has varied.[31]

Since the Gospels insist that Jesus knew and predicted that his earthly life would end on the cross[32] (Mark 8:31-33; 9:12-13, 31-32; 10:32-34;

---

[30] See ibid., 169–88.

[31] On historic modes of choice of leaders see Alexandre Faivre, *Naissance d'une hiérarchie: Les premières étapes du cursus clérical* (Paris: Ed. Beauchesne, 1977).

[32] See Raymond E. Brown, *An Introduction to New Testament Christology* (New York: Paulist Press, 1994) 46–7:

It is difficult to decide about Jesus' foreknowledge of his passion, crucifixion, and resurrection. Modern criticism would cast serious doubt upon a detailed foreknowledge. Yet we should not undervalue the general agreement of the Gospel tradition that Jesus was convinced beforehand that, although his life would be taken from him violently (see also Luke 17:25; Mark 10:45), God would ultimately vindicate him.

See also Brown's *The Death of the Messiah,* vol. 2, 1468–91, esp. 1489.

John 3:14 and parallels) it was necessary that he provide for the continuation of this leadership after he had departed. Although he would always be invisibly present to his Church in faith ("I am with you always, until the end of the age" Matt 28:20), nevertheless this headship of the Church must somehow continue visibly if the mission of the Church is to be accomplished as faith tells us it will be: "All power in heaven and on earth has been given me, go, therefore, and make disciples of all nations, baptizing them in the name of the Father, of the Son, and of the Holy Spirit, teaching them to observe all that I have commanded you" (Matt 28:18-19).

This is why Jesus so carefully chose and prepared the Twelve to whom he explained the full meaning of his teaching. "The knowledge of the mystery of the kingdom of heaven has been given to you, but to them [the crowds] it has not been granted" (Matt 13:10-11). He gave to the Twelve his own titles of shepherd (pastor, as when he said to Peter, "Feed my sheep," John 21:17), judge ("Whatever you bind on earth will be bound in heaven, and whatever you loose on earth will be loosed in heaven," Matt 16:19; cf. Matt 19:28), and teacher ("He who hears you, hear me," Luke 10:16).

It could be asked why in such texts no mention of the word *priest* is made.[33] Yet the apostles are commanded by Jesus (Matt 28:18-19, quoted above) to administer baptism as a cultic act essential to their office as sharers in Christ's own powers. Similarly they were commanded to celebrate the Eucharist, another cultic act, and to forgive sins (John 20:22), a power that only the Son of Man dare exercise. Thus it is clear that in preparing and leaving leaders in his Church, Jesus intended that they should share in his headship of the Church not only as shepherds and teachers but also as ministers of the sacraments, that is, as participants in his priesthood since he himself is the primordial sacrament.

It has also been objected that in the texts I have cited and other similar ones, it is not always clear whether Jesus is conferring powers exclusively on the Twelve and their successors or on *all* his disciples then and now. Vatican II answered this, as I have already shown, by teaching that while the whole Church is priestly in that it shares in Jesus' mission and his threefold ministry of shepherd, teacher, and priest, it cannot do so without visible leadership. These leaders are not outside and over the

---

[33] Jean Colson, *Ministre de Jésus-Christ ou le Sacerdoce de l'Evangile* (Paris: Beachesne, 1966), says the New Testament avoids the term "priest" for presbyters to avoid confusion with Old Testament priests, but the extra-biblical writers of the first two centuries can be understood to admit a priesthood instrumental to that of the one priest Jesus Christ. See page 346 for his conclusion. See André Lemaire, *Les ministères dans l'église* (Paris: Centurion, 1974); on the problem of sacerdotal language see 93–7.

Church, but are members of a living body as its head is also part of the body. They too receive their life from that body. Indeed, they live and act in the service of the unity and mission of that body only by the power of the Holy Spirit that animates the Church, head and members.

Hence those who are authorized by Christ to teach and govern are also authorized to lead the community in worship, especially by presiding at the Eucharist, the Church's supreme act of worship.[34] Only by this ordering of ecclesial leadership to presidency in worship can the essentially spiritual purpose of their leadership be manifest. In this way it fits the model set by Jesus at the Last Supper.[35]

Some have seen a reference in Hebrews to the Eucharist in the following text:

[34] The study of Hervé Legrand, "The Presidency of the Eucharist According to the Ancient Tradition," *Worship* 53:5 (September 1979) 413–48, agrees that in the early Church the president of the Eucharist is the one who presides over the community *in personae ecclesiae,* but questions whether this requires ordination in the modern sense. Apart from arguments *ex silentio* are two positive bits of evidence for such a doubt. (1) Didache ch. x (ca. 100) permits visiting "prophets" to "give thanks" *(eucharistein)* as they will. Yet in ch. xiii we read that "prophets" who have settled permanently in the community are to be supported with first-fruits "for they are your high priests." (2) The *Apostolic Tradition* (ca. 200) ch. ix seems to say that martyrs are presbyters without ordination. Paul R. Bradshaw, "Ancient Church Orders: A Continuing Enigma," *Fountain of Life,* ed. Gerald Austin (Washington, D.C.: Pastoral Press, 1991) 3–22, shows how ambiguous are such early documents that seem more concerned about the moral quality of the candidates than their official powers. Yet the *Apostolic Tradition* says that in Rome the bishop, presbyters, and deacons were ordained and that the bishop presided at the Eucharist.

[35] In *Ministers of Christ and His Church* (189), David Power says,

We seem to be moving into an era when there will be no question of defining a presbyter only in terms of his power to celebrate the eucharist, and when there will be a more vivid expression of the collegial nature of the ordained priesthood through a wider diversification of function, allowing for greater specialization, and made possible by a greater sense of collaboration and communion among pastors.

Yet it would be wrong to think the medievals defined priesthood only in terms of the power to celebrate the Eucharist. St. Thomas, *Summa Theologiae* III Suppl., q. 37, a. 2, only says that the orders are distinguished by their relation to the Eucharist as the supreme act of worship. Vatican II, *Lumen gentium* 28, describes the three ministries without explicitly ranking them, but *Presbyterorum ordinis* 2 says, "The ministry of priests is directed toward this work [offering the Eucharist] and is consummated by it. For their ministry, which takes its start from the gospel message, derives its power and force from the sacrifice of Christ." The council's *Sacrosanctum concilium* 10 also says, "Nevertheless, the liturgy is the summit toward which the activity of the Church is directed: at the same time it is the fountain from which all her power flows."

Do not be carried away by all kinds of strange teaching. It is good to have our hearts strengthened by grace and not by foods, which do not benefit those who live by them. We have an altar from which those who serve the tabernacle have no right to eat (Heb 13:9-10).

It is common today, however, for biblical scholars to see no more in these words than an allusion to the heavenly altar, that is, the eternal, once-and-for-all sacrifice of Christ.[36] This reading requires one to suppose that the text (in a rather strained fashion) uses "eating" to mean an act of faith in the cross. Does it not seem more natural to understand it as a comparison between the Old Testament sacred meal shared by those who offer a sacrifice in the Temple and the Eucharist as a sacred meal that commemorates and makes present the sacrifice of the cross? This is similar to St. Paul's comparison (1 Cor 10:14-22) of the eucharistic meal both to Jewish and pagan sacrificial meals.

Even if this text is not to be taken as a reference to the Eucharist, we need not be surprised that the author of Hebrews preferred to rest his arguments on Old Testament texts at a time that the New Testament was not yet written. His understanding of the shedding of Christ's blood as the inauguration of the New Covenant (Heb 9:18) seems to reflect the eucharistic words of institution in the tradition reported still earlier by St. Paul, "This cup is the new covenant in my blood" (1 Cor 11:25).

A final question that has been raised is why in the New Testament we find no talk of "ordination" for the priestly leaders of the early Church, such as the elaborately prescribed ritual in Leviticus 8 for the priests of the Old Law that was later to influence the developed Catholic rites. What should be noted about the sacrament of holy orders for bishops, priests, or deacons[37] is that these leaders in the Church do not act on their own

---

[36] Ellingworth, *The Epistle to the Hebrews*, 708–12, in discussing Heb 13:9-10 notes that Catholic exegetes have often understood the text as a warning against the Judaizers who insisted on the Old Testament dietary laws. Thus it says that such material food is of no spiritual profit, since Christians have the spiritual food of the Christian altar, namely the Eucharist. On the contrary Protestants often reject this and say that the "altar" is a metaphor for the cross. Ellingworth, a Protestant, notes, however, that it can mean both the cross *and* the Eucharist, since the Eucharist commemorates the cross. I would add that in the context of a final exhortation a veiled reference to the Christian Eucharist as a sacred meal replacing those of the Jews seems entirely appropriate.

[37] On the diaconate see Jean Colson, *La Fonction diaconale aux origines de l'Eglise* (Paris: Desclée Brouwer, 1960); on *diakonos* in the New Testament see esp. 8–81. He inclines to the view (p. 40), now common, that the seven in Acts 6 were presbyter-bishops for the Greek-speaking Jews since they also exercised ministries other than "serving at table." But if "serving at tables" means celebrating the Eucharist, how did

but precisely as members of Christ's body. They do not act in their own right or only *in persona ecclesiae,* that is, as representatives of the Christian community. They also and primarily act *in persona Christi* since their special role is to make Christ symbolically (sacramentally) visible within the worshiping community as its head just as the other sacraments are the signs that make the forgiving, healing, and feeding acts of the invisible Christ symbolically visible. Therefore, while the community can testify to the suitability of the candidate for priesthood and receive and acclaim him as legitimately their representative once that one is ordained, they cannot make the final decision as to that nominee's ordination, nor can they confer the sacrament of holy orders on their nominee. Only the bishops who have the fullness of the sacrament have the authority from Christ through their predecessors, the apostles, to confer this sacrament.

This conferring of the same apostolic authority that Jesus conferred on the Twelve must be by some public act that makes it clear to the flock who their shepherds are. Otherwise the flock will be scattered by "savage wolves" (Acts 20:29; cf. Gal 1:1-2, 9; Jude 3-4). While it has been argued by some that an isolated Christian Church that for a long time lacked a bishop might on its own authority choose one of its members as a priest, there would be no way to know that such a leader has this apostolic authority until it was recognized for the whole Church by such a regular ordination. Some theologians have speculated that an isolated Christian Church lacking a bishop for a long time might be able by right of its own participation as a Christian community in Christ's priesthood to appoint its own priests.[38] Nevertheless, if they were to attempt this in good faith, there would still be no way for them or the whole Church to know that such a leader has priesthood by apostolic authority until he would be ordained by a legitimate bishop in a certainly valid sacramental act. Although the ministry of this supposed priest might be even more pastorally fruitful than that of some ordained priests, this would not make him a sacramental sign or validate the sacraments he might attempt to perform.

---

this hinder the apostles from preaching? The complaints of the widows must have been about ordinary food for the poor. The traditional view, still accepted in the rite of diaconal ordination, is that deacons first of all carry out the charitable work of the Church (serving at tables) to the poor, but can share with priests preaching, baptism, and witnessing marriages.

[38] Among the very different reconstructions of the development of Church polity based on our scanty data see Kenan B. Osborne, *Priesthood: A History of the Ordained Ministry in the Roman Catholic Church* (New York: Paulist Press, 1988); and Patrick J. Dunn, *Priesthood* (Staten Island, N.J.: Alba House, 1990).

By valid ordination a priest sacramentally symbolizes Christ not merely in a hidden manner but as head of the historic Church in its unity throughout time and space. Of course, Christ can confer graces of ministry outside the sacraments as he instituted them, since his Holy Spirit reaches all humanity. Nevertheless, neither a Christian community lacking a bishop nor even the college of bishops or its head, the Bishop of Rome, can essentially change or replace the sacraments. The essential permanence of the sacraments incarnationally manifests the historic unity and continuity of the Church.

From very early in the Church's history this sacramental sign of ordination has been conferred by the "laying on of hands"[39] by those recognized to be successors of the original apostles (the bishops) with appropriate prayers expressing the rank and meaning of the office being conferred. This laying on of hands is a very natural sign, redolent of Jesus' own practice of conferring grace by reaching out and touching the one in need (Matt 8:15, etc.). In Acts 13:3 we read how the church of Antioch sent Paul and Barnabas on the first mission to the Gentiles. After fasting and prayer "they laid hands on them and sent them off," thus acknowledging the need of God's grace for such an impossible task.

While this laying on of hands was practiced in both the Eastern and Western churches, the claim that it is the essential act of ordination was not always recognized by theologians or formally declared until Pius XII did so in 1947. What is clear is that from the beginning it was always considered necessary that for Church leaders to have priestly as well as pastoral and teaching authority they must receive it by some form of public ordination performed by other leaders who could rightly claim apostolic authority.

Conclusion

The Bible confirms the natural law that some form of priesthood, that is, leadership in offering sacrificial worship to God, is a universal

---

[39] Acts 6:1-6; 13:3; 14:23; Tim 4:14; 5:22; 2 Tim 1:6; 4:1-8. On this see Power, *Ministers of Christ and His Church*, 26. The terms "order" and "ordination," although not New Testament terms and perhaps weighted with accidental connotations, essentially say no more than an empowerment to perform an ecclesial function. Recent Church documents have made a distinction between the sacramental "ordination" to the three sacred orders and the non-sacramental "institution" of other lay ministries. With this the "minor orders" generally considered not "sacred" have disappeared. One might, therefore, distinguish a sacramental ordination to perform a ministry from a non-sacramental one. Therefore, the question arises whether the "ordinations" of Paul and Barnabas and of the seven can be cited as sacramental and not merely non-sacramental. This can only be answered by determining the functions for which they were "ordained."

need of every community. Hence in the Mosaic Law such a priesthood was provided and regulated so that it would lead the people in such worship of the One True God. Nevertheless, because of the sinfulness of Israel and the inadequacy of the sacrifices it offered to God to express the true worship due him, the priesthood of the Old Testament could not fulfill its purpose. This perfect worship became possible only with the coming of the one true priest, Jesus Christ, the incarnate Son of God. His self-offering as victim for sin and manifestation of God's love has provided forever this adequate worship not only for the Jews but for all humanity. Moreover, his self-offering is not just a replacement for the inadequate worship of humanity. In harmony with the principle of incarnation and by the power of his Holy Spirit, Christ the priest by baptism and the other sacraments transforms the faith community into his mystical body. Therefore, his body the Church and all its baptized members truly participate in Christ's priesthood. Moreover, by this same principle of incarnation by which the working of God's grace is sacramentally embodied and made manifest within the community of the baptized some members are ordained to participate in Christ's priesthood. They are ordained primarily to represent sacramentally Christ as the mediator who represents both the people in the worship of the Father and the Father to the people as source of all gifts. Yet as Christ is mediator primarily as sent from the Father to intercede for the people, so within the community the ordained priest primarily mediates God to the people and consequently the people to God. In other words, priests act *in persona ecclesiae* only because they act *in persona Christi capitis.* The same is true of the general priesthood of the baptized; they witness and thus mediate the Gospel to the world *in persona Christi,* as Christ's body. As a consequence, but only as a consequence of their empowerment from God in baptism, they are also able to intercede for the world, *in persona populi.*

8

Reflections on the Priesthood in "Eastern Orthodoxy"

KENNETH PAUL WESCHE

In the Byzantine theological tradition, there are not many sources on the priesthood; those that do exist are not systematic. What come to mind beside certain texts from the New Testament are the Didache, the epistles of Clement of Rome and St. Ignatius, certain passages from Irenaeus' *Contra Haereses* IV, and certain texts from John Chrysostom, Nicholas Cabasilas, Simeon the New Theologian, and Dionysius the Areopagite. The influence of Dionysius on what one might consider an Eastern Orthodox understanding of the priesthood certainly is not negligible, but I am not persuaded that Dionysius can be upheld as the definitive authority on any question concerning the priesthood as it is experienced and understood in Eastern Orthodox tradition. He, like so many others, is simply laying an interpretation, in his case drawn from the Neo-Platonic character of his mystical theology, on an entity that exists just as it is, dependent neither on the interpretation of Dionysius nor that of anyone else for doing what it does or looking like it does.

This is to say that in Eastern Orthodoxy the priesthood is, like the air we breathe, the environment in which questions of theology and spirituality are conducted, and is so rudimentary to the fabric of the Church

---

that it has never occurred to anyone, until the modern era as far as I know, that its existence should require justification or that it could itself be the subject of theological scrutiny. To challenge the rightness of the priesthood in any of its aspects is to challenge the rightness of the Christian confession. This is not to suggest that such scrutiny is inappropriate or of no value; particularly if it is conducted by a thirst for genuine understanding the illumination it may offer might be most rewarding. It is simply to remember what we are dealing with, and to explain why I cannot offer the following reflections as the "Eastern Orthodox" understanding of the priesthood; they are rather the reflections of a man ordained to the priesthood in the Eastern Orthodox tradition on the priesthood as it is experienced in that tradition.

An important assumption governing the way I look at things is my understanding of the pure essence of "Eastern Orthodoxy." In its pure essence, Eastern Orthodoxy is not a dogmatic system or an ecclesiastical body politic. It is the mystery of the soul; its embodiment is the *Theotokos,* the "Glorious Gate of God, facing toward the East." The dogmas, hierarchical and sacramental structures, liturgical cycles and feasts, and everything else are all so many different icons that give form to, but do not exhaust, the incomprehensible mystery of the soul. They are so many aspects of the "gate facing toward the East" through which one enters to follow the soul to its natural destiny. Borrowing from St. Athanasius: Eastern Orthodoxy is the "road to God," and the "road to God is each one's soul and the mind within it."[1]

Following from this, I maintain that the forms of any "religion," if they are true at all, are so because they give manifest expression in timespace to the incomprehensible mystery of the soul, and so their substance is the nature of the soul in its pure, inviolable essence. If Eastern Orthodoxy is an icon of the soul, then it follows that the form the priesthood takes in Eastern Orthodoxy has its origin ultimately in the mystery of the soul. And so, after making some general observations on how the priesthood is experienced and understood in the liturgical theology of Eastern Orthodoxy, I shall want to go outside the field of Christian theology proper to reflect on certain data from comparative mythology—presupposing with analytical psychology that mythological images reflect something of the ontology of the soul—for the purpose of discovering what vision of human nature and destiny the priesthood as an icon of the soul may be setting forth.

[1] Contra gentes 30.

General Observations: *Laos* and *Cleros*

The Laos

In popular understanding the priesthood is associated with the "clergy" as an ecclesiastical, magisterial body set over the laity. A more nuanced understanding of the clergy, however, comes from considering the nature and identity of the laity, from the Greek λαος.

In mundane usage, the term *laos* may designate "the common people" as opposed to their leaders, and so perhaps from this it is extended to designate in certain instances slaves or the subjects of a prince. More generally, it can refer to a civil population as opposed to the priests and soldiers in Athenian society, or to an assembly, or more generally still, humankind. In the Septuagint it designates "the common folk" of Israel as opposed to the priests and Levites.

When incorporated into the christological vision of the Church, the term retains the integrity of its mundane sense even as it undergoes significant transfiguration. In baptism, of course, one is united with the mystery of Christ's death and resurrection and is born again as a "child of God." In chrismation, through the seal and gift of the Holy Spirit, one is brought into the company—the *laos*—of the "children of God." In biblical terms, the *laos* would be the "new Israel," and so the "new royal priesthood" in reference to Exod 19:5-6: "If you will obey my voice and keep my covenant, you shall be my people that is over and above [λαος περιουσιος] all the nations, for the whole earth is mine. You will be to me a royal priesthood [βασιλειον ιερατευμα] and a holy nation."

Thus, the *laos* of the Church is not "common," but a select people, a people ordained, set apart, made holy for a specific function: and that is to be a royal priesthood that, in the vision of the author of the epistle to the Hebrews, "offers gifts and sacrifices for sins" (Heb 5:1c). This is certainly at the heart of what the *laos* does in worship: "Thine own of thine own *we* [i.e., the *laos*] offer unto Thee, on behalf of all and for all."

St. Ignatius of Antioch (d. 110 C.E.) drew the image that became standard for the Christian ecclesia: the *laos* assembled round the bishop and his presbyters. But the bishop and his presbyters are gathered round the altar, on which rests the Living Bread that is Christ. At the center of the *laos,* then, is the mystery of Christ; this is where the mundane sense of *laos* undergoes transfiguration. For the leaders to whom the *laos* is opposed in Christian understanding are not the clergy as such but the Christ and the Theotokos: "The Queen stood on thy right side, arrayed in golden robes all glorious."[2] Thus, to say in this context that the *laos* is "opposed"

---

[2] From the Proskomedia, or Liturgy of Preparation.

to its leaders invites illumination as to the real character of the Church. In the Christ and his Mother, all opposition is healed, the wall of enmity is torn down. The two, God and man, are made one flesh through the self-emptying of the Christ and also of his Mother. The Church is a holy communion with the divine. Leadership in the Church becomes an "icon" of the self-emptying love of Christ for his bride, the Church. The character and structure of the *laos,* the "new royal priesthood," in all its aspects makes manifest the profoundest character of divine love in which and by which all of creation is made to exist.

The Clergy

The Greek κλήρος designates a sphere or a province, a piece of land, an allotment or that which is assigned by lot. As a sphere or a province or an allotment the term could be applied as a description of the *laos* set apart by God, according to Exod 19:5-6. In this sense, the Christian *laos* is *cleros,* or clerical. The term *cleros* refers also to an inheritance, and so it is equivalent to κληρονομια, which the Christian *laos* is said to be. "O Lord, save Thy people [λαος], and bless thine inheritance [κληρονομια]."[3] As a piece of land, the term *cleros* could be applied—by one who likes to play with the symbols of Scripture and of the Church as the Fathers liked to do—to the promise of land given by God as the fulfillment of the Abrahamic covenant. In this sense, the *cleros* or the *cleronomia* of the Church is the mystical land that is "not of this world"; i.e., the eschatological kingdom of heaven, in which the covenant of Abraham finds its perfect fulfillment through the ineffable "dispensation" of the Christ, the Second Isaac (cf. Gal 3:16).

Because of the innately clerical nature of the Christian *laos,* there can be drawn from within it certain individuals who are "assigned" to perform a certain function. This is the sphere (or *cleros*) of the "priesthood." It exists within the sphere (i.e., *cleros*) "assigned" to the *laos,* and so we can say that the clergy of the priesthood is the "clergy" of or within the "clergy" of the *laos.* One is reminded of Gregory the Great's description of the papacy: "Servant of the servants of God."

My interest in the present essay is on the character and function of the *laos,* or the "new royal priesthood" of God, in order to understand the character and function of the "clergy" whom we conventionally identify as the priesthood. I shall not appeal to the authority of tradition for a properly "Christic" understanding of the priesthood, since appeal to tradition is but a *petitio principii.* I want to look to a broader horizon to consider certain universal patterns that would indicate something about the

---

[3] From the troparion of the Cross.

nature of the soul and illumine the ontological vision set forth in the icon of the Christian priesthood.

Notes from Mythology

Priest and Priestess

Mircea Eliade makes the following observation concerning the religious "mind" of the primitive:

> For primitives as for the man of all premodern societies the *sacred* is equivalent to a *power,* and, in the last analysis, to *reality.* The sacred is saturated with *being.* Sacred power means reality and at the same time enduringness and efficacity. . . . Religious man deeply desires *to be,* to participate in *reality,* to be saturated with power.[4]

The term for *priest,* ιερευς, can mean sacred man. In pagan societies there was as well a sacred woman, ιερεια. Indeed, in the "mind" of the primitive the woman is sacred simply by virtue of her femininity.[5] Together with the sacred man she performed the sacred rites, including the most sacred rite of the *hieros gamos,* the sacred marriage: a union of opposites that ensures the emergence of life from death and the continuance of the cosmos. According to popular understanding, there would appear to be in the Christian religion sacred men but no sacred women; priests but no priestesses. If the sacred is, as Eliade says, equivalent to a power and, in the last analysis to reality, saturated with being, then the exclusion of women from the priesthood or, more accurately, from the possibility of being ordained to a "priestesshood"—an order of sacred women who are essential for the completion of the sacred rites—is equivalent to excluding women from the power of reality and real being.

That the woman is not inherently sacred is contrary to what the primitive mind feels instinctively about woman, and I think contrary to what the soul knows in its gut. But I think it is also contrary to the Church's vision of the priesthood. The priesthood is the *laos* set apart as the *cleros* of God, which requires both sacred men and sacred women to perform its liturgical function. I can guess in what direction you think I might be going with this; and if it is what I think it is, you are mistaken. Let me construct my case before you anticipate my conclusion.

[4] Mircea Eliade, *The Sacred and the Profane* (New York: Harcourt Brace, 1968) 12–13.

[5] See the studies of J. J. Bachofen, *Myth, Religion, and Mother Right,* trans. Ralph Manheim (Princeton, N.J.: Princeton University Press, 1967); and Robert Briffault, *The Mothers: A Study of the Origins of Sentiments and Institutions* (New York: Macmillan, 1927).

Cult of the Goddess

Immediately on the broader horizon of human experience there is what appears to be, from archaeological and mythological evidence, a more original experience of divinity than what we find in the Old Testament. The evidence of artifacts dug up from Spain to the eastern coasts of Russia and from the lands of the Norwegian Sea to the Mediterranean, many of which date back to 25,000 B.C.E. and earlier, is compelling and indicates that over an extensive area of the world an original experience of the divine was of a "Great Goddess," an uroboric figure[6] containing both masculine and feminine aspects, but in whom the feminine aspects are predominant.[7] The deity whom man first worshiped was apparently a sovereign all-encompassing *Magna Mater* manifested in many forms and under many different aspects, who begets, nourishes, and sustains the world, her body, and its creatures, all of whom are her children. The Goddess was worshiped for millennia in all parts of the globe as the Great Mother. She was the *mysterium tremendum* that permeates nature, emanating from some profound, invisible depth and whose power is manifest in the living, throbbing, potent forces of nature that bring creatures into being, animating and agitating them, inspiring them with uncanny powers by which they are able to thrive.

On an ancient Sumerian tablet, the Mother Goddess is Nammu; her name is written with the ideogram for *sea*. She is "the mother, who gave birth to heaven and earth";[8] she is "mother, first one, who gave birth to the gods of the universe"; she is "Mother of Everything." She is a goddess without a spouse, the self-procreating womb, the primal matter, the inherently fertile and fertilizing waters of the "sweet ocean."[9] She is also called Ninhursag, Goddess of the Earth, in an ancient creation myth from

---

[6] A circle with the beginning and ending mutually penetrating, symbolized in the serpent, curved in a circle, swallowing its tail.

[7] See the studies of Marijas Gimbutas, *Goddesses and Gods of Old Europe* (Berkeley: University of California Press, 1990); Elinor Gadon, *Once and Future Goddess* (New York: Harper & Row, 1989); Joseph Campbell, *The Masks of God,* 4 vols. (New York: Viking Press, 1959–68); Merlin Stone, *The Paradise Papers: When God Was a Woman* (New York: Harcourt Brace, 1978); Anne Baring and Jules Cashford, *The Myth of the Goddess: Evolution of an Image* (London: Viking-Arkana, 1991); Erich Neumann, *The Great Mother* (New York: Pantheon Books, 1955).

[8] Samuel Noah Kramer, *Sumerian Mythology* (Philadelphia: The American Philosophical Society, 1944) 39.

[9] Gwendolyn Leick, *Sex and Eroticism in Mesopotamian Literature* (London: Routledge, 1994) 14–15.

Old Babylon (1750–1550 B.C.E.): "Thou, O Ninhursag, art the mother-womb, the one who creates mankind."[10]

In the very beginning "all the lands were sea," explains a text from the Neo-Babylonian period (ca. 600 B.C.E.) called the *Eridu Story of Creation.* By the time this creation story was recorded, Marduk had become the supreme God, but Marduk himself is but the great-grandson of Tiamat.[11] The same is true of the creator God in Egypt. In a creation hymn from Memphis, dating probably from 1550–1350 B.C.E., the chief God, Ptah, is said to be the creator of the universe and everything in it, but Ptah himself comes from out of the primeval waters; that is, he is born from the primordial Mother.

> He sought a place for his foot. The god sought a place for his foot in the primeval waters because he had grown old [referring to the time of his being delivered from the womb?]. He found that a place was in this land. There he came forth from the primeval waters.[12]

You will recall that the primal element, in the teaching of the Seven Sages, out of which the world is composed is water, and that is the ancient ideogram of the goddess. According to Damascius, Night was the original element in the religious cosmogony of Orphism, and Night is a symbol of the ancient Goddess' womb. From these myths, the primordial beginning is the Mother Goddess. But what does that mean? What experience of reality is coming to expression in the cult of the Goddess?

The Uroboros

The Great Mother is all that is, and so she is both masculine and feminine. Among her many ancient symbols is the uroboros: a serpent swallowing its tail. The uroboros shows its feminine character in receiving its tail into its mouth, its masculine character in the tail that penetrates the mouth as the phallus the womb.

The uroboros is a symbol of the primordial pair from whom the world and all that is in it come to be. In the *Enuma Elish,* perhaps the most famous of the ancient Near Eastern myths, all things come from the primordial pair: the masculine Apsu, the ocean, which perhaps may be taken as a symbol of the male semen, and the feminine Tiamat, the primeval waters, perhaps a symbol of the uterine waters of the "universal

---

[10] Barbara C. Sproul, *Primal Myths: Creating the World* (San Francisco: Harper and Row, 1979) 114.

[11] Ibid., 120–1.

[12] Ibid., 87.

Mother." But the Mother is supreme; her waters surround and embrace Apsu just as the uterine waters surround and embrace the seminal waters in sexual intercourse.[13] From the eternal mingling of the waters of Apsu and Tiamat are produced all the divine and natural forces that make up the world: all things visible and invisible.[14]

Pherecydes the "theologian," one of the first to write about the nature and generations of the gods,[15] wrote a book entitled *Theocrasia*. The term means divine mingling and so it must have dealt with some form of the Babylonian myth of Apsu and Tiamat.[16] Another pre-Socratic, Acusilous of Argos (sixth century B.C.E.), lists chaos as the first principle, another ancient symbol of the goddess as one can discover from the opening lines of Hesiod's *Theogonia*. Then for Acusilous comes forth a type of uroboros: Erebus, the male, and Night, the female. From their union spring Air, Eros, and Metis (which sounds rather like the Babylonian goddess Tasmetum, or Intelligence).[17] According to Aristotle, the ancient theologians of Greece named Ocean and Tethys (sea) the parents of creation—an ancient Greek version of the Babylonian Apsu and Tiamat.[18] In yet another version of Orphism, that of Hieronymus and Hellanicus, the first two elements are water and earth, uroboric symbols again of the Mother Goddess. A third element is begotten of these two, a serpent called Ageless Time, or Unchanging Heracles.[19] The second version may be more ancient because it shows Time as the product of a masculine

---

[13] Cf. Mircea Eliade, *Patterns in Comparative Religion,* trans. Rosemary Sheed (New York: World, 1963) 191ff.; and Neumann, *The Great Mother.*

[14] Sproul, *Primal Myths,* 91. Cf. Leick, *Sex and Eroticism in Mesopotamian Literature,* 19–20.

The notion of a watery matrix was the most widely accepted one [in Mesopotamia] and it is generally linked with a female creative principle. But while the actual control over the process of primary creation could be ascribed to various agents or gods, depending on the theological slant of the text, the dynamic process of creation, the unfolding diversification, is always symbolized by a male-female pair who mate to produce further offspring and so on. This view recognizes the fundamental purpose of sexuality as a means of reproduction and creative organization of the universe.

[15] Hermann Diels, *Die Fragmente der Vorsokratiker,* 4th ed. (Berlin: Weidmann, 1922) I.A.1; p. 43.

[16] Kathleen Freeman, *Ancilla to the Pre-Socratic Philosophers* (Cambridge, Mass.: Harvard University Press, 1948) 13.

[17] Diels, *Die Fragmente der Vorsokratiker,* I.B.1, p. 53.

[18] Cf. Aristotle, *Metaphysics* I.iii.983B and Diels, *Die Fragmente der Vorsokratiker,* I.B.10, p. 9.

[19] Freeman, *Ancilla to the Pre-Socratic Philosophers.*

deity, the serpent, which is itself born of an androgynous deity, water and earth, recalling again the ancient myth of Babylon, of Apsu and Tiamat, or Ocean and the primeval Waters.

The ancient symbol of the uroboros conveys the primordial experience of the Great Mother in which all things are united in one Great Round of life and death. Birth is the prelude to death, and death is the prelude to new life. The One in whom all opposites are united is the Great Mother. She is the birthgiver of all things, her womb is the tomb of death and the matrix of regeneration. Her chief mystery is sex, not in its lascivious aspect but in its biological and generative aspect. Her central act is the *hieros gamos,* the union of male and female, opposites that comprehend the totality of all that is.

This explains why man and woman are sacred in the cult of the goddess, and why her cult requires a priest and priestess. The forces that the masculine and feminine embody must be joined together through sympathetic magic to complete the whole and to generate life. If they are sundered, the whole withers and the energy of life dissipates for lack of vital forces to renew it. But in their union, death is the matrix of new life even as life presses ceaselessly toward death as the womb of its regeneration and renewal. Above is the gateway to the below, and the below is the entrance to the above. Light and dark, life and death, day and night, revolve endlessly on their axis, the Great Mother, each opposite alike a natural component of the Great Round of Life.

The goddess' spiritual depths are profoundly felt but her principal epiphany is the concrete world: animals, plants, celestial bodies (particularly sun and moon), man, and above all woman. Her images are the cave, the moon, the stone, the serpent, bird, and fish; the spiral, meander, and labyrinth; the wild animals—the lion, bull, stag, bison, goat and horse; rituals concerned with the fertility of the earth and of animals and human beings.[20] Each is a part of the natural world, experienced as incarnations or epiphanies of an invisible dimension inseparable from the visible dimension of existence. The symbol of the uroboros gives expression to the intuitive sense that life is a unity and that everything is integrally connected as parts of a living whole. Death, darkness, the below, the visible, and body are inseparable from life, light, the above, the invisible, and spirit.

> The Mother Goddess, wherever she is found, is an image that inspires and focuses a perception of the universe as an organic, alive and sacred whole, in which humanity, the Earth and all life on Earth participate as "her children."

[20] Baring and Cashford, *The Myth of the Goddess,* 40.

> Everything is woven together in one cosmic web, where all orders of mani-
> fest and unmanifest life are related, because all share in the sanctity of the
> original source.[21]

The children of the goddess face the darkness of death in the security of her arms, knowing that to be buried in the tomb of her body, the
earth, is to be conceived in her life-generating womb, that as surely as
day follows night and the green life of spring follows the death of winter,
so each death is the prelude to new life in the Great Round of Life.

The Omnipresent Goddess

There is strong evidence that the ancient cult of Israel's YHWH either emerged from or was overlaid on an earlier cult of the goddess. One
recognizes the goddess in the formlessness and void that was "in the beginning" from which God creates the heavens and the earth. She would
be, in the alphabet of the ancient mythological symbols, the "darkness
covering the face of the deep," the primordial waters over whom the Spirit
of God hovers. One sees the primordial couple of ancient mythology
when God, like the Sumerian god En-lil, God of the air, separates the
light from the darkness,[22] or when he separates the "waters" from the
"waters" (Gen 1:6), in other words, Apsu from Tiamat. The goddess is
clearly visible in the second creation story of Genesis (chapter 2) as the
"ground" from which YHWH Elohim brings forth the plants, the animals,
the tree of life and the tree of the knowledge of good and evil, and finally
man himself.[23] The tree is another one of her major symbols, so the tree
of life and the tree of the knowledge of good and evil would be different
aspects of her being. She is thinly veiled as Eve, the "Mother of all Living." She can be found in the cosmogony of the psalmist: "The earth is
the Lord's and all it contains, the world, and those who dwell in it. For
he has founded it upon the seas, and established it upon the waters" (Ps

---

[21] Ibid., xi.

[22] Cf. the Sumerian myth: "When An had carried off heaven, after Enlil had carried off earth." Kramer, in *Sumerian Mythology,* 74, translates this Sumerian mythological theme into contemporary theological language. "The union of An and Ki
produced the air-god Enlil, who proceeded to separate the heaven-father An from the
earth-mother Ki." This mythopoeic motif belongs to the theme of the "separation of
the world parents" and is interpreted as a symbol for the rise of consciousness. Cf.
Erich Neumann, *The Origins and History of Consciousness,* trans. R.F.C. Hull, Bollingen
Series XLII (Princeton, N.J.: Princeton University Press, 1973) 102–27.

[23] For fuller description of the symbols of the goddess in the Old Testament
creation accounts, see the relevant chapters in Baring and Cashford, *The Myth of the
Goddess.*

24:1-2). The symbolism recalls that of the *Enuma Elish* in which Marduk creates the earth and the heavens from the vanquished body of the great sea monster, Tiamat, and Tiamat is the primeval sea from which all the gods and goddesses, or the forces of nature, come forth.

There seems to be something irrepressible about the goddess. She cannot be gotten rid of, and the more one tries to destroy her or run from her, the more one gets caught in her web. Take, for example, her very strong presence even in the "patriarchal" religion of Israel. The railing of the prophets against the Asherah, the Canaanite consorts of Ba'al, suggest that Levitical Judaism fought a never-ending battle against Israel's popular adoration of the goddess in her Canaanite version. She was adored by people, kings, and priests as the consort of YHWH Elohim.[24] If the Great Mother Goddess in her Canaanite and Babylonian forms was rejected in Levitical theology, she found an entrance into the "pantheon" of official Judaism in the forms of Chokmah or Sophia, and the Shekhinah or the presence of God. So powerful was she in the Israelite psyche, apparently, that "Israel"—the name of the patriarch, Jacob—was feminized by the prophets to become the bride of God.

There is not the same resistance to the "divine feminine" in the apostolic traditions of Christianity, of course; and it is interesting to note that adoration of the Theotokos is generally an essential aspect of dogma and spirituality where a strong liturgical and sacramental life are present. The ancient goddess is found in the Christian dogma of the *creatio ex nihilo* where *nihilo* is but a philosophical version of the mythopoeic Chaos. The Theotokos (Mater Dei) is venerated as the "Queen of Heaven," the "Bride and Mother of God," the "Temple truly divine." The divine feminine appears as well in those Christian movements of a more dubious reputation. She is Bythos, the consort of Sige in Valentinus' primordial pair; she is manifested in her various aspects as the different female partners in the syzygies of the Gnostic pleroma, and, of course, as the wandering Sophia who gives birth to the demiurge, maker of the world. It is most interesting to observe how Sophia comes forth with great power in most every form of Christian mysticism, especially among those Christian groups where the Theotokos is ignored or figures not at all in the "official" dogmatic structures. I am thinking, for example, of the mysticism of Jacob Boehme, Gottfried Arnold, and of the whole alchemical tradition that was such a powerful force in those mystical movements coming out of the "protestant" reformations of the sixteenth and seventeenth centuries.

[24] See Raphael Patai, *The Hebrew Goddess* (Detroit: Wayne State University Press, 1980).

How are we to account for the goddess' irrepressible power as clearly shown by her omnipresence in the history of human religious experience? The ancient philosophers were among the first to realize that the goddess in fact is a symbol for the cosmos and for the human soul. In terms of analytical psychology, she would be a symbol by which the contents of the human soul are projected onto the screen of divinity, enabling the primitive mind, by engaging the symbol, to engage to some degree unknown contents of the soul. Her power, then, comes from the fact that she is the mystery of the soul. She cannot be gotten rid of because her mystery is the mystery of *us* in the unknown depths of our being.

If that is so, then it is of the highest theological interest that in her cult, man and woman are sacred because they embody the opposites that comprehend the totality of our being, and in their sacred union they make manifest some mystery that pertains by nature to our soul. What is the cult of the goddess telling us about ourselves, about our nature and destiny? I want to look more closely at the drama of the *hieros gamos* and the myth that sets forth its inner content, because I think it is here that we begin to get to the heart of the goddess' cult, and therefore to the heart of our question regarding the character and function of the Christian priesthood.

The Hieros Gamos

For millennia, the god was carried in the Mother's womb as the Mother's masculine aspect. During the Bronze Age, he emerges as her son. He grows to manhood to become her husband, her lover. Annually he copulates with her in the holy rites of the sacred marriage, the ιερος γαμος. Having expended fully the creative energy of his Eros, planting himself in her womb as the fecundating seed, the Lover God succumbs to death and descends into the dark regions of hell in the bowels of the earth, the maternal womb of the Great Mother. There, he awaits his regeneration, symbolized in the new moon or in the rebirth of spring, when he is resurrected, bringing in his train new life. At this stage, the core of male personality seems to be the genitalia, for in them are localized the energies of life and regeneration that constitute the core of each individual.

The myth of a sacred union accompanied by the death and resurrection of a son/lover is repeated throughout the Mediterranean world.[25]

---

[25] I am laying aside here the myth of the daughter's descent because of the schematic character of the present study. The descent of the daughter, Persephone, rehearses the theme of resurrection, the continuation of the cycle of birth-death-rebirth, of βιος (sustained by Ζωη). The myth of the son/lover adds another important theme which is more immediately germane to this study, and that is the union of opposites in the sacred marriage.

But in the Bronze Age there appears another myth, that of the god's contest with the Mother, the monster of the sea, who is destroyed by the god and whose vanquished body is used to fashion the world and the race of men. The myth is present in Old Testament texts; the Lord God slays the great sea monster, Leviathan, and establishes his sovereignty over the earth (Isa 27:1; Job 3:8; 41:1; Pss 74:14; 104:26). But the myth is given for us in greater detail in the ancient Babylonian festival dedicated to the exploits of Marduk.

This feast took place in the spring during the month of Nisan, our March and April, and lasted for twelve days. On the fifth day of the feast, a sheep or lamb was immolated and thrown into the Euphrates as an expiatory offering, taking away the sins of the people. The sheep may be the symbol of the shepherd king, Tammuz. Throwing the lamb into the waters of the Euphrates must have to do with a re-creation of the world, for the rite is immediately followed on the sixth and seventh days of the feast with a rehearsal of the creation epic, the *Enuma Elish,* in which everything comes into existence from out of the primeval waters, together with a liturgical drama probably depicting the death of Marduk and his descent into the infernal regions. The original chaos of the beginning is enacted in the village, where there is general affliction and disorder. The eighth day of the feast celebrates Marduk's victorious combat by which he frees the spirits who had fallen into the clutches of the infernal regions. Again, the *Enuma Elish* is recited recounting Marduk's contest with Tiamat, the primeval waters of chaos. There follows the celebration of Marduk's resurrection and his triumphal return, which takes place on the third day of his death and descent into hell. The feast ends with the celebration of a sacred marriage of Marduk and his paramour Sarpanit.[26]

I find most interesting this conclusion of Marduk's conquest of the great sea monster. The original conflict between male and female is resolved in the sacred union between Marduk and Sarpanit. The uroboros is established again, but not in its original uroboric state. Rather, the primordial uroboros of Apsu and Tiamat has been reconfigured, as it were, by the victory of Marduk, and in his union with Sarpanit the opposites of cosmic being have become integrated on a higher plane of existence ruled no longer by raw instinct but by law and social order. From the drama of Marduk and Sarpanit, and others like it, I would interpret the union of priest and priestess in the dramatic rite of the *hieros gamos* as a mythopoeic symbol giving expression to an underlying, essential capacity of the soul for integration and transformation resulting in a higher consciousness

[26] Jean Bottéro, *La Religion Babylonienne* (Paris: Presses Universitaires de France, 1952) 126–7.

and manner of existence. Here at this point the christological vision of the Church reveals within the mystery of the *hieros gamos* a seed of even profounder capacities inherent to the soul.

Notes from Christology

Israel's Marduk

The mythologem illustrated in the Babylonian myth of Marduk has a Hebraic counterpart. Israel's God, too, engages a dark, watery foe in a cosmic contest, set in terms virtually identical to those of Marduk's contest with Tiamat. The most detailed version is from Psalm 74:

> God my king is from old,
> He works deeds of deliverance in the midst of the earth [the goddess]
> Thou didst divide the sea by thy strength
> Thou didst break the heads of the sea-monsters in the waters.
> Thou didst crush the heads of Leviathan;
> Thou didst give him as food for the creatures of the wilderness
> Thou didst break open springs and torrents;
> Thou didst dry up ever-flowing streams.
> Thine is the day, Thine is the night;
> Thou hast prepared the light and the sun.
> Thou hast established all the boundaries of the earth.
> Thou hast made summer and winter (Ps 74:12-17).

Like Marduk, YHWH conquers the primordial waters of the deep and the monsters dwelling in them; like Marduk, he despoils the body of the monster. Marduk fashions the world from the monster. YHWH here does something similar: he gives the monster to the world for food. Then, like Marduk, YHWH unites all the opposites by the power of his own command, establishing his sovereignty over heaven and earth. Marduk and YHWH are invincible, independent, all-powerful. Neither one "needs" the feminine, which, in the symbol of the great sea monster, poses an ever-present threat to the cosmic order that has been established by the power of *logos,* divine intellect. As sea monster and as the threat of stifling darkness and chaos, the feminine is vanquished; yet, her body and its latent energy, interestingly enough, are used to fashion and nourish creation: a mythologem expressing the concept of philosophy that we and the world are the goddess.

The myths of Marduk and YHWH are similar because, as I have suggested, they express the same underlying principle: the soul contains by nature a capacity for integration and transformation, resulting in a higher consciousness and manner of being. But beneath the similarities is a critical difference that places one on the threshold of the Church's christological vision of being, as expressed in the clerical nature of the *laos,* the "new royal priesthood."

Marduk comes forth from the abyss of Tiamat; that is, from cosmic being. Marduk then is a supreme cosmic power. But in the prophetic vision of the Bible, the God of Israel dwells in "light unapproachable." In the beginning, his Spirit is already brooding over the waters. Sun and moon and stars—supreme deities in the mythologies of antiquity—are God's handiwork. He comes, in other words, from beyond and "outside" the goddess. In liturgical texts, he is "immaterial" [αυλος]. I take this to mean more than that he is incorporeal. It means that he is not of the materia, not of the world, not of the primordial *hyle* from which all things derive. This means that he is not of the Mother; he is not another version of the father god of mythology, and so he is not a cosmic power; he is not the uroboros of cosmic life. He is in his own being "supra-cosmic": altogether beyond everything that is, infinitely transcending and embracing within himself the goddess and all the opposites of cosmic being that she embraces in *her* womb: visible and invisible, light and dark, above and below, masculine and feminine.

This gives immediately quite a different character to the contest between YHWH and Leviathan. The contest between Marduk and Tiamat could be taken as a contest between the opposites of cosmic being latent within the waters of chaos, specifically the opposites of unconscious instinct and the potential for consciousness—or perhaps, if you like Freud, between the id and an emerging superego. But the contest of YHWH and Leviathan is over the orientation of cosmic movement: that is to say, over the *telos* that will determine the manner in which the opposites of cosmic being shall find their integration. Leviathan is the sea monster, a sea serpent; and so he is the uroboros. YHWH's contest with Leviathan, then, is against the power of the serpent's seduction to draw the opposites of cosmic being away from their origin and *telos* in YHWH and into themselves to create the closed uroboric existence of self-love that is "against nature." YHWH's victory over Leviathan means that he has established the cosmic movement in which the opposites of cosmic being exist in himself, and so has established the opposites of cosmic being at their core in an *ecstasis* that draws cosmic being outside the uroboros of self-love, outside of itself and into the supra-cosmic Other in whom it was made to exist and in whom it finds its true, natural perfection.

Alongside the myth of YHWH and Leviathan, the Old Testament has also its Sarpanit with whom YHWH unites as with his bride. But she is not some mythical Goddess "out there." She is the people Israel; and this, together with the vision of who YHWH is relative to cosmic being, changes everything.

The Hieros Gamos *of the Old Testament*

The union between YHWH and Israel is itself the Abrahamic covenant: "I passed by you and saw you, and behold, you were at the time for love; so I spread my skirt over you and covered your nakedness. I also swore to you and entered into a covenant with you so that you became mine" (Ezek 16:8).

The covenant of Abraham centers on the child, Isaac, the child of promise in whom is to be realized the covenant's promise of land and progeny; that is, a prosperous, free life. In every particular, we have here a *hieros gamos* in which Abraham and Sarah are a kind of Apsu and Tiamat, for they are the primordial pair from whose union comes forth the whole nation of Israel in the person of Isaac, the fruit of their union. But there are critical and profound differences that point to the emergence of a fundamentally different vision of human nature and destiny.

To begin with, the three main players—Abraham, Sarah, and Isaac— are ordinary mortals, not gods and goddesses. It follows from this that the "myth" of the Abrahamic covenant pertains to an event on the same plane as the here and now, not in *illo tempore* or in the "dream-time." The ancient projection of the myth has been withdrawn, giving to the banality of historical events themselves an inherently mythical, or, if you prefer, a mystagogical (sacramental) power.

If they are ordinary mortals, then in the terms of the *hieros gamos* myth Abraham and Sarah would be the priest and priestess, the magical embodiments of the primordial goddess in her masculine and feminine aspects, the opposites of cosmic being that constitute the totality of cosmic being. But the fruit of their union, Isaac, really does not come from them. His origin lies beyond them in a God who is not an aspect of the goddess. Isaac therefore originates in some source that transcends the opposites of cosmic being, lying outside the goddess altogether beyond all that is.

Consider the details of the story of Isaac's birth. Abraham and Sarah are barren and Sarah is past the age of child-bearing. They are for all practical purposes, according to the logic of ancient Near Eastern culture, dead. When Sarah conceives the child in her womb, both she and Abraham are, in effect, raised from the dead. Consider further the way in which the sacred text describes the conception and birth of Isaac. In Gen 18:10: "The Lord said, '*I will surely return to you* at this time next year; and behold, Sarah your wife shall have a son'"; and in 21:1-2: "Then the Lord *visited* Sarah as he had said, *and the Lord did to Sarah* just as he had said, and Sarah conceived and bore a son to Abraham." Nowhere does the sacred text say that Abraham knew Sarah. The significance of Abraham's apparent absence in the conception of Isaac comes into view against the backdrop of the ancient *hieros gamos.*

In the ancient *hieros gamos,* the child comes from the union of priest and priestess who are each one an aspect of the goddess; and so the child of the ancient *hieros gamos* is the product of cosmic being copulating with itself. It is the life of the cosmos recycled, a life destined to return to the grave whence it came and, in the grave, destined to be raised up into the same life it just left in death. From the perspective of the Church's christological confession, the child of the *hieros gamos* stands for the life of cosmic being that has fallen out of its origin and *telos* in that which is beyond itself, the Lord God, and has collapsed in on itself into the closed narcissism of the uroboros.

Isaac comes from an altogether different kind of union. Abraham's apparent absence in the conception of Isaac means that Isaac is not the product of the uroboros; the life in and by which Isaac is made to exist lies outside the uroboros. It lies in the God who conquers Leviathan and establishes cosmic being at its core in a movement of ecstasis, drawing it out of the uroboros, out of itself and into an Other who is its true origin and *telos* (goal and perfection). Yet Isaac's birth marks not the *telos* but only the *beginning* of the covenant's fulfillment. His birth therefore points beyond itself to a fulfillment that lies beyond the present, beyond cosmic being.

The promises given in the covenant are land and progeny, which are not yet possessed by Abraham and Sarah. But in Isaac they possess the *seed* of what is to be the fulfillment of the covenant's promise. Any healthy child is a child of promise and blessing. But if *this* child, Isaac, originates from a power and life "not of the world," then the land and progeny of the covenant's promise cannot be land and progeny, for these are things of this world. Land and progeny must be icons of a substance that is not of this world: power, freedom, and life that are in God alone.

The Bride of God

In the prayer of the Church, the Theotokos is hailed as the "Land of promise flowing with milk and honey."[27] She is the fertile ground born of soil that was formerly barren.[28] The Theotokos is also the child of promise: she is the "glorious fruit born of a holy seed," a "flower blossomed

[27] From the Akathist hymn to the Theotokos, the second Stanza for the Second Friday of Great Lent.
[28] From the feast of the Nativity of the Theotokos.

from Jesse, a branch sprung from his root." She is the child of God, daughter of the king. If Isaac is the beginning of the covenant's fulfillment, then the Theotokos is its *telos,* for it is in the Theotokos that the world is united with God. She is the "Queen and spotless Bride of the Father," the "Bridal Chamber of the King" in whom the "marvelous mystery of the ineffable union of natures comes together in Christ."[29] In her, the whole creation is made new and like God (cf. Gen 3:5), for she is the glorious gate facing toward the east through whom God alone passes, the bridge and ladder that reaches up to heaven, in whom heaven and earth are joined in the mystery of her Son, Jesus Christ.[30]

Implicitly, the Theotokos is given in liturgical and patristic texts as the Church and as the embodiment of the soul. For the Theotokos, the Church and the human soul are all said to be the "bride" of God. There is then a *hieros gamos* in the Church. Indeed, a *hieros gamos* is the substance of the Christian mystery. Christ's death is a sacred marriage,[31] our union with Christ in baptism is a sacred marriage,[32] and the Eucharist is the marriage feast, celebrating the successful nuptials of the Lamb and his bride, the Church, accomplished in the death and resurrection of Christ.[33] In this *hieros gamos* of the Church, Christ is the bridegroom, the Church is the bride. That means, in the language of ancient mythology, that Christ is the priest and the Church the priestess.

In the earliest documents of the Church, those who preside at the eucharistic table are called bishops and presbyters; they are not called priests. Is this terminology informed by an understanding of Christ as the priest and the Church as his priestess? This is what the biblical and patristic descriptions of Christ and the Church as bridegroom and bride would mean in the language of the ancient *hieros gamos.* The *laos,* then, would be the bride of God, and so the priestess in the schema of the *hieros gamos.* The roles of bishop and presbyter, then, would also be of a bridal character since they are drawn from the *cleros,* the sphere, of the *laos.* Indeed, in the Eastern Orthodox tradition, the priest says as he vests:

[29] From the feast of the Nativity of the Theotokos.

[30] From the feast of the Theotokos' Entry into the Temple.

[31] See St. Augustine, *Sermo Suppositus* 120.8: "Like a bridegroom, Christ went forth from his chamber. He went out with a foreshadowing of his wedding into the field of the world. . . . He came to the marriage bed of the cross and there, in mounting it, he consummated his marriage."

[32] See the baptismal instructions of John Chrysostom 6.23–25: "I exhort those deemed worthy of baptism to keep the marriage robe in its integrity, that with it you may enter forever into this spiritual marriage [πνευματικος γαμος]. And what takes place here [the movement from baptism to Eucharist] is a spiritual marriage."

[33] Cf. Rev 19:7-8.

"As a bridegroom he has set a crown on me; as a bride adorns herself with jewels, so he has adorned me."

The bridal character of the Christian priesthood gives concrete form to the Gospel proclaimed by the Church. It bears witness to a *hieros gamos* in which cosmic being is not uniting with itself but is drawn out of itself. For the bridegroom of this *hieros gamos* is "not of this world," and the Theotokos, the bride of Christ with whom God unites in an ineffable union, is the world opened to God and liberated from the self-love of the uroboros. In this union, the bride receives into herself the seed not of "man" but of the "immaterial" God, and in that she is made truly fertile; that is to say, she is given the capacity to bring forth a life that is not of this world. This is the life of the Spirit, which infinitely transcends the integration of unconscious and conscious symbolized in the union of Marduk and Sarpanit. In its bridal character, the Christian priesthood bears witness to the profoundest capacity of human being to be made one with that which is not itself and to be taken up into the mystery of the divine life of the incomprehensible God.

Conclusion

From the baptismal font, the *laos* comes into being. It would follow that the structure of the *laos* would conform to the substance of the mystery in and by which it was brought into being, so that its phenomenal structure makes manifest its mystical substance. The "phenomenal structure" of the *laos* is its "liturgical form": this is the form the *laos* naturally conforms to in its worship, for in worship the *laos* becomes mystically the divine being in which it has been made graciously to live. On the one hand, then, the liturgical assembly manifests its bridal character, which pertains to the entire *laos:* to the laity and to the clergy. On the other hand, the liturgical assembly makes manifest, in the icon of the priesthood as it is conventionally called, the presence of the bridegroom who is "in our midst" as the mystery of our regeneration in the life of his Spirit that is "not of the world."

I would distinguish between the liturgical structure of the Church and her administrative structure. The administrative structure is the sphere, the *cleros,* of political and magisterial power and authority. That structure, it seems to me, owes its present character almost wholly to the historical phenomenon of Roman-Byzantine culture and is not necessarily in conformity with the mystery of the Church's *hieros gamos*— particularly in regard to the manner in which political and magisterial power are exercised by that structure. But the liturgical structure does owe its form wholly to the substance of the Church's mystery. In her liturgical substance, the Church is of a bridal character oriented to a bridegroom who is not an aspect of her own being because he is "not of the world." In her liturgical substance, the whole *laos* is saturated with power and real being because the entire *laos*—together with all the clerical and monastic ranks within it—is drawn from the baptismal font. And the liturgical structure of the Christian priesthood as it has existed from the beginning makes manifest why it is that the whole *laos* is saturated with power and real being: it is because the bridegroom who has made himself one with her and has infused her with the seed of his Spirit that is not of the world is in her midst. In the mystagogy of the Church's liturgical worship, he is always present "today" in the mystery of his Spirit, and his Spirit is the mystery of a love that has the power to transform the world because it is the love of God the Father that has conquered the self-love of the uroboros with the love of his Son who is "not of the world."

In the structure of her "liturgical priesthood," then, the Church bears witness to the most fundamental ontological reality inherent to the soul: the life by which we are made to exist and in which we find our natural destiny lies outside of ourselves and outside the cosmic being in which we exist. It is to be found in that God who is "not of the world." Cosmic being exists by nature in an essential movement that would take it beyond itself and into an Other, because its origin and *telos*—its goal and perfection—lie not in itself but in the mystery of the God who is "not of this world."

In the vision of the Church's christological confession, sexuality becomes an icon of the *pneumatikos gamos* of the Church: a union with God that has its center not in the genitalia, but in the depths of the spirit, at the point of the spiritual core of our being; that is, in our true self, the *pneuma*, the κατ᾽εικονα.[34] Sexuality becomes an icon in the sacrament of marriage; for it is in the fidelity of marriage, in the fiery furnace of personal commitment to a love that transcends uroboric instinct, that husband and wife, through the trials and afflictions endemic to the spiritual warfare of the sacramental life, transfigure the uroboros of instinctive self-love to become one in spirit, and in this, an icon of the mystical spiritual marriage of Christ and his Church.

From the baptismal waters, the *laos* come into being as the royal priesthood of God, the bride of God, the priestess, assigned the *cleros* of offering "unto Thee, O God, Thine own of Thine own, on behalf of all

---

[34] I am thinking of Origen's definition of the primary substance [*hypostasis*] of human being that becomes standard in the theological tradition of Alexandria. See his commentary on John XX.

and for all." And in its priestly structure, the *laos* is a *martyria,* an epiphany revealing within cosmic being a profound capacity to be made one with the "immaterial" God, and in that union to become more than what it is by nature, and in that to realize its natural destiny.

9

Priest, Prophet, King:
The Ministry of Jesus Christ

DONALD J. GOERGEN, O.P.

In the theology of the letter to the Hebrews, Jesus Christ is the supreme high priest (Heb 4:14-15). I take this to mean that Jesus Christ is also the supreme exemplification of what it means to be priest within a Christian context, whether we refer to the priesthood of all the baptized or to the priesthood of the ordained. In other words, we ought not take some pre-conceived understanding about priesthood and apply it to Christ, in the manner that "priests do this, therefore Christ did such and such," but rather, the other way around: "This is who Christ is; this is therefore who we as baptized or ordained should be." Christ is the model, the exemplar, the one from whom we learn what being priestly is all about. In other words, the question of priesthood among Christians is first of all a christological question about Jesus Christ.

Both ordained ministry and lay ministry take as their model the mission and ministry of Jesus. Both baptism and the sacrament of orders have to do in distinct ways with ministry, even if the priesthood of the ordained and the priesthood of all the baptized are essentially different. They are different, but that does not mean that the word *priest* is equivocal when applied to all baptized Christians and to ordained ministers in the Church. Each comes to understand something about priesthood from

---

*Scripture quotations in this chapter are taken from the New Revised Standard Version Bible, Catholic edition, © 1989 by the Division of Christian Education of the National Council of Churches of Christ in the USA. Used by permission. All rights reserved.

the other.[1] Yet for both the starting point is Jesus Christ. Who do we say that Jesus is (Mark 8:27-29)?

Kenan Osborne, in his historical study of ordained ministry in the Roman Catholic tradition, recognizes the need to ground a theology of priesthood in christology.[2] Few would disagree. The difficulty, however, is that many who search for a contemporary Catholic theology of priesthood do not begin with contemporary christology and its manifold insights. If christology is indeed to be the starting point for a Catholic theology of priesthood, it is with contemporary Catholic christology that we must begin. Otherwise our theology of the priesthood will be out of step with what students of theology are learning about Jesus Christ. We can't put our christology over here, and our theology of priesthood over there, and never shall the two meet. The theology of ordained ministry must be integrated into the rest of theology and not set off by itself.

Now, of course, there are many contemporary christologies. Yet there are common threads among them as well. Christology today is particularly cognizant of the fact that there are stages to the story of Jesus. While affirming the two natures of Jesus Christ, christology unfolds the story of Jesus in stages: the risen Jesus, the earthly Jesus, the pre-incarnate Word, in whatever order one might choose to allow the story and mystery of Jesus to disclose itself. And the earthly Jesus' history develops around two crucial foci: the public ministry of Jesus and his death on a cross. What do each of these tell us about the priesthood of Jesus Christ, since, according to Hebrews, he was/is our chief High Priest even though the rest of the New Testament does not speak of him in those terms?

When we are talking about the priesthood of Jesus Christ *today,* we are clearly talking about the risen Christ. The risen Christ is the only Christ there is. As Osborne wrote: "The risen Jesus continues his ministry in and through the Church's ministry, and therefore a study of Church ministry is in reality a study of the ministry of the risen Lord."[3] The risen Jesus' ministry is not confined to his work within the Church, but ministry in the Church still remains the ministry of Jesus. Thus ordained ministry works out of a theology of the resurrection. We are the ministers of the risen Christ.

The risen Christ, however, is the earthly, historical, and crucified Jesus. That is the Jesus whom God raised from the dead. We cannot speak

---

[1] For further reflection on this complementarity between the two, see Jack Risley's article "The Minister: Lay and Ordained" in this volume.

[2] Kenan Osborne, *Priesthood: A History of the Ordained Ministry in the Roman Catholic Church* (New York: Paulist Press, 1988) 3–29, 317–8.

[3] Ibid., 29.

of the risen one apart from the earthly one; these titles refer to the same Jesus. Jesus is always the risen and crucified One.[4] There is only one Jesus. While the whole of Jesus is not historiographically accessible, and while portraits of "the historical Jesus" widely diverge one from the other, nevertheless the broad outlines of Jesus' mission as an itinerant preacher, teacher, and healer are abundantly attested, as is Jesus' death on the cross, even if not all the details of the passion narratives are to be taken as historical. No Jesus researcher denies Jesus' public execution by crucifixion. The ministry of the earthly Jesus teaches us about the continuing ministry of Jesus as risen Christ and becomes paradigmatic for those who follow Jesus, his disciples, and thus especially those called to ministry, lay or ordained, in the Church.

But the mission and ministry of the earthly Jesus, both as manifest in his life as well as his death, is but the extension into time and space of the mission of the Word. Jesus' mission and ministry are the mission and ministry of the incarnate Word. His was and is a ministry of the Word. A theology of ministry is thus also a theology of the Word as well as a theology of the resurrection. It is the Word who came to set up its tent among us in whose ministry we collaborate. Ministry is ultimately a sharing in the Trinitarian life, a partaking of the very life of God. Ministry is "God-with-us."

All ministry is thus ministry of the Word, and that expression is to be understood as both an objective genitive and a subjective genitive. The Word, as eternal, as incarnate, as risen Christ, is the one who ministers, who comes to be with the people. And it is also the Word as enfleshed in Scripture and community that we serve. The Word has a primacy. All ministry is grounded in giving witness to the Word. The ordained minister gives witness and proclaims the gospel in distinctive ways. He can excuse himself from neither witnessing nor preaching.[5] But we look at that Word through the prism of the earthly Jesus. What was Jesus as God's Word doing in the world, or what was God's Word in the world doing? In what does the mission of the Word in the world consist?

Jesus certainly preached God, a God of great compassion. He sought to bring people to God, to break down the barriers between God and people. He proclaimed God as longing for his people and made God's solidarity with people manifest. Jesus sought to establish a solidarity among people as well as with the God who loves people. "Love of neighbor" (Lev 19:18) was a commandment like unto the "first and great" commandment

---

[4] See James Alison, *Knowing Jesus* (London: SPCK, 1993) 3–30.

[5] For the primacy of preaching in the ministry of the presbyter, see Stephen DeLeers' chapter "The Place of Preaching in the Ministry and Life of Priests" in this volume.

(Matt 22:38-39), that of loving God with all our soul (Deut 6:4). Which is more important: love of God or love of neighbor? For Jesus, you can't have one without the other. And Jesus' love for the people, that is, God's love for the people, was manifest in Jesus' prophetic preaching, healings, exorcisms, fellowship at table, as well as the wisdom expressed in his sayings and stories. The symbolic action par excellence that manifested his own heartfelt, soulful love of his God as well as self-offering on behalf of his people was his death on the cross as servant of God and servant of humanity.

There developed a post-biblical theological interpretation of the mission and ministry of Jesus that has been both problematic and productive, namely that of the threefold ministry of Jesus as priest, prophet, and king.[6] This approach has a biblical basis in the naming and proclamation of Jesus as the Messiah. As "the Anointed One of Israel," Jesus sums up within himself all the anointed ones of Israel. The prophets (1 Kgs 19:16; Sir 48:8), the priests (Exod 29:7; Lev 8:10), and the kings (1 Sam 10:1; 16:12-13) were anointed messiahs in the sense in which that would have been understood early in Israelite history. Jesus as the Messiah par excellence, the awaited one, was a prophet like Moses, a new high priest (the Levitical Messiah), as well as king, like David descended from the house of Judah. The question of course remains what these mean when applied to Jesus, for Jesus was clearly not a king like David, or a priest like the priests of old, or exactly another Moses either, although the parallel here is stronger. So the language is applied to Jesus, but it is Jesus who helps us to understand the language rather than the other way around. Jesus teaches us what it means to be prophet, priest, and king within the Christian context—and Jesus' kingdom and priesthood were not like those of this world, or of his world. Nevertheless, there is a theological sense in which Jesus as Messiah came to be understood as having incorporated into his ministry dimensions of priesthood, prophecy, and kingship.

---

[6] One of the difficulties is that this paradigm can be seen as a less historically conscious theological approach. For instance, Jesus was not in fact in history perceived as a priest or king. Also, if one follows the Old Testament roles, the "sage" has a claim to equal consideration, which then creates more of a fourfold paradigm. In fact, the historical Jesus was both prophet and sage, a prophet like the prophets of old and a teacher of wisdom. The only suggestion I have seen for incorporating this fourth function into our interpretation of Jesus is that of John E. Johnson of the Baptist International Church in the Netherlands, "The Old Testament Offices as Paradigm for Pastoral Identity," *Bibliotheca Sacra* 152 (April–June 1995) 182–200. For a significant critique of the approach to the mission of Jesus via these three offices see Wolfhart Pannenberg, *Jesus: God and Man* (Philadelphia: Westminster Press, 1968) 212–25.

The Second Vatican Council used this threefold typology for understanding episcopal, presbyteral, and diaconal ministry as well as the ministry of all the baptized (*Lumen gentium* 10–13, 20–1, 25–31, 34–6). This trilogy has an interesting history.[7] In the fourth century Eusebius of Caesarea spoke of Jesus Christ in this threefold way. John Chrysostom, among others, applied the three roles to all the baptized. Thomas Aquinas applied the three titles to Christ (*In Mattheum* 1:1, 28:19-20; *Ad Rom.* c. 1, lect. 1; *ST* III, q. 31, a. 2). John Calvin was the first to give an extended treatment to this tripartite way of interpreting the ministry of Jesus and he also applied it to all the baptized.

Both at the Council of Trent and among Catholic theologians of that period there are references to this threefold way of speaking. However, Trent defined the power of consecration and the power of absolution or keys as the main powers of the priest with no emphasis on the preaching or prophetic office. During the next centuries priority was thus given to the act of consecration as defining priesthood. John Henry Newman, in a sermon of 1840 from his Anglican days, developed and applied the teaching on the threefold office to Christ.[8] Later, in 1877, in the Catholic preface to the *Via Media,* he saw the threefold office worked out in the life of the Church, in her government, devotion, and schools.[9] Cardinal Manning manifested the earlier theology by saying that, with the two powers of consecration and absolution, the priesthood was complete. Pius XII used the threefold way of speaking to discuss the roles of the bishops. Yves Congar applied the three titles to all the baptized as had been done in the patristic period. The Second Vatican Council was indebted to Newman. By applying the paradigm widely in its teaching about ministry, the council significantly enlarged our understanding of presbyteral ministry as comprising more than the two powers.[10] The Second Vatican Council gave emphasis to the presbyter as preacher and the primacy of preaching in his ministry and life.[11]

[7] See Yves Congar, "Sur la trilogie: Prophète-Roi-Prêtre," *Revue de sciences philosophiques et théologiques* 67 (1983) 97–115; Joseph H. Crehan, "Priesthood, Kingship, and Prophecy," *Theological Studies* 42 (1981) 216–31; Peter J. Drilling, "The Priest, Prophet, and King Trilogy: Elements of Its Meaning in *Lumen gentium* and for Today," *Eglise et Théologie* 19 (1988) 179–206; and L. Schick, *Das Dreifache Amt Christi und der Kirche* (Frankfurt: Peter Lang, 1982).

[8] Sermon V, "The Three Offices of Christ," *Sermons Bearing on Subjects of the Day* (London: Longmans, Green and Co., 1898) 52–62.

[9] Preface to the *Via Media,* 3rd ed. (London: Longmans, Green and Co., 1891).

[10] For a critique of the theology of the "potestas" approach to priesthood see Congar, "Sur la trilogie: Prophète-Roi-Prêtre."

[11] For the development of this see DeLeers, "The Place of Preaching in the Ministry and Life of Priests."

If we follow through with this threefold paradigm taken up by Vatican II, our first concern still remains the ministry of Jesus. Does this threefold way of describing his ministry do justice to Jesus? That must be determined before the approach can be applied elsewhere, say to ordained or lay ministry in the Church. It is certainly valid to speak of the risen Christ as priest, prophet, and king, as Eusebius of Caesarea had done. Jesus is the heir of all three traditions, although it still remains to be interpreted what those terms as applied to Jesus mean. When we take the earthly Jesus as our model, the problem emerges. Jesus was historically neither king nor priest in the ways those roles were understood within the Judaism of his day. Jesus would have seen himself neither as priest nor king. So when we apply those titles to Jesus, we are making a theological assertion about Jesus and we need to indicate what that "new theology" intends. And that theology has to be grounded in Jesus, in the mission and ministry of the earthly Jesus. We cannot simply take theological constructs and apply them to Jesus; Jesus has to elucidate, illuminate those constructs for us. They must have something to do with "the real Jesus." Jesus must not be conformed to a pre-conceived theology of priest, but rather the priest must conform himself to Jesus Christ. Therefore, before proceeding further, we must ask what priest, prophet, and king mean when we apply them to Jesus Christ. Or what does Jesus tell us about who a priest, prophet, or king is? How are we to understand priest, prophet, and king as christological titles?

In answering these questions, I will turn to African theology for assistance. Something illuminating for me occurred while I was teaching a course on Jesus in East Africa, focusing on who Jesus is in Africa today, for Africans and among African theologians. Within African theologies of inculturation and liberation, specifically African ways of naming Christ have emerged, for example Christ as Proto-Ancestor or Brother-Ancestor, Christ as witchdoctor or elder brother or chief, to name only a few. Doing theology in that particular context helped me to appreciate in a new way the traditional titles of priest, prophet, and king as associated with Jesus. Three ways of speaking about Jesus Christ in Africa that are both traditional and yet African emerged. These are Jesus as healer, as liberator, and as king. Let me discuss each of these first,[12] and show how they help us to put content into the traditional titles we apply to Jesus, and then I will return to the relationship between these titles and their implications for a theology of ministry.

---

[12] Much of the following material I take from another article which I have completed on African christology, to be published by *African Christian Studies*.

Doing Christology in an African Context

Jesus, the Healer

We are dealing here with the African concept of *nganga*.[13] Suggestions vary as to how best to convey this in English, from healer[14] to diviner[15] to medicine man or witchdoctor.[16] In the West some may find witchdoctor jarring given negative associations with the word *witch*. Yet witchdoctor itself is not a negative word, anymore than doctor is. The witchdoctor is a doctor who treats witches, whose expertise is knowledge of witchcraft and how to deal with it. He is not a sorcerer.[17] In contemporary terms, he practices alternative medicine. In Africa, the witch is the most powerful image of what not to be. Thus Christ is a non-witch, an anti-witch, a witch healer or doctor, a physician who has power over the powers of evil. "Jesus is a healer" may be the best way to communicate this.

[13] See R. Buana Kibongi, "Priesthood," *Biblical Revelation and African Beliefs,* ed. Kwesi Dickson and Paul Ellingworth (London: Lutterworth, 1969) 47–56; and also the excellent treatment of Matthew Schoffeleers, "Folk Christology in Africa: The Dialectics of the *Nganga* Paradigm," *Journal of Religion in Africa* 19:2 (1989) 157–83, as well as his earlier "Christ as the Medicine-Man and the Medicine-Man as Christ: A Tentative History of African Christological Thought," *Man and Life,* Journal of the Institute of Social Research and Applied Anthropology, Calcutta, 8:1 and 2, 11–28. Pashington Obeng, *Asante Catholicism* (Leiden: E. J. Brill, 1996) 203–5, speaks of the *duyefoo* (medicine man, healer, witchdoctor) among the Asante Roman Catholics of Ghana and how it is applied to Christ as a pan-ethnic *duyefoo* in Catholic ritual. He also speaks about Christ as *oaagyefoo* (warlord or liberator) and as *kurotwiamansa* (leopard) in Asante Catholicism.

[14] Kibongi, "Priesthood"; Cécé Kolié, "Jésus Guérisseur?" *Chemins de la christologie africaine,* ed. Kabasélé, Doré, and Luneau (Paris: Desclée, 1986) 109–25, translated and reprinted in *Faces of Jesus in Africa,* ed. Robert Schreiter (Maryknoll, N.Y.: Orbis Books, 1991) 128–50. Bénézet Bujo, *African Theology in Its Social Context* (Maryknoll, N.Y.: Orbis Books, 1992) 85, also considers "Healer of Healers." See Emmanuel Milingo, *The World in Between: Christian Healing and the Struggle for Spiritual Survival* (Maryknoll, N.Y.: Orbis Books, 1984). Milingo was the Catholic archbishop of Lusaka, Zambia, until 1982.

[15] Michael Kirwen, *The Missionary and the Diviner* (Maryknoll, N.Y.: Orbis Books, 1987). Kirwen is a North American Maryknoll missionary who has been in ministry in East Africa since 1963.

[16] Aylward Shorter, *Jesus and the Witchdoctor: An Approach to Healing and Wholeness* (Maryknoll, N.Y.: Orbis Books, 1985). Shorter is a British-born missionary of Africa. Also see his "Folk Christianity and Functional Christology," AFER 24 (1982) 133–7. For the particular relationship between this christological concept and folk Christianity see Schoffeleers, "Folk Christology in Africa."

[17] On divination and witchcraft, see among others Laurenti Magesa, *African Religion: The Moral Traditions of Abundant Life* (Maryknoll, N.Y.: Orbis Books, 1997) esp. 179–91, 209–34.

The title "healer" resonates well with what we know about the earthly Jesus. Healing was a significant dimension of his ministry,[18] although perhaps less emphasized in post-Enlightenment studies of Jesus given their skepticism about miracles at all. But healings and exorcisms are widely attested in the New Testament, and in material that meet critical biblical criteria. Nor should the healings and exorcisms be separated from the preaching. They were preaching in deeds rather than words. Words and deeds are always integrated in Jesus for whom praxis was never separated from proclamation. Nor does healing need to be limited to the ministry of the earthly Jesus. The risen Jesus continues to heal and give hope following upon his resurrection in the work of the disciples and the mission of the Church.

In addition to the parallel that exists between Jesus as an African healer and the biblical Jewish Jesus, an even stronger advantage to this title for Jesus in African theology is the need for it within African life and society, and not in Africa alone. There is great need in all of the two-thirds world, as well as throughout the world, for personal healing: physical, mental, emotional, and spiritual. The wounds are many. Yet, we must look beyond even personal healing; there also exists the need for economic, political, social, tribal, and national healing. Can Jesus' healing power reach these wounds? As we ponder this question, Jesus the healer becomes Jesus the liberator, whom we will consider shortly. But the two are not totally separate. Healing need not imply only personal needs, and in an African context always implies something communal.[19] The nations of Africa have been wounded by the slave trade, colonization, the post-colonial formation of the nation-states, neo-colonialism's economic dependency, intertribal violence and war, the corruption of many post-independence national leaders, and on and on. The healing Jesus has a strong appeal in Africa today and has that same capacity to speak to the needs for healing of the entire global community as well as the environment. The "Messiah," particularly as "priest," is first and foremost a healer.

Christ the healer has a parallel in the tradition of Christ the Priest.[20] Michael Kirwen has indicated that in African society and African traditional religion the diviner is really the African counterpart of priest:

[18] See Donald J. Goergen, *The Mission and Ministry of Jesus* (Collegeville: The Liturgical Press, 1986) esp. 170–6. Stevan Davies, *Jesus the Healer: Possession, Trance, and the Origins of Christianity* (New York: Continuum, 1995), places primary emphasis on Jesus as a spirit-possessed healer. Graham Twelftree, *Jesus the Exorcist* (Peabody, Mass.: Hendrickson, 1994).

[19] See Bénézet Bujo, *The Ethical Dimension of Community: The African Model and the Dialogue Between North and South* (Nairobi: Paulines Publications Africa, 1998), among others.

[20] See Kibongi, "Priesthood," where *nganga* is translated as priest.

In retrospect, the African people had to understand the Christian priests as diviners. There was no other role or model into which the Christian priest could fit. A great deal of the respect and interest of the people in the Christian priesthood, no doubt, came from this linkage. The more the Christian priest takes on the role of the diviner—the divinely inspired healer—the more effective and meaningful he becomes in the lives of the Africans.[21]

Jesus Christ is the supreme priest, that is to say healer par excellence, the healer of healers.[22]

This means not only applying a title, an African name, to Jesus, naming Jesus in an African way, but also applying the name in a new way, which is the nature of metaphorical language. We must remind ourselves with all the titles, traditional and new, African or Asian or Western, that their character is metaphorical. They are not like steno-language,[23] one-to-one equations, but they are rather intended to be revelatory of who Jesus is within the confines of human language. Thus they can best be understood with something of a yes-no-yes structure.[24] This is true of each title. We must be critical if they are applied literally. For example, in a very literal way Jesus is not an ancestor as one speaks of ancestor within the various African cultures, and yet Christ as ancestor is a very helpful inculturated approach to interpreting Jesus in Africa today. Nor is Jesus strictly speaking a king, not even the Christ in the way that "Messiah" was ordinarily understood within the Judaism of Jesus' time.

Metaphorical speech goes through a yes-no-yes pattern as we attempt to deepen our understanding. Yes, Jesus is an ancestor. No, Jesus is not an ancestor (not in that way). But yes, Jesus is our ancestor, both in a deeper sense of what we mean by ancestor and in the sense that *Jesus* is ancestor. Jesus tells us, reveals to us, as much about what it means to be ancestor as the category of ancestor tells us something about Jesus. The two illuminate each other. This is true of Jesus as healer, liberator, king, or even Christ, shepherd, son of God. Jesus both is and is not ancestor in the African sense, both is and is not healer-diviner in the African sense. On the one hand, the names or titles or metaphors tell us something real and significant about who Jesus is. But on the other hand it is Jesus who tells us

---

[21] Kirwen, *The Missionary and the Diviner,* 106, also 80–106.

[22] See Bujo, *African Theology in Its Social Context*, 85.

[23] See Philip Wheelwright, *Metaphor and Reality* (Bloomington: Indiana University Press, 1962); Philip Wheelwright, *The Burning Fountain: A Study in the Language of Symbolism* (Bloomington: Indiana University Press, 1954). Also Donald J. Goergen, *Jesus, Son of God, Son of Mary, Immanuel* (Collegeville: The Liturgical Press, 1995) 186–8.

[24] See Gail Ramshaw-Schmidt, *Christ in Sacred Speech* (Philadelphia: Fortress Press, 1986) 23–6.

what being an ancestor, a healer, a priest is all about. And this is the traditional Christian way of naming Jesus even with the biblical titles. Jesus is the prime analogate.

The letter to the Hebrews itself had to rethink the meaning of priesthood in order for the metaphor "priest" to fit Jesus. The earthly Jesus was not historically a priest in the sense in which that would have been literally understood within the Judaism of Jesus' day; nevertheless to the author of the letter to the Hebrews, Jesus was not only a priest, but the only true priest. Likewise with the expression *Messiah* or *Christ* as applied to Jesus: Jesus was not the Messiah in the varied ways in which that was understood within Judaism at that time. These names could not be applied to Jesus literally without any flexibility, without theologizing the names, without realizing that they were functioning as metaphors for Jesus. The content of such titles comes as much from who Jesus is or was as from the prior understanding of them within the cultural milieu of which they were a part.

So where does this leave us in our exploration of Jesus as priest? As priest, Jesus is one who heals, who drives out demons, who dines with sinners, who gives hope to people. He is the medium of spiritual power and energy, a mediator between God and God's creation, between God and God's people. He stands in solidarity with people and not apart from them. He is not confined by codes of exclusion. He offers himself on behalf of others as God's servant.

To return to our earlier question about what priesthood means when derived from the life and ministry of Jesus, and after having looked at "Jesus, the priest" within an African context, the priest *(nganga)* is primarily a healer, mediator, reconciler, a practitioner of rites and rituals. This is well testified in the ministry, healings, and exorcisms of Jesus. Following the example of Jesus then, the ordained minister is called to be a healer, exorcist, and, by means of Christian rituals, a mediator of reconciliation and communion. Priestly ministry consists of healing and reconciliation. To be a priest is to be a healer. We learn this from the ministry of Jesus Christ. And we retrieve that insight by the emphasis placed on Jesus as healer in African christology.

Jesus Christ, Liberator

Another significant title for Jesus emerges from within praxis-oriented, context-aware, socio-politically conscious liberation theologies. Sometimes these theologies have been placed at odds with the theologies of inculturation in Africa, although this is less and less true as one sees the interconnectedness between cultural analysis and social analysis. In the end, one is not possible without the other. Liberation must be a liberation of the African cultures as well as being social and economic. At the same time, however, contemporary Africans cannot become culturally conscious, genuinely African, as well as profoundly Christian without addressing the human deprivations in African life. Hence there is the growing awareness that there can be no inculturation apart from sociopolitical liberation, and no liberation apart from true inculturation and the Africanization of Christianity. Of course, the motif of Jesus as liberator emerged first within Latin American theology and is Latin America's major contribution to christology.

A criticism of the early theologies of liberation was their almost exclusive emphasis or overemphasis on liberation in socioeconomic terms to the neglect of the whole human person. But how can one overemphasize the need for Christian theology and the churches to be attentive to this facet of human existence? Is it not that the Church in the past spoke of salvation in almost exclusively spiritual or other-worldly terms to the neglect of the whole human person? So perhaps a shift in perspective had to go far in another direction in order to achieve a balanced appreciation and truly integral liberation that is attentive to both the interiority and the exteriority of human personhood.[25]

Jean-Marc Ela, Africa's first liberation theologian of note outside South Africa, a Cameroonian and Catholic priest, has written, "The Bible, which speaks of God and human beings in the same breath, always includes in the deliverance of God's people their political, economic, and social liberation—without, however, its being reduced to these."[26] For Ela, Jesus Christ is the ultimate liberator. "The faith cannot be lived atemporally: It must be inscribed in a historical context and be expressed in a praxis, for it must manifest, in comprehensible signs, the Christian message of liberation in Jesus Christ."[27] Inculturation isn't the only requirement for an ongoing incarnation of the gospel and of Jesus Christ in the world. As is true of its Latin American counterparts, Ela's theology emphasizes Jesus' roots in the prophetic tradition and his solidarity with the poor. But not only do the people need liberation, the gospel itself does as well. "How can we 'liberate' the gospel so that it can become the leaven of liberation in a socio-religious context where we discover that the God of

---

[25] On the integration of these two dimensions of life see Xavier Irudayaraj, "Interiority and Liberation," *Leave the Temple,* ed. Felix Wilfred (Maryknoll, N.Y.: Orbis Books, 1992) 116–24.

[26] Jean-Marc Ela, *African Cry* (Maryknoll, N.Y.: Orbis Books, 1986) 90. Also see Jean-Marc Ela, *My Faith as an African* (Maryknoll, N.Y.: Orbis Books, 1988).

[27] Ela, *African Cry,* 87.

Jesus Christ refuses to accept the role the Church has assigned to him, by sanctifying powers which, in fact, he opposes."[28]

If Jesus as healer in African theology helps us to understand what it means to speak about Jesus as priest, liberator aptly describes the prophetic Jesus. Liberation in African theology is liberation as it is understood by the prophets—as wide or as narrow as that might be. It is religious liberation to be sure, but it is also a socially-conscious liberation. For just as religion and society could not be separated in Jesus' world, so it cannot be separated in our world. Liberation for Jesus is grounded in a right relationship with God, but it is not confined to one's relationship with God, precisely because a relationship with God cannot be so confined. To love God with one's whole heart is to love God's people as well, to desire justice, and to stand in solidarity with those disadvantaged by the social structures of our world. Jesus reached out to social outcasts and those branded as sinners. He challenged rigidity in the observance of the Law. Jesus stands within this prophetic tradition.[29]

Jesus gave particular attention to women as well as others and challenged the taboos of his world that had negative effects on human dignity and equality. Africa's women theologians see Jesus as liberating rather than seeing his maleness as an obstacle. Jesus means freedom and equality for women as well as men. Jesus is talking about another way of being human other than that into which patriarchal societies enculturate us.[30]

In spite of negative factors associated with Christianity in Africa, Mercy Amba Oduyoye sees the continued appeal of Christianity in its response to the primal and African cry for salvation. Christ is Savior, the *Agyenkwa,* the rescuer.

> The *Agyenkwa,* the one who rescues, who holds your life in safety, takes you out of a life-denying situation and places you in a life-affirming one. The Rescuer plucks you from a dehumanizing ambiance and places you in a position where you can grow toward authentic humanity. The *Agyenkwa* gives you back your life in all its wholeness and fullness.[31]

[28] Ela, *My Faith as an African,* 112, also 102–12.

[29] Goergen, *The Mission and Ministry of Jesus,* 146–76. Also Albert Nolan, *Jesus before Christianity* (Maryknoll, N.Y.: Orbis Books, 1978).

[30] Enculturation here refers to the socialization of the individual by a society rather than inculturation, which is the insertion and incarnation of the gospel and Jesus Christ into the particular cultures of world, christianizing cultures and inculturating the gospel. See Aylward Shorter, *Toward a Theology of Inculturation* (Maryknoll, N.Y.: Orbis Books, 1988) 3–16.

[31] Mercy Amba Oduyoye, *Hearing and Knowing* (Maryknoll, N.Y.: Orbis Books, 1986) 98.

Liberation and redemption are not two opposing concepts; both restore the image of God in us and restore our human dignity to us. African liberation and feminist theologies depict Christ as liberator with the understanding that the liberation that Christ embodies needs to be still further articulated. It is the liberation of which the Hebrew prophets spoke, liberating us for the kind of humanity that God intended for us.

If we are to speak of Jesus as prophet, we must realize what being prophetic means. Jesus was in fact perceived by many who followed him as being a prophet (Mark 8:27-28), and it is most probable that he even saw himself in prophetic terms (Mark 6:4). This does not mean that *prophet* as applied to Jesus is simply attributing to him prophecy as it had been understood or practiced within the Hebrew traditions that were his heritage. But neither can Jesus, as prophet, ignore that history. There is kinship between being a prophet and being a liberator. A prophet is first and foremost grounded in God, but, from that vantage point, is socially and eschatologically aware. Jesus was God-conscious, socially-conscious, and eschatologically-conscious, the latter always being grounded in the former. God-consciousness leads to social consciousness; and social consciousness leads to eschatological consciousness. One's concern is both this world and beyond our present experiences of this world. Jesus' ministry was liberating for those who followed him because his was a prophetic praxis, the praxis of God.

So then, likewise, the ordained minister. His ministry ought to be prophetic, liberating, grounded in the gospel. To be a prophet is to be a preacher,[32] but prophecy says something about the character of that preaching, that it is a word of consolation to the socially and ecclesially marginal, and a word of challenge to those who place self-interest or group-interest or institutional interests prior to the interests of the reign of God. Jesus preached God, and aligning ourselves with God, and praxis in accord with the reign of God; so, likewise, the prophetic preaching to which the ordained minister is called. This clearly presents a challenge to those whose preaching takes place in a society in which Church and state are to be "separate," or in a Church where "speaking the truth with love" (Eph 4:15) can be interpreted as disloyalty. The presbyter must be a prophetic preacher, liberator of those without status, a voice for the voiceless.

Christ, the African King

Ukachukwu Chris Manus, a lay Nigerian theologian, has developed a king christology. It is the specifically African concept of kingship that Manus suggests as a way of interpreting Jesus, not simply Christ the king,

---

[32] R.B.Y. Scott, *The Relevance of the Prophets* (New York: Macmillan, 1971) 14.

but Christ the African king.[33] Manus' suggestion of kingship as a hermeneutical key is grounded in his own ethno-historical studies of African
kingship as well as in his New Testament studies. In neither are there
traces of triumphalism; rather one has the notion of a servant-king. Manus
studied, in particular, how kingship functioned among the Yoruba (in
southwest Nigeria), the Baganda (of Uganda), the Shilluk (of southern
Sudan), and the Zulu (of South Africa). He studied the manner of selecting and installing the king, the sacral nature of the kingship, and the
king's role as mediator between God and the people, as well as concomitant priestly functions. African kingship is (among the Yoruba and Shilluk)
and was (among the Baganda and Zulu) a sacralized institution; incumbents fulfill their sacral duties as divine agents for the good of their subjects. The theology of kingship in the Old Testament and its understanding
of YHWH as king (e.g., Isa 43:15; Pss 5:2; 10:16; 84:3), the kingdom of
God in Jesus' preaching, and the New Testament's understanding of Jesus
as the Messiah, the anointed servant-king, all manifest parallels. They
are not exact parallels, but, nevertheless, are significant parallels to the
African understanding of kingship. Manus emphasizes that "the kingship of Jesus is never exactly like any of the earthly African kingships,"[34]
that the kingship of Jesus transcends African traditional religious cultures. At the same time there is a similarity between the kingship of Christ
and African kingship.

What is the value of a christology focused on Christ as king? Jesus is
servant-king or servant-leader. Manus' is as much a servant christology
as it is a king christology and it offers a model for African leaders, both
civil and religious. It is better to include *servant* in the title "Christ the
African servant-king" because the greatest challenge facing a royal or king
christology is that the title can so easily connote oppressor. Given the
concept of African kingship as interpreted by Manus, it becomes an ap-
pealing way to speak of Jesus Christ. It is biblical. It unites within it varied significant African themes, including among others the relationship
of the king to the ancestors, Jesus as the founding or foundational ances-
tral king. The king as protector of the people, as for the people and yet
one of the people, shows ready application to Jesus. Of course, the image
of Jesus the king completes the threefold way of speaking of Christ as
prophet-liberator, priest-healer, and servant-king.[35]

[33] Ukachukwu Chris Manus, *Christ, the African King* (Frankfort: Peter Lang,
1993) esp. 117–67, 210–38.

[34] Ibid., 233.

[35] Concerning this threefold paradigm in reference to African christology, see
Douglas Waruta, "Who Is Jesus for Africans Today? Prophet, Priest, Potentate," *Jesus*

The threefold way in which Jesus' ministry had been theologically interpreted as far back as the fourth century and most recently at the Second Vatican Council is one way in which we can talk about Jesus and ordained ministry. It is not the only way. However, in using that schema the question is not so much whether the framework is in fact the best one to use but rather what these titles or images mean as illuminated by the mission, ministry, death, and resurrection of Jesus. Placing these traditional titles in an African context has allowed us to infuse them with significant meaning. Jesus as risen from the dead remains a healer, liberator, and servant-leader of God's people. Jesus means health and wholeness, freedom, and being at the service of humanity. Jesus is Son of God and son of humanity. Jesus heals through word and deed, in private and in public, at table. Jesus manifests freedom, proclaims freedom, and liberates people from varied levels of bondage. He came not to be served but to serve (Mark 10:45). As Jesus, so the ordained minister, in his presbyteral and sacerdotal roles.[36] The presbyter or ordained minister is one who heals, liberates, and serves. As priest, prophet, and king, his is a ministry of reconciliation, liberation, and servant-leadership. A theology of ordained ministry or priesthood must be a theology of healing and reconciliation, liberation, and servanthood, if it is grounded in Jesus Christ.

The Three Offices or Ministries and the Baptized

There are pros and cons in the efforts to discuss the mission of Jesus as well as ministry in the Church in the light of this threefold structure. It can do justice to Jesus but runs the risk of being historically less conscious. The value and validity of this schema depends upon the content we bring to the three offices. Their content need not be limited to Hebrew, Israelite, and Judean traditions prior to Jesus, nor as these were manifest at the time of Jesus. Yet their content must have some real connection to the earthly and risen Jesus at the same time that he is allowed to fill them with new meaning and we are allowed to develop them theologically.

My experience with African christology allowed me to see these three titles as genuinely illuminative of who Jesus Christ is for us. Biblically, Jesus was a healer. Healing and mediation were and are constitutive of his mission. Here African christology can rightly challenge some historical

---

in African Christianity, ed. J.N.K. Mugambi and Laurenti Magesa (Nairobi: Initiatives Publishers, 1989) 40–53, reprinted in *Faces of Jesus in Africa,* 52–64.

[36] On the language we use in discussing ministry and priesthood, see Frank C. Quinn's chapter "Ministry, Ordination Rites, and Language" in this volume.

reconstructions that diminish the degree to which healing and Jesus' contact with the world of spirit are paramount in the New Testament. Healing is Jesus' priestly ministry—at a wide variety of levels. The priesthood of Jesus Christ is about healing. We retrieve this insight into the Jesus of the New Testament from the emphasis placed on this "priestly" ministry within African christology.

Being in the presence of Jesus was experienced as liberating, and not only due to the personal wholeness and communion with God that he effected. He was a critic of those structures of society, religion, and consciousness that prevented God's people from truly experiencing God's love for them. He prophetically denounced all that held people in bondage—for bondage was a work of the evil one, not of God. Aligning oneself with God, solidarity with God, the praxis of God requires a new way of being in the world and ultimately a new world. Jesus the prophet is Jesus the liberator—God-conscious, socially conscious, eschatologically conscious, cosmically conscious. The urgency and need for liberation in our world, as manifest in liberation theologies throughout the world, prevents us from domesticating the prophetic character of Jesus' life and the genuine scandal in his associating with the socially and religiously marginalized. Prophecy, God's word, liberates and speaks truth.

And Jesus is king, not like the kings of this world, but rather the paradigm for rulers of this world. He did not come to be served. More will be said of Jesus the servant later. The cross is often associated with Jesus' priesthood, but biblically it is even more so associated with Jesus' prophetic mission, and even more than that with the nature of Jesus' messiahship. It symbolizes the kind of Messiah Jesus came to be: God's servant, a servant of all, Son of God, son of humanity. When James and John spoke of being at his side in the kingdom, Jesus knew that they had not yet understood the kind of kingdom God had in store for them. All leaders, religious and civil, are called to take their cue from Jesus. A ruler is one who comes to serve.

As we see this content in the mission and ministry of Jesus, in Jesus the healer, the liberator, the servant—the priest, the prophet, the king— we then have seen some implications for ministry in the Church, particularly ordained ministry. The presbyter as healer, liberator, and servant, as presider at ritual, preacher of the gospel, and pastor of people: this is the threefold office. We have suggested some implications for ordained ministry as we proceeded. But we can also see implications here for the lives of all the baptized. We are all called to be followers after Jesus, and the Second Vatican Council has asked us to consider these in relationship to all the faithful as did John Chrysostom centuries ago. Thus I would like to indicate a few implications of how we as baptized in Christ might understand these three challenges within our discipleship.[37]

How do we as baptized share in the priestly office of Christ? In other words, how do we participate in the ministries of healing and reconciliation?

We remind ourselves of the universal call to holiness, to wholeness, and therefore to healing and reconciliation. We are called to live the Christian life in its fullness, the moral, sacramental, and contemplative dimensions of that life. Christian life is life "in the Spirit." Each of us is a channel of God's Spirit. We, too, mediate the Spirit within the community of the faithful and beyond. We, too, are called to be healers, in our relationships, in society, and among peoples. We can exercise the ministry of healing in many and varied ways.

We heed the call to worship and our obligation to participate actively in the Eucharist and liturgical life of the Church. By contributing our gifts, we build up the body of Christ. Through our own life of prayer we share in the priestly prayer of Christ. We can exercise liturgical ministries and be extraordinary ministers of the sacraments.[38]

Congar also speaks about "a priesthood of the fathers and mothers of families" and "the priesthood of Christian husband and wife."[39] Partnering and parenting are a dimension of the priesthood of the laity. And in one theological understanding, the husband and wife are the ministers of the sacrament of marriage. We need to recognize how marriage and family life are truly priestly in character. They don't survive or flourish apart from healing and reconciliation.

How do we as baptized share in the prophetic office of Christ? How do we participate in the ministry of liberation? We are all called to give witness. Paul VI referred to witness as the primary form of preaching.[40] The laity, too, preach, and not only through witness. Lay preaching has a

---

[37] A very developed treatment of this topic is Yves Congar's *Lay People in the Church* (London: Geoffrey Chapman, 1963). He follows the threefold structure in his discussion of the roles of the laity.

[38] Perhaps here we think of baptism, which any lay person can administer. But Congar (*Lay People in the Church*, 217–18) refers also to the role of the laity with respect to confession:

> Another tradition that was commonly received for five centuries (about 800 to 1300 in the East; about 1000 to 1500 in the West) allowed a practice which, if it still be in existence at all, must be exceedingly rare—confession to lay people. Among theologians, St. Thomas took an exceptionally favourable attitude to this practice, and he expressly bracketed it with the administration of baptism: it appeared to him that in both cases necessity for salvation justified maximum faculties.

[39] Congar, *Lay People in the Church*, 192–3.

[40] *Evangelii nuntiandi*, par. 21, 41.

significant role to play in the Church. The preaching mission of the baptized includes the profession of faith, the evangelization of the market as well as cultures and civilization as a whole, as well as the call for some to martyrdom. All of these are prophetic dimensions in the lives of the baptized.

Not only is there a role for the laity in the Church's preaching, but also a significant role as teachers. Here we can think of lay theologians, professional theologians, but within the approaches of contextual theology, all the people do theology. There is also the important role of catechist. But laity also teach in the other disciplines, at various levels of instruction, and in varied ways. These too are the exercise of ministry. We include here also the *"sensus or consensus fidelium,"* or "the infallibility of the believing Church," as Congar puts it.[41] All the baptized are a part of the teaching church and have a role to play in that teaching. And also, of course, there are the many significant ministries that pertain to peace and justice in our churches and in society. Here too all the baptized play a crucial and essential prophetic role and have a significant vocation. As Christians we not only preach and teach by what we say but even more so by what we do.

How do we as baptized share in the servant kingship or leadership of Christ? How do we exercise our call to leadership?

We are called to exercise leadership in our world. Here we can mention social engagement, solidarity with the poor, the ministries of resistance and empowerment, the political offices and economic roles to which some are called, as well as a ministry to all of creation. Simply put, the laity are the world's leaders. Many of the contemporary lay movements in our world did not have their origins within the Church proper, but are clearly the workings of the Holy Spirit: those movements on behalf of civil rights, the equality and dignity of women, the peace movement, and so forth. In these movements the laity exercised their role as servant-leaders.

Lay leadership is exercised not only in the world, but also in the Church as well. An active laity is the sign of a healthy local church. Lay leadership is exercised in parochial life in many ways; without it the parish suffers. To be baptized is to be called to ministry. There is the ministerial nature of work itself, what we might think of as secular work, but there is also the growth in ecclesial lay ministries that manifest the priestly, prophetic, and pastoral activities of the faithful. The former might be seen as ministry *ad extra, ad mundum,* and the latter as ministry *ad intra, intra ecclesia.* Here one could even speak about two lay priesthoods: the priesthood of all the faithful and the priesthood of the ecclesial lay ministers, both of these a participation in the threefold ministry of Jesus Christ.

[41] Congar, *Lay People in the Church,* 433, 275–81.

The threefold office is about mission and ministry, whether that be of Jesus Christ, the ordained, or all the baptized. Both baptism and orders are sacraments of ministry. We are baptized and ordained to serve.

Ministry as Servanthood

Jesus' life is paradigmatic for all baptized Christians. This is eminently true of all those called to ordained ministry in the Church. Jesus is the exemplar, the model, the paradigm. No one image of Jesus by itself alone does justice to who Jesus is. Different images, different theologies bring out different facets of who the presbyter is as an ordained minister in the life of the Church, as well as who the lay minister is. We must avoid a theology that sees the presbyter as all things to all people. People are served by many and varied professionals as well as by other ecclesial ministers in the Church. The priest is not super-human or a super-Christian.[42] Still, the presbyter is called to live out the call to discipleship in an exemplary way.

Servanthood permeated Jesus' own consciousness as well as became a prominent way in which the New Testament interpreted him and particularly his death on the cross.

> Jesus' servant consciousness manifested itself at his last meal with his disciples (Mk 14:24). It also clearly manifested itself when disputes about greatness and position and status surfaced among his disciples (Lk 22:24-27). "Here am I among you as one who serves!" has a claim to authenticity (Lk 22:27). And so does: "For the son of humanity also came not to be served but to serve, and to give his life as a ransom for many" (Mk 10:45/ Mt 20:28).[43]

Although in the previous section on African images of Jesus servant was particularly applicable to the servant-king, the concept of servant is also applicable to the prophet and priest, to the liberator and healer. As prophet, priest, and king, Jesus is servant. The prophets, priests, and kings of Israel and Judah were all called to be servants of the Lord. Just so, the

---

[42] See James D. Whitehead, "Priestliness: A Crisis of Belonging," and Evelyn Eaaton Whitehead, "Accountability in Priesthood: Telling the Story of an Emerging Ministry," *Being a Priest Today,* ed. Donald J. Goergen (Collegeville: The Liturgical Press, 1992) 17–49. Also Donald B. Cozzens, *The Changing Face of the Priesthood* (Collegeville: The Liturgical Press, 2000).

[43] See Donald J. Goergen, *The Death and Resurrection of Jesus* (Wilmington, Del.: Michael Glazier, 1988) 39–70, for a discussion of servanthood and Jesus. With reference to the text of Mark 10:45, see p. 65, n. 31.

priest or presbyter is servant-prophet (prophetic preacher, teacher of wisdom, one who preaches and teaches in deeds as well as words, a liberator for people socially and personally), servant-priest[44](healer, discerner of spirits, master of rites, mediator, reconciler, offerer of sacrifice including a sin-offering), and servant-king (pastor, leader, animator of community, facilitator of the gifts or charisms within the community). It is not a question of whether the presbyter is a leader, but rather what kind of leadership he exercises.[45] What does it mean to be a servant of the people?

The servant in the Scriptures is first of all a servant of the Lord. The starting point for the servant is God, the kingdom of God, the gospel of God, simply God. The servant is God-conscious; a mission begins within a life of prayer. But one who is called by God is also sent by God to God's people. The People of God are as vital a concern to the servant as is God. Jesus' solidarity with God is manifest in his solidarity with people. The servant of God becomes by the very fact of being God's servant a servant of the people. The "Son of God" becomes the "son of humanity." The servant sees clearly God's love for people and that God is a God of people. To be a servant means to live "for the other." Jesus was a man for others; so likewise are all women and men who are his disciples. We live not for ourselves alone. Hence status, prestige, privilege, power, greed, and arrogance have no place in the lives of God's servants and no place in the vocation of the ordained or the baptized.

The servanthood of the Hebrew Scriptures makes it possible for the New Testament to interpret the mission and ministry of Jesus as one of servanthood, which in turn makes it possible for the Christian Church to understand ministry within it as one of servanthood as well. Ministry is service, *diakonia.* We are all deacons, all the baptized and all the ordained. Servanthood and clericalism, whether that be found among the ordained or among lay ministers, are incompatible.

The presbyter is a part of a community who has been called to be of service to the whole community. There is more to the community, more gifts, more ministries, than those of the presbyter alone. The presbyter is not the community, nor intended to dominate the community, but is es-

[44]We must always keep in mind when we use the threefold paradigm for talking about "priesthood" that we are using the word *priest* in two ways: as the umbrella category, and as one of the descriptive terms falling underneath that umbrella. Thus the priest is prophet, priest, and king. Therefore, priesthood is only one facet of the life and ministry of the priest. We are always using *priest* in two ways. This is another reason to prefer the word presbyter for the ordained minister. The presbyter is prophet, *sacerdos,* and servant-leader.

[45] Perhaps the best exposition of the priest as servant is Bernard Häring's *Priesthood Imperiled* (Ligouri, Mo.: Triumph Books, 1996).

sential to the life of the community. It is a question of seeing a relationship between whole and parts.[46]

The presbyter is ordained and then becomes part of a community of the faithful. The presbyter is complete within himself, and yet incomplete apart from the community of which he is a part. He is both whole and part, and it contributes to dysfunction to deny one or the other. Without the former, the presbyter will show excessive dependency upon those whom he serves due to his own neediness. He will lack a sense of identity, confuse his boundaries, be lacking in wholeness. Without the latter, the presbyter will display excessive independence, seeing himself as the center of the community, needing to dominate or be the center of attention, unable to be a part. Servant-leaders need to be whole; they need to be parts.

We must always return to the christological foundation. When we talk about ministry, it is first of all Jesus of whom we speak. He is the exemplar for ministry in the Church. The presbyter is called to leadership in the Christian community. Yet ordained ministry is not the only form of leadership in the Church, albeit an essential one. Leadership is a process of being drawn more deeply into the paschal mystery of discipleship. The equality of disciples does not rule out the call to leadership. The question is not whether the gospel requires leaders but whether leadership is exercised in accord with the gospel.[47]

The gospel requires a certain integrity, yet not one that lapses into self-righteousness. It requires recognizing one's own vulnerability, fragility, and fallibility. Yet it also calls for wisdom and strength. One needs to be strong and yet human. One needs the humility to hear criticism, but the strength to lead after having heard it. Gospel does not at all mean being middle of the road. Sometimes it may require that one be radical, and at other times moderate. Sometimes it may look an awful lot like the right or like the left. As gospel, it cannot be pre-defined. The challenge is to be able to let the gospel lead, to let the Spirit in.

Whether we are talking about the baptized or the ordained, we need to let the Spirit in. Ordained ministry is not only an ecclesial reality, it is also a pneumatic reality. Ecclesiology and pneumatology can too easily be severed from each other. The Church itself is a work of the Spirit, and leadership in the Church is accountable to the Spirit, not the Spirit to ecclesial leaders. The preacher of the Word, the presider at Eucharist, the pastor of people must first and foremost be a man of the Spirit. The

---

[46] See Ken Wilber, *Sex, Ecology, and Spirituality* (Boston: Shambala, 1995) esp. 3–31.

[47] Donald J. Goergen, "Religious Life and the Gospel," *Letters to My Brothers and Sisters* (Dublin: Dominican Publications, 1996) 137–42.

presbyter mediates the work of the Spirit, not confining it but mediating it. In the end it is the Spirit who gives birth to the word, who makes Christ sacramentally present, who vivifies and sanctifies God's people. The christological foundations of ordained ministry become a pneumatological foundation. Christology and pneumatology are inseparable from each other.[48] For St. Paul, the risen Christ was practically speaking indistinguishable from the Spirit. The ordained minister has *both* an ecclesial *and* a pneumatic role in the body of Christ.

The ordained leader's life must be not only evangelical (centered on the gospel), and spiritual (a living out of the life of the Spirit), but also ecclesial. We are clearly in the Church and of the Church. There needs to be among us a genuine affection for the Church. Catherine of Siena models what it means to be an ecclesial woman, someone who loved the Church and who at the same time struggled for reform in the Church, someone who knew evil in the Church and yet could embrace the Church as a source of both joy and pain. Catherine can teach us to love the Church even when the Church disappoints us—an essential thing to learn in human life whether we are talking about human relationships or human institutions. How do we reach out and embrace that which causes us pain?

The dangers are two: to fail to be critical or to fail to love. We simply accept the Church as it is, or we react angrily against it. Catherine challenged the Church all the way from the papacy to the people. She had an ecclesial consciousness in the best sense of that word. Leadership must strive to elicit this among members: not to promote hostility toward Church, nor to foster complacency about it; not to be defined by reactivity to flaws in the Church, nor to let ecclesial identity supersede evangelical identity.

The Roman Catholic priest is someone ordained for presbyteral and sacerdotal ministry, leadership, in the life of the Church. How this plays itself out for the secular clergy and for those who function as priests from within the context of religious life will naturally vary. But the ordained minister is prophet, priest, and king, that is to say liberator, healer, and leader, or rather preacher, presider, and pastor. All three reflect the threefold ministry of Jesus Christ. All three are grounded in the life and workings of the Holy Spirit. In each the priest acts *in persona christi.* In each the priest acts in the Spirit, who comes from the Father through the Son. Pneumatology, christology, ecclesiology, and the theology of ministry come together as the servant-leader facilitates our truly being Church for the world. Jesus Christ, a gift of the Spirit, is the supreme priest, re-

---

[48] Donald J. Goergen, *Jesus, Son of God, Son of Mary, Immanuel* (Collegeville: The Liturgical Press, 1995) 221–49.

ally the one and only priest, in whose priesthood we share, of whose body we are members. We are a priestly, prophetic, and royal people because we are in Christ, because we too have been anointed with the Spirit.

10

In Conclusion: Ordained Leaders for the Body of Christ

PAUL PHILIBERT, O.P.

As the preceding pages make clear, we have lived through several decades in which cultural, pastoral, and theological developments have emerged side by side—not in tandem, but in spurts and jumps. Culturally, the young adult and youth generations of the Church in North America are coming of age in a society in which the link between family religiosity and the Catholic tradition is very tenuous. The Lilly Endowment, for example, is so concerned about the possible loss of religious leadership to future generations of the Christian denominations that it is funding programs in seminaries and universities to spark interest in vocations to religious leadership. Pastorally the Church is experiencing the evolution of widespread interest in ecclesial service (see O'Meara and Risley).[1] Theologically the Church has benefitted from the extension of biblical and liturgical renewal to many enclaves of small Christian communities and committed adult Catholics, but it is also experiencing a cautionary attitude and skepticism on the part of Vatican officials and more recently appointed bishops about the effects of post-conciliar renewal. To bend a familiar metaphor into new shape, more than one drum is beating right now . . . and many people are unclear about which direction they are being called.

[1] Philip J. Murnion and David DeLambo, *Parishes and Parish Ministries: A Study of Parish Lay Ministry* (New York: National Pastoral Life Center, 1999); see also the research reports on Catholic pastoral life in the United States in *The CARA Report* (Washington, D.C.: Georgetown University) 1995–2000.

As a result, it is perfectly possible that well-meaning Catholics (ordained or lay) can understandably have seriously differing perspectives on the meaning of priesthood, depending upon their particular experience or their own theological culture. The goal of this summarizing chapter is to pull together a statement of major viewpoints that emerge from the arguments of the authors of this volume and to synthesize the vision that they have contributed. While there is not always complete agreement among the contributors to this volume, there is an overall recognition that we are in a new position, based on our examination and analysis of the Church's evolving understanding of ordained leadership for the body of Christ.

In an attempt to summarize the developing consensus about directions for a theology of priesthood, I propose the following three propositions, which I will use as organizing points to bring together some summary positions from the chapters. These points have been made in various ways in the different chapters, so I will refer to several authors under each one of these points. The three propositions are: (1) Presbyteral ministry must be defined in broad pastoral, not uniquely cultic terms; (2) the meaning of ordained ministry is radically embedded in the meaning of Christ's unique priesthood; (3) it is wrong to separate "ministerial priesthood" from the context of "spiritual sacrifices," which the baptized offer to God along with the body of the Lord. Likewise, it is wrong to imagine the apostolic ministry of the ordained apart from the context of the apostolic fruitfulness of the baptized.

In examining the significance of each of these propositions, I will try to show how they represent both a consensus of the theological views of the authors as well as an advance upon previous understandings of priesthood in the Tridentine and Baroque periods.

A Broad Pastoral Vision of Presbyteral Ministry

Presbyteral ministry must be defined in broad pastoral, not uniquely cultic terms. Several of our authors have pointed out the strong influence of Old Testament images of priesthood on the formation of priesthood in the Christian world (Philibert, Ashley, Quinn). This is one element that led to a dominantly cultic understanding of priestly ministry in the pre–Vatican II period. In addition, the medieval concern for the ontology of the sacraments, especially the sacrament of the Eucharist, leading to the doctrine of "real presence," meaning a real transformation of bread and wine into the real body and blood of Christ, brought about the decisive move in medieval and post-Tridentine theology to so emphasize the eucharistic body of Christ as to lose the context of the mystical body as the purpose of Eucharist (see Philibert, Quinn, Wesche).

Other historical factors, as we have seen, loaded on to the ritual of the Mass a theological and psychological urgency that disconnected the celebration of the sacrament from the pastoral life of the community. The most notable example of this phenomenon was the desire for Masses to be offered for the dead in the fourteenth and fifteenth centuries in the wake of the Black Plague.[2] So-called "absolute ordinations" of priests without parishes, who were given stipends to recite Masses for the dead, aggravated the tendency to imagine the Eucharist as a ritual reality more or less disconnected from the building up of a local community of faith and directed toward persuading God to a difficult mercy. Finally, the adversity that the Church experienced in the revolutionary period left many priests and faithful alike feeling weak and vulnerable in the social order, and this tended to induce a mystique of spiritual escapism (Philibert). On the other hand, as Rausch shows above, strong missionary movements in the seventeenth and eighteenth centuries affirmed the evangelizing nature of presbyteral service, even though the majority of the missionaries were clerical religious, rather than diocesan clergy.

Stephen DeLeers shows the central importance of the role of preaching to the developing understanding of the ministry of presbyters. As he notes, Vatican II clearly understood preaching as the first task of the Church and the primary responsibility of the ordained. The Church's preaching transmits the tradition of the word of God that leads us to the table of the Lord. Thus primacy of preaching in presbyteral ministry fundamentally contextualizes the meaning of the ordained priest's eucharistic service by showing that the eucharistic rite arises from the word of God as well as by enhancing the possibilities for catechesis that will link the eucharistic body of the Lord to the mystical body.

In similar fashion, Rausch distinguishes between a primarily cultic priesthood and a more prophetic one. Focused on the ministry of the word in its fullest sense, prophetic priesthood is kerygmatic rather than liturgical. As John O'Malley and Michael Buckley have likewise insisted, this prophetic model is thought to be closely linked to the ministries of clerical religious, while the cultic may be more characteristic of diocesan clergy.[3] Rausch, like O'Malley, reminds us that the prophetic form of

---

[2] Consult, for example, Philippe Ariès, *The Hour of Our Death,* trans. Helen Weaver (New York: Knopf, 1981); also John Bossy, *Christianity in the West 1400–1700* (Oxford: Oxford University Press, 1985).

[3] John W. O'Malley, "One Priesthood: Two Traditions," *A Concert of Charisms: Ordained Ministry in Religious Life,* ed. Paul K. Hennessy (Mahwah, N.J.: Paulist Press,

priesthood expresses itself in apostolic ministries that include education, spiritual formation, social ministries, and many other forms of apostolic life. Observe, however, that as DeLeers develops his reading of the role of the presbyter in the documents of Vatican II, the diocesan clergy appear called into the dynamics that these other authors describe as a prophetic priesthood.

Other authors (especially O'Meara and Risley) highlight the generative and mentoring functions of presbyteral ministry. The awakening of the apostolic sensibilities of the laity has created a new situation in the life of the contemporary Church, a situation that calls for the promotion and discernment of apostolic vocations for all the baptized, their formation, and the coordination of their expression.

These are some of the reasons for claiming that presbyteral ministry must be defined in broad pastoral terms. In my view, we are probably at the beginning of a period of theological and pastoral development that will lead us into *terra incognita* that will ultimately produce a living church whose apostolic center of gravity will be outside the Sunday assembly, not inside. Grace detonates in the marketplace, not in the sanctuary. Such at least is the logic and the dream of many of the documents of Vatican II. Such is the warrant for imagining priesthood fundamentally as broadly pastoral and seeking to awaken and support pastoral vocations in all Christians.

The Unique Priesthood of Christ

The meaning of ordained ministry is radically embedded in the meaning of Christ's unique priesthood. There are divergent pathways we can take to understand ordination and the priesthood of Christ. One pathway—called the univocal—would lead us to imagine that Christ was a priest who offered sacrifice (like the sacrifices of the Old Testament priests in the temple) and who has called (ordained) others to be priests like him. This univocal pathway imagines the need for endlessly repeated sacrifices to placate the wrath of an angry God. But that is not Catholic teaching.

Benedict Ashley shows, following Hebrews, that Christians believe that Christ is not only a priest, but the only true priest. The fundamental offering that Jesus Christ extended to the Father in sacrifice and that constitutes his priesthood is not exclusively the bloody hours of his crucifixion on the cross, but the whole of a lifetime of incarnation of the eternal word of God. At the heart of the biblical understanding of priest-

---

1997) 9–10; Michael J. Buckley, "Jesuit Priesthood: Its Meaning and Commitments," *Studies in the Spirituality of the Jesuits* 8 (1976).

hood is mediation, which places the "priest" between a supplicant people and a merciful god. As Hebrews insists (and Catholic theology following it), Christ is the only mediator between the Church and the Father. So the perspective and understanding offered by Frank Quinn in his discussion of metaphor as the language of the rites is of central importance.

Metaphorically, we can understand all the baptized as a priestly people, because through their baptism they offer "spiritual sacrifices" to the Father along with the body of the Lord (see 1 Pet 2:5). Also metaphorically, we can understand the ordained priesthood of presbyters and bishops as priestly because of the mandate it gives them to act in the name of the body of Christ *(corpus mysticum)* and of the person of Christ *(in persona Christi)* in calling together, presiding over, and ministering to the People of God.

To affirm that ordained "priesthood" is metaphorical is not to diminish either its reality or its importance. It is rather to clarify what is so frequently misunderstood: there is only one priest, Jesus the Christ. Roman Catholic "priests" are ordained to celebrate the rites of the Church which we perform "in memory of me [Christ]," so that the Holy Spirit can "make us one body, one spirit in Christ." We can use the formula yes-no-yes that arises in measuring the meaning of metaphors: yes, Christ is the priest who offers humanity to the Father in the mystery of his incarnation; no, Christ is not a priest who repeatedly offers sacrifices of blood like temple priests; but yes, Christ continues the offering of spiritual sacrifices acceptable to the Father both in the universal priesthood of all the baptized (see *Lumen gentium* 34) and in the ministerial priesthood of the ordained who are called to lead the Church in this most important reality of its life.

We have become so familiar with the accretions laid over the New Testament roots of ordained leadership that it is refreshing to refocus the lens and see afresh. Donald Goergen allows us to do that by leading us through a reflection on three titles for Jesus from contemporary African christology. All three of these—healer, liberator, and king—are expressions that can help us to appreciate what the function of Jesus' priesthood means for the living church. To see Jesus as healer par excellence is to give valid new content to the idea of his priesthood. As healer he is the medium of spiritual power for God's people: a powerful rephrasing of the idea of mediator—one who stands in solidarity with sisters and brothers and at the same time speaks as God's servant. The goal of healing is wholeness, and this is linked to Christ's pastoral function of caring for those entrusted to him, guiding them safely toward their divine destiny.

In an African context, Jesus as liberator plucks believers out of a "life-denying" situation and places them in a "life-affirming" one. His prophetic power—able to speak for the Father and reveal the mystery of true life—is the basis and source of his liberating power. As prophet, Jesus literally liberates believers from darkness (including magic and idolatry) and illumines their understanding. It is interesting that many early documents of the Church called baptism "illumination." In such light there is freedom.[4]

Finally, Christ as king (as seen through African eyes) links him to the ancestors, marks him as the protector of the people, and interprets him in a privileged servant role for the community. These African images can help us to re-imagine the beneficent qualities of Jesus' role in the life of the Church as we interpret and affirm that his unique priesthood is the source of all mediatorship and priestly service in the Church.

These reflections likewise help to clarify that not only ordained priesthood, but also the universal priesthood of the baptized are embedded in Christ's unique priesthood. Thus it is not the ritual of the Mass and its great treasure of the eucharistic bread that is the central object of the Church's concern, but the transformed humanity of those who both offer and receive the Eucharist. As the Constitution or the Church puts it: "In the celebration of the Eucharist, [the lives of the laity] are offered to the Father along with the body of the Lord" (§34).

Paul Wesche's unique perspective from Orthodox theology shows us another reason to consider the priesthood of Jesus as unique and essential for the mystery of the Church. Emphasizing the importance of icons for the Church's mystagogy (i.e., catechesis of the holy mysteries), he reviews the many archetypal and mystical dynamics that enter into the structure of the icons. Orthodox theology is ultimately all about theosis, that union of the many (creatures) with the One (creator) that is the revealed goal of all Christian theology and the fruit of eucharistic life. Liturgy is the celebration of a mystical marriage between the Church and the super-cosmic, super-essential God leading to a shared life that allows believers "to live as God lives."

The role of Christ as priest is the unique role of the one who knows both these realities and who stands between them: who is God and is man; who is in the bosom of Father and is the first born of all sisters and brothers transformed by theosis; who is—in other words—the icon of transformation. In our colloquium, Wesche's language and images were difficult and a stretch for most of us, but they led us to a new grasp of the

---

[4] Freedom is a fundamental issue for Christian anthropology, one linked to the radical purpose of human living and therefore linked also to the Christian's "spiritual sacrifices." See Thomas Merton, *New Seeds of Contemplation* (Norfolk, Conn.: New Directions, 1961); also John Paul II, *Fides et ratio* (Washington, D.C.: N.C.C.B., 1998).

most fundamental point here, that is, that the humanity of Christ is the icon of all transformed humanity, and the mysteries that we celebrate in our liturgy are our invitation and sacramental means to surrender ourselves, here already, to the promised transformation of theosis. This is what Christ—the one priest—can do for us.

Leadership in Apostolic Fruitfulness: Baptized and Ordained

It is wrong to separate "ministerial priesthood" from the context of "spiritual sacrifices," which the baptized offer to God along with the body of the Lord. Likewise, it is wrong to imagine the apostolic ministry of the ordained apart from the context of the apostolic fruitfulness of the baptized. Thomas O'Meara develops the powerfully rich phrase "liturgy as the nourishing sacrament of wider ministry." Correctly, he insists that the vision and logic of the sacramental theology of Vatican II is intended to confirm and nourish ministries in the world. He has clearly indicated the great shift from the Baroque period (from the late sixteenth to the early eighteenth centuries), wherein the priest was considered the sole liturgist or officiant of the Eucharist, to the vision of Vatican II (essentially recaptured from New Testament and patristic theologies) in which the People of God offer themselves, with Christ, to the Father. An important and essential part of this sacramental theology is (as St. Augustine so clearly taught) that the "whole Christ" is offered to the Father by the "whole Christ"—the Lord Jesus and all of his members. In this way O'Meara shows that the apostolic fruitfulness or "ministries" of the whole assembly both flow from the Eucharist and are brought back in loving gratitude to the Eucharist.

Jack Risley explains this dynamic in a parallel way. The laity, he says, exercise their priesthood in both eucharistic and non-eucharistic settings. As the assembly, they are present in the Eucharist both as those who offer this mystery to God ("We come to you Father in praise and thanksgiving . . .") and as the gift itself—whose lives are spiritual sacrifices offered to the Father. They exercise their priesthood in non-eucharistic settings by expressing the power of word and sacrament in the justice, integrity, and fruitfulness of their lives. Homes, offices, factories, meeting places, neighborhoods—all these are places where the gospel becomes life. The *Catechism of the Catholic Church* teaches that the priesthood of the ordained is ordered to the priesthood of the laity. This affirms, as Risley does here, that the presbyter must understand the target of the word of God and of the rites to be the transformation of the baptized into living and apostolic members of the body of Christ and the redemption and illumination of the world they share with one another and the wider cosmos.

Concluding Thoughts

Despite the different perspectives of our authors on distinct aspects of the history, theology, pastoral context, and changing forms of Catholic presbyteral life, we have traced these three common themes that all of our authors have supported in various ways. We have affirmed the broad pastoral structure of presbyteral ministry, the embeddedness of all priesthood in Christ's unique priesthood, and the solidarity of the universal priesthood and the ministerial priesthood in a common apostolic fruitfulness in the world. A fitting way to conclude these reflections, it seems to me, is to turn to the words of Yves Congar, who wrote in 1968 these insightful and reconciling lines about the problem of a potential conflict between cultic priesthood and apostolic mission:

> It is impossible to speak in a valid way about the Christian ministerial priesthood without speaking at the same time of the spiritual sacrifices that Christians are called to offer and of the gift of God in Christ Jesus which has to be communicated to the faithful. It is impossible to isolate Christian cult—especially eucharist—from the building up of the Body of Christ, which is the end and goal of all ministry (Eph 4:12-13). In sum, it is the apostolate that gives meaning to Christian cult in a pilgrim church still on its way to fulfillment; yet, by the gift of the Holy Spirit, this pilgrim church already possesses the deposit of the eschatological Jerusalem and is already spiritually the body of the Risen Christ.[5]

The priesthood of the Old Testament was essentially cultic; the priesthood of the New Testament is essentially prophetic: all Christian worship arises from faith, and faith arises from preaching. It is not too strong to say that Jesus replaced the Levitical priesthood with the apostolate. That is another way of saying that the ministry of word and sacrament is the fundamental way in which the Church's prophecy is sown as a seed in the life of the faithful, and apostolic fruitfulness is the fundamental way in which that seed bears fruit. The ordained are called to give their lives to assure the continuation of this graced ecology, offering—like Christ himself—all their gifts and their whole being to this mystery.

---

[5] Yves Congar, "Le Sacerdoce du Nouveau Testament: Mission et Culte," *Les Prêtres, Unam Sanctam* 68 (Paris: Cerf, 1968) 256.

Contributors

BENEDICT M. ASHLEY, O.P., Ph.D., S.T.M., is professor emeritus of moral theology at Aquinas Institute of Theology, St. Louis, Missouri, and adjunct faculty at the Center for Health Care Ethics at St. Louis University.

REV. STEPHEN VINCENT DeLEERS, D.Min. in Preaching, is assistant professor of homiletics at Saint Francis Seminary and Director of Continuing Formation of Clergy for the Archdiocese of Milwaukee.

ANN GARRIDO is a lay ecclesial minister from St. Louis, Missouri, pursuing her doctorate of ministry in preaching at Aquinas Institute of Theology, while serving as the school's Director of Field Education, Placement, and Parish Relations.

DONALD J. GOERGEN, O.P., Ph.D., a preacher and lecturer in theology, is currently a member of the Friends of God community, a Dominican ashram in Kenosha, Wisconsin.

THOMAS F. O'MEARA, O.P., Ph.D., holds the William K. Warren Chair in Theology at the University of Notre Dame, Indiana.

PAUL PHILIBERT, O.P., S.T.D., is prior of St. Dominic's Priory and Distinguished Visiting Professor of Church and Society at the Aquinas Institute of Theology in St. Louis, Missouri.

FRANK C. QUINN, O.P., Ph.D., is professor of liturgical theology at Aquinas Institute of Theology, St. Louis, Missouri, and occupies the Fra Angelico Chair of Liturgical Studies.

THOMAS P. RAUSCH, S.J., Ph.D., is the T. Marie Chilton Professor of Catholic Theology and chair of the department of theological studies at Loyola Marymount University in Los Angeles.

JACK RISLEY, O.P., spent many years as a missionary in Bolivia, including teaching at the Superior Institute of Theological Studies in Cochabamba. He is presently chaplain at the Dominican Motherhouse, Sinsinawa, Wisconsin.

KENNETH PAUL WESCHE, Ph.D., currently serves as the pastor of St. Herman's Orthodox Church (OCA) in south Minneapolis.

Index

African christology, 192–201
Angrisani, Joseph, 10, 11, 21
Apostles/apostolic, 4, 7, 14, 15, 74, 89, 90
Apostolic Tradition, 64, 73, 160
Aquinas, 7, 17, 18, 34, 36, 50, 52, 59, 80, 112, 142, 155, 191, 203
Ashley, Benedict M., 139, 212
Augustine, 17, 96

Baptism/the baptized, 36, 47, 54, 56, 61, 62, 63, 66, 67, 69, 74, 75, 76, 77, 81, 87, 91, 92, 100, 121, 134, 139, 149, 152, 153, 157, 159, 162, 164, 167, 182, 187, 191, 201–05, 206, 207, 212, 215, 216, 217
Baroque, 75, 212
Berry, Thomas, 41
Bishop, 4, 7, 8, 10, 14, 15, 18, 19, 22, 26, 27, 43, 45, 57, 58, 60, 62, 65, 76, 79, 88, 89, 95, 105, 109, 140, 161, 162, 163, 167, 182, 215. *Also see* episcopacy.
Brown, Raymond, 11, 13, 14, 15
Buber, Martin, 127
Buckley, Michael, 106, 107, 213, 214
Burrell, David, 50
Byzantine. *See* Eastern Orthodoxy.

Calvin, John, 19, 191
Campbell, R. Alastair, 143
Catechism of the Catholic Church, 6, 7, 8, 9, 10, 29, 217

Catherine of Siena, 69, 208
Celibacy, 23, 25, 36
Character, 9, 39
Charism, 69, 72, 73, 80, 81, 83, 106, 134
Christifideles laici, 90, 121
Christ. *See* Jesus Christ.
Clergy/*cleros*, 6, 73, 167–9, 183, 184
Coffey, David, 30, 31, 32, 33, 34, 122
Congar, Yves, 21, 37, 71, 73, 76, 79, 83, 191, 203, 204, 218
Cooke, Bernard, 19
Cultic, 29, 38, 44, 45, 47, 48, 53, 56, 57, 72, 106, 109, 113, 130, 148, 149, 151, 159, 212, 213

Daly, Robert, 46
Deacon/deaconess/*diakonos*, 6, 9, 15, 19, 47, 59, 62, 64, 67, 68, 73, 74, 79, 80, 89, 108, 121, 140, 153, 158, 160, 161, 191
DeLeers, Stephen V., 87, 99, 189
Denis, Henri, 71
Discipleship, 14, 125, 126, 127
Dominicans, 17, 28, 68, 107–10, 111, 114, 116, 129, 140, 156
Donovan, Daniel, 26
Dulles, Avery, 13, 31

Eastern Orthodoxy, 9, 23, 73, 163, 165–6, 216
Eliade, Mircea, 169

Episcopacy/episcopal/episcopate/*epis-copos*, 5, 6, 8, 14, 15, 21, 41, 47, 65, 94, 191

Eucharist, 3, 6, 11, 15, 16, 18, 19, 24, 26, 27, 33, 34, 35, 36, 37, 38, 39, 40, 44, 52, 53, 54, 55, 57, 58, 59, 63, 65, 71, 79, 82, 87, 93, 100, 106, 107, 111, 112, 113, 116, 119, 135, 142, 144, 147, 150, 152, 156, 159, 160, 161, 182, 203, 207, 212, 213, 216, 217, 218

Evangelization, 16, 21, 26, 27, 28, 66, 73, 96, 99, 102, 111, 115, 116, 117

Faivre, Alexander, 70, 71
Fawcett, Thomas, 51, 54
Fink, Peter, 132–3
Franciscans, 107–10, 114, 116, 140

Gaudium et spes, 21
Goddess, 170–78
Goergen, Donald J., 18, 123, 141, 187, 215
Gospel, 5, 8, 9, 23, 37, 61, 88, 89, 90, 91, 94, 95, 96, 102, 108, 109, 111, 114, 115, 116, 128, 133, 137, 158, 202, 206, 207
Gy, Pierre-Marie, 66, 79

Healer, 192, 193–6, 198, 200, 201, 202, 208, 215
Hebrews, letter to, 13, 54, 55, 129, 132, 145, 146, 147, 148, 149, 150, 152, 153, 156, 158, 160, 161, 167, 187, 188, 196, 214, 215
Hierarchy/hierarchical, 9, 10, 16, 17, 18, 19, 20, 26, 27, 46, 54, 69, 76, 83, 125, 134, 153, 154, 155, 156, 166
Hieros gamos, 169, 173, 176–8, 180–1, 182, 183
Hilkert, Mary Catherine, 115
Hippolytus, 58
Holy Orders, 6, 7, 8, 9, 11, 18, 21, 27, 31, 39, 41, 58, 59, 63, 112, 125, 135, 139, 157, 158, 161, 162, 187

Holy Spirit, 2, 6, 7, 8, 9, 21, 23, 30, 33, 35, 39, 47, 60, 61, 62, 65, 70, 72, 73, 80, 81, 83, 84, 90, 92, 94, 102, 123, 125, 153, 154, 159, 163, 164, 167, 184, 203, 204, 207, 208, 215, 218
Homily, 87, 97, 99–102,

ICEL, 62
Ignatius of Antioch, 7, 14, 15, 140, 167
in persona christi, 7, 18, 26, 29, 30, 31, 32, 34, 35, 36, 106, 162, 215
in persona christi capitis, 7, 21, 158, 164
in persona ecclesiae, 29, 30, 31, 32, 34, 35, 36, 158, 162, 164
Inculturation, 197

Jesuits, 28, 110–12, 114, 116
Jesus Christ/Christ, 2, 6, 9, 10, 11, 14, 15, 20, 32, 33, 35, 39, 43, 44, 53, 54, 55, 56, 62, 63, 64, 66, 84, 88, 89, 90, 92, 122, 127, 130, 132, 133, 135, 147, 149, 151, 153, 154, 156, 159, 160, 161, 163, 164, 182, 187, 192, 193–201, 214, 215
John Paul II, 5, 21, 28, 77, 121, 124, 137
Jordan, Mary Ann, 135

Kavanagh, Aidan, 56, 57, 121
Kilmartin, Edward J., 31
King, 7, 52, 143, 152, 190, 192, 199–201, 202, 208, 215
Kirwen, Michael, 194, 195

Laity/lay/*laos*, 2, 3, 4, 10, 11, 19, 41, 52, 54, 73, 80, 83, 89, 108, 119, 121, 125, 128, 132, 134, 156, 167–9, 182, 183, 184, 185, 203, 204, 217
Lathrop, Gordon, 47
Leader/leadership, 14, 24, 66, 73, 122, 126, 217
    cultic, 1, 38
    ordained, 1, 4, 5, 32, 212, 215
    presbyteral, 2, 5, 36, 38, 39, 41, 84
Leclercq, Jean, 17

Legrand, Hervé, 79
Léon-Dufour, Xavier, 55
Liberator, 192, 196–9, 200, 201, 202, 203, 208, 215
Liturgy/liturgical, 2, 3, 79, 80, 105, 111, 131, 135
Lumen gentium, 2, 29, 38, 119, 126, 144, 154, 191, 215
Luther, 19, 24

Manus, Ukachukwu Chris, 199–200
May, Rollo, 127, 128
Metaphor, 39, 43, 44, 48–54, 55, 56, 57, 58, 63, 65, 66, 73, 155, 195, 196, 215
Minister/ministry, 14, 17, 25, 26, 46–8, 68, 69, 73, 78, 80, 81, 82, 83, 84, 105, 110, 125, 135, 163, 188, 201, 205
  language of, 46
  lay, 141, 187, 189, 192, 204
  of the Word, 22, 66, 93, 99, 105, 107, 111, 113, 114, 116, 117, 189, 213
  ordained, 2, 6, 7, 10, 24, 35, 43, 44, 48, 54, 57, 58, 114, 121, 126, 128, 134, 157, 187, 188, 189, 192, 196, 199, 201, 202, 205, 207
  presbyteral, 29, 32, 40, 201, 212–4, 218
  priestly, 97, 98
  sacerdotal, 48
  theology of, 79, 192
Möhler, Johann Adam, 80

Newman, John Henry, 191
Nolan, Albert, 131
Nouwen, Henri, 127, 128

O'Malley, John W., 26, 27, 28, 29, 40, 107, 109, 111, 213
O'Meara, Thomas F., 17, 19, 20, 67, 121, 211, 214, 217
Orders. *See* Holy Orders.
Ordination/*ordinatio*/ordained, 5, 6, 8, 15, 17, 18, 28, 43, 52, 54, 56, 57, 58,
  59, 60, 61, 62, 65, 66, 73, 80, 82, 93, 106, 107, 110, 113, 121, 125, 126, 132, 134, 158, 160, 162, 163, 164, 206, 207, 208, 214, 215, 217
  episcopal, 63–6
  presbyteral, 61–3, 66
Orthodoxy. *See* Eastern Orthodoxy.
Osborne, Kenan, 125, 126, 162, 188

Pastores dabo vobis, 5, 121,137
Paul VI, 21, 23, 61, 76, 84, 85, 103
Philibert, Paul J., 1, 18, 28, 211, 212, 213
Pius XII, 61, 119
potestas, 18, 112
Power, 18, 25, 59, 113, 119, 120, 122, 123, 124, 125, 126, 127, 128, 129, 134, 169, 191
Power, David, 17, 18, 29, 34, 35, 47, 53, 54, 114, 160
Preach/preaching, 8, 13, 14, 17, 22, 23, 27, 42, 61, 63, 66, 82, 84, 87–103, 108, 111, 112, 114, 115, 117, 144, 148, 150, 156, 158, 162, 189, 191, 194, 199, 200, 202, 203, 204, 207, 208, 213
Presbyter/presbyteral/*presbyteros*, 2, 3, 5, 6, 10, 14, 15, 17, 19, 20, 25, 29, 31, 36, 39, 40, 43, 44, 45, 47, 59, 60, 61, 62, 63, 64, 66, 67, 72, 73, 79, 83, 87, 88, 89, 95, 96, 102, 128, 131, 133, 134, 135, 137, 140, 143, 144, 153, 155, 160, 167, 182, 191, 199, 201, 202, 205, 206, 207, 208, 213, 215, 217
Presbyterate, 6, 22, 57, 64, 66, 70, 107, 149, 153
Presbyterorum ordinis, 8, 11, 21, 22, 24, 25, 26, 27, 28, 29, 38, 87, 91, 102
Priest, 4, 5, 7, 8, 10, 11, 12, 16, 21, 23, 25, 31, 33, 35, 37, 39, 44, 45, 54, 55, 72, 75, 78, 79, 82, 87, 91, 93, 97, 99, 100, 101, 102, 141, 142, 143, 145, 147, 150, 151, 157, 159, 161, 169, 182, 187, 190, 192, 196, 208, 214, 215

Priesthood, 1, 2, 5, 7, 8, 10, 12, 13, 14, 17, 18, 21, 24, 28, 36, 47, 48, 54, 55, 56, 57, 58, 61, 62, 63, 67, 71, 72, 75, 105, 109, 110, 113, 116, 129, 130, 132, 134, 141, 142, 146, 149, 165, 166, 183, 191, 196
    celibate, 10
    common, 7, 18, 25, 26, 119, 120, 123
    cultic, 44, 46, 150, 218
    ministerial, 6, 7, 26, 119, 120, 131, 212, 215, 218
    of Christ, 6, 11, 119, 120, 121, 137, 139, 158, 164, 188, 212, 214–17
    of the baptized/baptismal, 6, 19, 119, 120, 121, 132, 137, 139, 150, 152, 164, 187, 215
    of the ordained, 25, 119, 120, 122, 123, 129, 132, 135, 137, 139, 153–63, 156, 158, 160, 187, 216
    prophetic, 112, 114, 115
    religious, 105–17
    theology of, 1, 9, 10, 23, 28, 40, 78, 112, 188, 201, 212
    universal, 19, 152, 215, 216
Prophet/prophetic, 7, 12, 13, 23, 29, 52, 106, 110, 121, 128, 143, 144, 148, 152, 190, 192, 197, 199, 202, 208, 213, 216
Puglisi, James, 65

Quinn, Frank C., 43, 142, 201, 212, 213

Rahner, Karl, 80, 81, 82, 93, 106
Ratzinger, Joseph, 21, 23, 24, 31
Rausch, Thomas P., 105, 213
RCIA, 68, 139
Religious life/religious orders, 16, 20, 26–9, 105–17

Risley, Jack, 119, 211, 214, 217
Rouet, Albert, 32, 33

sacerdos/sacerdotal, 1, 8, 15, 16, 43, 44, 45, 46, 55, 56, 57, 58, 59, 60, 61, 62, 63, 65, 66, 87, 106, 113, 142, 144, 152, 201, 208
Sacrifice, 6, 7, 9, 12, 13, 16, 19, 22, 24, 45, 46, 47, 48, 49, 52, 53, 54, 56, 57, 58, 60, 62, 132, 142, 148, 150, 153, 163, 164, 214
Schillebeeckx, Edward, 24, 25, 38, 39, 40, 153
Servant/servanthood, 157, 200, 201, 202, 205–09
Signs of the times, 41
Sobrino, Jon, 129–32
Spirit. *See* Holy Spirit.

Theology. *See* priesthood, theology of. ministry, theology of
Theotokos, 166, 167, 175, 181, 182
Twelve, 14, 15, 147, 159, 162

Uroboros, 171–74

vita apostolica, 108, 109

Wesche, Kenneth Paul, 165, 213, 216
Whitehead, James and Evelyn, 124, 126, 128, 205
Women, 5, 38, 39, 74, 122
Word, 19, 25, 27, 36, 37, 40, 44, 47, 66, 80, 82, 87, 88, 89, 90, 91, 92, 94, 95, 96, 99, 106, 114, 115, 131, 134, 135, 148, 156, 189, 202, 207, 208, 213, 217
Worker-priest, 25